THE GREEK TEXT OF EZEKIEL
An Examination of Its Homogeneity

SOCIETY OF BIBLICAL LITERATURE
SEPTUAGINT AND COGNATE STUDIES SERIES

Edited by
Claude Cox

Number 18

THE GREEK TEXT OF EZEKIEL
An Examination of Its Homogeneity

by

Leslie John McGregor

THE GREEK TEXT OF EZEKIEL
An Examination of Its Homogeneity

by
Leslie John McGregor

Scholars Press
Atlanta, Georgia

THE GREEK TEXT OF EZEKIEL
An Examination of Its Homogeneity

by
Leslie John McGregor

Library of Congress Cataloging-in-Publication Data

McGregor, Leslie John.
    The Greek Text of Ezekiel.

    (Septuagint and cognate studies series ; 18)
    Bibliography: p.
    1. Bible.   O.T.   Ezekiel.   Greek--Versions.
I. Title.   II. Series: Septuagint and cognate studies series ; no. 18.
BS1544.G7M34   1985   224'.4048   85-18482
ISBN 0-89130-902-0
ISBN 0-89130-903-9 (pbk.)

Printed in the United States of America
on acid-free paper

PREFACE

This study is a slightly revised version of a doctoral thesis submitted at the Queen's University of Belfast in 1983. In the course of producing it I have had to seek the advice and direction of a number of people. I now wish to express my thanks to all of them for rendering that advice. In particular, I would like to thank Mr. D. F. Payne, my supervisor, and Dr. G. J. Wenham, who was interim supervisor when Mr. Payne was on sabbatical, for their careful and constructive comments. No less appreciation must be given to Prof. D. W. Gooding for his equally sound guidance and penetrating analysis.

Most of my research work was carried out at the Queen's University of Belfast. For a period too I was able to study at Tyndale Library, Cambridge. I would like to express my thanks to both institutions for the use of their facilities.

I wish also to acknowledge the help of the Thesaurus Linguae Graecae, who supplied me with a (copyright) computer-readable text of the Septuagint of Ezekiel. The aid and advice of the Queen's University Computer Centre and the Cambridge Computer Laboratories must be acknowledged too. For most of the examples cited in the thesis I have relied on standard concordances. However, material for examples about syntax or prepositions has been obtained through the use of my own concordance programs on the TLG text. The responsibility for the accuracy of this material is mine alone.

CONTENTS

Contents ix

ABBREVIATIONS AND CONVENTIONS

A. Transliteration Scheme

Greek:

α	β	γ	δ	ε	ζ	η	θ	ι	κ	λ	μ	ν	ξ	ο	π
a	b	g	d	e	z	è	th	i	k	l	m	n	x	o	p

ρ	σ	τ	υ	φ	χ	ψ	ω
r	s	t	u	ph	kh	ps	ò

Hebrew:

א	ב	ג	ד	ה	ו	ז	ח	ט	י	כ	ל	מ	נ	ס	ע
'	b	g	d	h	w	z	h	t	y	k	l	m	n	s	'

פ	צ	ק	ר	ש	ת
p	ṣ	q	r	ś/š	t

Transliterations are presented in double angular brackets:
<<>>. Hebrew transliterations are usually given without
vowels. The Greek rough breathing is given as an "h" before
vowels.

B. Abbreviations

1. Periodicals:

APF   Archiv für Papyrusforschung
BASP   Bulletin of the American Society of Papyrologists
Bib   Biblica
BIOSCS   Bulletin of the International Society for Septuagint
         and Cognate Studies
BWAT   Beiträge zur Wissenschaft vom Alten Testament
CBQ   Catholic Biblical Quarterly
ETL   Ephemerides Theologicae Lovanienses
GRBS   Greek, Roman and Byzantine Studies
HUCA   Hebrew Union College Annual
JAOS   Journal of the American Oriental Society
JBL   Journal of Biblical Literature

JTS   Journal of Theological Studies
OTS   Oudtestamentische Studiën
RevQ   Revue de Qumran
RSPT   Revue des Sciences Philosophiques et Théologiques
RTL   Revue théologique de Louvain
StP   Studia Papyrologica
SVT   Supplements to Vetus Testamentum
VT   Vetus Testamentum
ZAW   Zeitschrift für die Alttestamentliche Wissenschaft
ZDMG   Zeitschrift der Deutschen Morgenländischen
        Gesellschaft

        2. Other Abbreviations and Sigla

BHS   Biblia Hebraica Stuttgartensia
            (edited by K. Elliger and W. Rudolph)
LXX   Septuagint
MT   Massoretic Text
PG   Patrologiae cursus completus, series Graeca
            (edited by J.-P. Migne)
PL   Patrologiae cursus completus, series Latina
            (edited by J.-P. Migne)
TDNT   Theological Dictionary of the New Testament
            (edited by G. Kittel)
TDOT   Theological Dictionary of the Old Testament (revised)
        (edited by G. J. Botterweck and H. Ringgren)
Ez   Ezekiel
nF   neue Folge
n.s.   new series
o.s.   old series
vol   volume
ed.   editor
edn.   edition
ch.   chapter(s)

a'	ch.1-27 (of Ezekiel)	S1	ch.1-25
b'	ch.28-39	S2	ch.26-39
g'	ch.40-48	S3	ch.40-48

Other abbreviations follow standard English usage.

C. References

Bibliographical references are given in parentheses in the text. Normally they contain the author's name, date of publication of article/book, and page(s) referred to. The name may be omitted when the context allows. Works of the same author occurring in the same year are differentiated by adding a letter to the date. Thus, for example, Thackeray (1903c: 590) refers to page 590 of one of three articles which Thackeray published in 1903. An author's works are listed in chronological order in the bibliography.

Foreign language quotations have been translated into English.

Biblical references follow the MT.

D. Format of Translation Examples

The evidence of the translation of a given term is normally presented in a fixed format. This is illustrated in the following example:

<5.2> סביב

5.5	וסביבותיה	και ... κυκλω αυτης	κ. κ. της (5)
5.15	סביבותיך	κυκλω σου	<> (2)/ <σου> (4)
11.12	סביבותיכם	<>	περικυκλω υμων (2,3)
12.14	סביבתיו	κυκλω αυτου	<> (4)
19.8	סביב	κυκλοθεν //	//

| 23.22 | מסביב | κυκλοθεν | — |
| 42.15 | סביב סביב | κυκλοθεν
διαταξει | // |

The first column contains references according to the MT. The second column contains the MT reading. (With some examples this column is omitted). The third column shows the LXX translation according to the Ziegler text. The fourth column displays the variants as collected in Ziegler's apparatus. Only the variants to the word under consideration are cited. Transpositions, haplography and the addition or omission of <<kai>> and the definite article are sometimes ignored.

The enumeration of examples is done by giving first the chapter number and then the number of the example within the chapter. For instance, ex. <5.2> means the second example to be cited in chapter five.

The heading of an example of a verb may be followed by:
.ּפ, .נ, .פ, .ה, .הת,
which indicate the Qal, Niphal, Piel (with Pual where relevant), Hiphil, (with Hophal where relevant), and Hithpae respectively. These show which forms of the verb are being considered. If all forms are listed, no abbreviation follows the example heading.

<> indicates omission of the whole term by the text, bu if the brackets enclose something, then only that which they enclose is omitted. The use of three stops ... means that so words in the text have not been cited. When the double line // appear with a reading they indicate a degree of uncertai about the identification of the reading, though it is thoug to be possibly correct. When double lines appear alone they signify greater uncertainty about the identification of a reading. Double lines with variants indicate that a closer examination of the context might be necessary.

The numbers in round brackets represent a compromise between clarity and detail. In noting the manuscript attestation it was difficult to give an evaluation of the importance of a variant. Ziegler had classed the witnesses to the Septuagint text into six groups, which have been numbered as follows:

(1) B 967 988 La Bo Sa Tyc. This group, the B-group, is assessed by Ziegler to be the most reliable set of witnesses to the LXX of Ezekiel.

(2) A 26 106 410 544 Arab Aeth. This group ranks next in importance to the B-group, though its members have undergone some hexaplaric influence.

(3) Q 88 Syh 62 147 407 Hi. This group contains the hexaplaric witnesses. MS 62 exhibits Aquila-type readings. At times 147 and 62 go together.

(4) 22 36 48 51 96 231 763 311 538 V 46 449 Zv 456 Constit Chr Tht. These are witnesses to the Lucianic recension.

(5) 87 91 490 49 90 764 130 233 534. This is the Catena group of witnesses.

(6) This group contains all that does not find a place with any of the other five, namely the "codices mixti": 86 198 239 306 380 393 403 611 613 710 770 927, some marginal readings, and various citations.

Only the number of its group is cited after a variant. This has the advantage of giving a sense of the spread of manuscript support for a reading, but has the disadvantage of not showing the spread of support within a group.

Further information about the MSS themselves is given in Appendix B.

INTRODUCTION

It has long been accepted that the corpus of material loosely called the "Septuagint" is far from homogeneous in nature. Different Old Testament books are seen to exhibit widely different styles of translation, and even different manuscripts of the same book may contain different translations. This is only to be expected. Both what we know about ancient book production and what we are told in traditional accounts of Septuagint origins lead us to anticipate such a situation. Yet while the concept of finding differences between books or between manuscripts of the same book is fully admitted, that of finding differences within a book meets a less ready acceptance. Although there have been attempts to divide up many individual Septuagint books, the validity of the methods employed and the results achieved have often been questioned.

This study is concerned with the issue of the differences within the text of one book, namely, the Greek translation of Ezekiel. It deals with the problem of whether the text as we now have it is homogeneous or not. It asks whether it is possible to divide the book up into different sections and what the relationship of each of the main sections to the others might be.

The historical background to the discussion about the homogeneity of the Greek Ezekiel text is given in Chapter I. There the development of views is traced from the pioneering work of Thackeray at the beginning of this century up to present-day suggestions. It is seen that the issue has now split into three: a) the still unresolved problem of the main divisions of the text, b) the question of the significance of the divine names, and c) the matter of the small section

36.23c-38 and its implications for the history of the text. The main focus of the present study is on the first of these, although the other two are given some consideration also.

However, there is one major issue which has largely been ignored in past discussions of translation homogeneity. This is the question of the whole methodology behind breaking up a translated text into different units on the basis of translation technique. Chapter II examines this area in detail and attempts to supply guidelines. In the course of discussion, examples used in earlier studies on Ezekiel are evaluated. Many examples cited to support the case for dividing up the text turn out to be invalid.

The problem of the divine names in the book of Ezekiel is dealt with next because of its prominence in previous discussions and its significance from a methodological point of view. Chapter III discusses the involved historical development of arguments concerning their value. Chapter IV then proposes a new solution to the problem. The chief implication of this solution for the present study is that the use of the divine names as a criterion to distinguish translation technique is invalid.

Several appendices pertaining to the nature and distribution of the nomina sacra are given at the end of the book.

The next three chapters — V, VI and VII — attempt to show however that there are still grounds for saying that the Greek text of Ezekiel is not homogeneous. Chapter V contends that 1-39 can be split into two main sections, 1-25 and 26-39. It is argued that the differences between these two are still best explained as due to two different translators, rather than due to partial revisions of some kind.

Introduction

Chapter VI deals with the remainder of the book, 40-48. This is seen to be distinct as a translation from 26-39 and to have had a textual history different from that of 1-25. It is maintained that the evidence is compatible with the suggestion that 1-25 and 40-48 were the work of the same translator. However, lack of conclusive data precludes dogmatism on this point.

One unexpected result was that, like 36.23c-38, chapter 16 seemed to be quite different from its surrounding text. The evidence for this is given in Chapter VII, where the nature of 36.23c-38 is discussed briefly as well.

In Chapter VIII the conclusions from the preceding chapters are drawn together and their implications discussed.

CHAPTER I

HISTORICAL BACKGROUND

The History of Research on the Greek Text of Ezekiel

The history of study on the composition of the Greek text
of Ezekiel can be divided into three phases, the beginning of
each phase corresponding roughly with the beginning of each
third of this century. Initially, there was the pioneering
work of H. St. J. Thackeray, along with the reaction that work
produced. Later, in the second phase, the evidence of Papyrus
967 tended to dominate the issue. Later still, in the most
recent phase, the discoveries in the Dead Sea area displaced
967 in significance, even though further fragments of the
papyrus came to light also. However, very little of the text
of Ezekiel itself, either in Greek or in Hebrew, was recovered
from the Judaean desert finds.

1. Thackeray and contemporaries

Although some nineteenth century commentators had
examined the textual value of the Greek witnesses to the book
of Ezekiel, the homogeneity of the Greek text itself was not
called into question until H. St. J. Thackeray investigated
the matter. Initially, Thackeray was concerned with the
unusual features exhibited by the Septuagint text of Jeremiah.
His conclusion that the bulk of the book had been divided
between two translators led him to examine the LXX of Ezekiel
(1903a: 253), where he found that this too exhibited
discontinuities. In an article entitled "The Greek Translators

5

of Ezekiel" (1903b: 398-411) he set out his views in detail.

He argued that that the LXX of Ezekiel could be divided
into three main sections:
1) a' - comprising ch.1-27,
2) b' - comprising ch.28-39,
3) g' - comprising ch.40-48.
These sections were the work of two translators. One
translator, the more competent of the two, tackled a' and the
difficult g' section, leaving the middle section to his
contemporary. Thackeray saw this as corroborating Epiphanius'
statement that the translators worked in pairs /1/. However,
Thackeray's view of what exactly took place was somewhat
inconsistent. At one point, when attempting to explain an
apparent mixing of vocabularies in ch.26-27, he suggested that
the "second translator, before beginning his own work, read
over the last portion of the work of his predecessor ..."
(1903b: 406). A little later, though, he expressed the view
concerning Ezekiel and Jeremiah that "each book was divided
into two parts, and two translators were set on to the work
simultaneously." (1903b: 410).

Thackeray also isolated a much smaller unit the Greek of
which stood out "markedly" from its immediate context. This
unit, 36.24-38, seemed to resemble the work of Theodotion.
Thackeray conjectured that these fifteen verses might have
come from a lectionary of some sort. It was possible that this
passage could have been used as a reading in the Jewish
synagogue and that the translators had incorporated it into
their text. A less likely possibility was that it might have
been a Christian lectionary which had somehow supplanted the
original text.

The method by which Thackeray arrived at his conclusions
was by an analysis of vocabulary and grammar. He listed

expressions which were common to certain sections but absent
in others. He was also aware of the possibility that variant
readings might point to a different picture, but his
examination of variants seems to have been limited to B, A and
Q, with the witness of B being strongly preferred. His
criterion for the location of the boundary between a' and b'
was the rendering of the name of Tyre. He relates that:

> it was the difference between the appellation of
> the city in the earlier part of this section
> [ch.26-28], where it is rendered <<Sor>>, and that
> in the later part, where it becomes <<Turos>>,
> that first drew my attention to the change in the
> Greek style. (1903b: 400; cf. 1921: 37)

In a later article (1903c: 578-585) Thackeray extended
the basis of his arguments to include the Minor Prophets and
came to the conclusion that the first half of Jeremiah,
sections a' and g' of Ezekiel, and the whole of the Minor
Prophets were translated either by one individual or by a
small group of collaborators. At the same time, he was not
blind to the possibility that copyists could have caused some
discrepancies between sections of books too. Indeed he
suggested that the Greek texts of Exodus, Leviticus and Psalms
showed a change in orthography just around the mid-point of
each (1907b: 88-98).

The one feature which gave Thackeray difficulty was that
of the divine names. The MT of Ezekiel is unique in having a
very large number (over 200) of occurrences of the form <<'dny
yhwh>>. The Greek rendering of this form varies considerably,
both from section to section and from manuscript to
manuscript. As the rendering in section a' was quite different
from that of section g', Thackeray was forced to explain this
discrepancy in order to protect his two translator theory.
This he did by adopting an earlier suggestion that the Hebrew

Vorlage of ch.40-48 (g') read <<yhwh 'lhym>> instead of <<'dny yhwh>>.

However, it was on this very issue of the divine names that much debate was to ensue. In 1909 J. Schäfers used the rendering of the divine names alone as a basis for dividing the book into three sections: 1-11, 13-39, and 40-48. Each of these sections was the work of a different translator. On the same basis, J. Herrmann (1913) suggested that the book should be divided into 1-27, 28-39, and 40-48. This was the same division as Thackeray had suggested, but Herrmann believed that 40-48 was the work of a third, different translator and not that of the translator of 1-27 /2/.

Despite Herrmann's suggestion, Thackeray remained convinced that a' and g' were the work of one translator. As he stated in his Schweich Lectures (published as "The Septuagint and Jewish Worship" in 1921):

A roughly equal division of labour, with the
resumption of the task by the leader at a point
where it seemed beyond the capacity of a
subordinate, adequately accounts for the facts.
(1921: 38)

Nevertheless, he now offered a different explanation for the apparent difference in the divine names. Here he suggested that the first translator found only <<yhwh>> in the first section, but <<'dny yhwh>> in the third section. Again, he altered his views on the origin of the unit 36.24-38. On the basis of style, he surmised that this lectionary unit was later than the surrounding text, a viewpoint he had already taken up in his Grammar (1909: 12). The "outstanding peculiarity" of this passage was the witness of B to the transliteration of <<'dny>> into Greek (1921: 125). He also mentioned in passing that the "unedifying chapter xvi was perhaps omitted by the Alexandrian company, and the Greek in our texts is a later supplement." (1921: 38; cf. 26). However, he did not attempt to substantiate this suggestion.

Herrmann's initial article had not attempted to argue the translator issue in detail, but this omission he rectified in a subsequent article entitled "Die Septuaginta zu Ezechiel das Werk dreier übersetzer" (1923: 1-19). As its title implies, this reasserted the view Herrmann originally suggested, namely that a', b' and g' each had a different translator. He attempted to vindicate his position by listing instances where each section differed from the other in its rendering of certain words. Although an awareness of certain uncial variants is indicated, the possible effect of textual variation is not discussed. Herrmann also noted, as Thackeray had done, the apparent mixing of material in ch.26-27, but accepted Thackeray's reliance on the <<Sor>>/<<Turos>> differentiation in order to fix the boundary between a' and b'.

Herrmann's position was further supported by W. Danielsmeyer in his dissertation "Neue Untersuchungen zur Ezechiel-Septuaginta" (1936). Danielsmeyer reinvestigated the issue by looking at the translation of phrases, rather than individual words, and came to agree entirely with Herrmann's conclusions. W. W. Baudissin (1929) and later J. B. Harford (1935) also agreed with Herrmann that the book gave evidence of three translators. However, they did not consider the double form of the divine name original, either to the Greek or to the Hebrew texts. In addition they preferred a different division of the text (1-20/ 21-39/ 40-48), although Herrmann's divisions were not totally discounted.

2. The Effect of Papyrus 967

In the early nineteen thirties a collection of papyri leaves came into the hands of a certain Alfred Chester Beatty. The text of these leaves was published in a series of fascicles by F. Kenyon entitled "The Chester Beatty Biblical Papyri: Descriptions and Texts of Twelve Manuscripts on Papyrus of the Greek Bible" (from 1937 to 1941). Among these papyri were texts attesting part of the LXX of Ezekiel. The Chester Beatty Ezekiel papyrus classified by Rahlfs as Papyrus 967 /3/ was apparently of Egyptian provenance, and was dated not later than the third century A.D. /4/. It contained the most of ch.11-17 of Ezekiel, written on about 16 pages of a codex /5/. Kenyon published its text in 1937, but gave no detailed appraisal of its value as a manuscript witness.

Other parts of the same papyrus found their way into the collection of John H. Scheide. These fragments were published in 1938 as "The John H. Scheide Biblical Papyri: Ezekiel", edited by A. C. Johnson, H. S. Gehman and E. H. Kase. This part of the codex consisted of about 21 leaves, and contained the text of parts of ch.19-39 /6/.

The Scheide volume contained an evaluation of 967 and an investigation of the issues it raised. In examining the textual affinity of 967 Gehman concluded:

> Of all our Greek MSS, the Scheide text of Ezekiel
> appears to be closest to the original LXX.
> (Johnson, Gehman, Kase 1938: 79)

He went on to say:

> The authority of B as our best source for the
> original Septuagint must yield to this new
> evidence. (1938: 79)

This concluding statement he endorsed (indeed repeated

verbatim) in two other separate articles on the textual
character of 967 (Gehman 1938a: 102; 1938b: 287). His high
evaluation of 967 was to be corroborated by Ziegler (1946:
93-4) and Barton Payne (1949).

Kase observed that 967 was very close to the Vetus Latina
witnesses, especially Codex Wirceburgensis. He was led to the
conclusion that:

> the original translation of the Old Latin version
> was made from a text closely resembling that of
> the Scheide papyri and probably of Egyptian
> origin, and the text of the Codex Wirceburgensis,
> although it gives evidence of some revision and
> has suffered much at the hands of an ignorant
> copyist, stands close to the fountainhead of the
> Old Latin tradition. (1938: 47-48)

One of 967's most notable features was its attestation of
the divine name. Out of 82 instances where the corresponding
passage in the MT usually gave a <<'dny yhwh>>, the Scheide
papyri read <<kurios o theos>> only 6 times. In the other 76
instances the text had just <<kurios>>. (All forms of the
divine names were given in the usual contracted manner. For
example, <<kurios>> was abbreviated to <<ks>>.) This was to
have important implications for the multiple translator
theories. The almost total absence of double divine name forms
in the earliest, apparently most reliable, Greek manuscript
strongly suggested that the double readings in other
manuscripts were later expansions, added to bring the LXX into
line with a Hebrew text similar to the MT. This in turn meant
that such double readings were invalid as criteria for
establishing multiplicity of translators. One of the main
supports for such arguments had apparently been removed.

In addition to this, 967 showed indications of sporadic

11

alteration of other forms, including those used to support
differences between sections e.g. <<oti>>/<<dioti>>, and
<<Turos>>/<<Sor>>, (Johnson, Gehman, Kase 1938: 14-15, 69-70).
This led Kase to suggest that there had originally been one
translator for the whole of the book, but that ch.1-27 had
undergone a revision "in the interest of supplying a more
literal rendering of the Hebrew." (1938: 73). The reason for
only half of the text being affected was the practice of using
two rolls for each large book. At some point the text of a
revised first scroll had come to be linked with that of an
unrevised second scroll.

Another important feature of 967 was its apparent
omission of 36.24-38 (more precisely 36.23c-38) and the
transposition of chapter 37 to the end of chapter 39. Johnson
noted that the Vetus Latina Codex Wirceburgensis (W) exhibited
a similar type of transposition and possibly had a similar
omission. Filson (1943: 27-32) judged the omission in 967 to
have been accidental, while Irwin (1943: 62-64) maintained
that the passage had been a very late addition to the Hebrew
text and had not been in the LXX Vorlage.

The assessment of 967 by Johnson, Gehman and Kase was in
the main accepted by J. Ziegler. He saw the text as
pre-Hexaplaric and as exhibiting the earliest attainable form
of the Ezekiel Septuagint. He agreed with Kase that the nomen
sacrum in the Greek text originally was only a single
<<kurios>> and observed that there was evidence of a sporadic
revision of the Greek towards the Hebrew text:

> Papyrus 967 is important chiefly for demonstrating
> that in the pre-Hexaplaric period (perhaps even in
> the first century A.D.) the Septuagint text of
> Ezekiel was being corrected toward the Hebrew text
> ...
> The vocabulary of Papyrus 967 shows that the

revision of the text of Ezekiel occurred at such
an early date that it has affected the entire
manuscript tradition, and is consequently
difficult to detect. The translator was far more
consistent in his rendering of the Hebrew exemplar
than has long been suspected ... Even his
rendering of the divine name <<kurios>> seems to
have been consistent. This makes it less likely
that several translators shared in its
preparation. (1946: 93-4) /7/

It should be noted that Ziegler does not clearly state
that he envisages the same type of revision as Kase suggests.
Indeed, he seems to view the second section (b') rather than
the first (a') as exhibiting signs of alteration (1946: 88).
He sees it as a sporadic correction, and not a thorough
revision.

Ziegler realised the relevance of the translator issue
for text-critical analysis. This was not just out of
theoretical considerations, but out of the practical problem
of compiling the Göttingen Septuagint edition of Ezekiel
(1952), of which he was the editor. He had already examined
the issue of the unity of the text in Isaiah (1934: 31-46) and
the Minor Prophets (1934/5: 1-16), and was thus well aware of
the importance of context and textual variation:

It is important when establishing the text to examine thoroughly the c h a r a c t e r i s t i c s
of the E z e k i e l t r a n s l a t i o n.
We must ascertain whether the translator gave an
exact or a loose translation. To begin with, it
must be accepted that he does not exhibit any
rigid consistency in the rendering of identical
words and expressions; this is a mark of Aquila. In
Ezekiel the examination of the translation tech-

nique is made difficult when several renderings
point to different translators; thus Thackeray and
Herrmann assume there to be three translators ...
In spite of this, the three translator thesis cannot be honestly maintained, as the investigations
on Pap. 967 show above anything else, cf. E.H.
Kase's essay, "The Translator(s) of Ezekiel", in
the edition of the papyrus (Princeton 1938)
p. 52-73. If it can be proved definitely that
one part comes from another translator, then we
must take into consideration that part's characteristic features. This holds true for 36.24-38,
which Thackeray regarded as a later lectionary
text. (1953: 440)

Ziegler went on to give examples of translation technique
which he believed indicated that the translator of the book
often rendered the same words in a multiplicity of ways, even
when the words lay within a few verses of each other.

In 1950 C. H. Roberts published the texts of part of a
collection of papyri found at Antinoopolis. Among this
collection were a few parchment fragments containing part of
Ez 33-34. The textual similarity between these fragments and
967 was so close that Roberts believed that they must have had
a common ancestor (1950: 19-23).

The weight of Ziegler's verdict against multiple
translators was considered impressive by P. Katz in his review
"Septuagintal studies in the mid-century" (1956a). Ziegler's
"master method of determining whether more than one translator
worked on a single book" (Katz 1956a: 196-7) had eclipsed
Thackeray's earlier hypotheses.

Ironically, in the same year (1956), N. Turner proposed
another variation of the three translator theory. Apparently

unaware of the debate engendered by 967, he contended in an
article entitled "The Greek Translators of Ezekiel" that the
text did indicate the work of three translators. However, he
felt that a different division should be made: 1-25; 26-39;
40-48. He rested his case on grammatical issues such as the
ratio of <<apo>> to <<ek>> and <<en>> to <<eis>>, as well as
on general vocabulary considerations.

Turner also believed that the seeming inconsistencies in
rendering words could indicate the presence of earlier
lectionary passages. He found examples of this in chapters 1,
3, 5, 6, 7, 9, 10, 14, 16, 18, 20, 23, 28, 33, 34, 36, 38, 40
and 44. His view of how the text had come to be was summed up
as follows:

> I suggest that in each of Thackeray's divisions
> there are sections which represent very early
> versions; that these versions, or fragments, were
> adopted and collated by three contemporary
> translators who collaborated to some extent; and
> that in this way, or by means of some subsequent
> editor, a unifying process was applied to the
> whole book. (1956: 23)

3. After Qumran

The caves of Qumran have produced only a few fragments of
the Hebrew text of Ezekiel /8/. However, certain finds in the
Dead Sea area have had at least an indirect influence on
thinking towards the Greek text of the book.

One general result of the Qumran finds was an elevation
of the text-critical value of the LXX. Certain readings

exhibited by Hebrew manuscripts from Qumran seemed to agree
with the LXX against the MT, and hence indicated that a number
of the LXX's differences with the MT might stem from a
different Vorlage rather than from the idiosyncracies of the
translators.

Furthermore, D. Barthélemy's study of the fragments of
the Minor Prophets scroll ("Les Devanciers D'Aquila": 1963)
showed that the Septuagint text had already undergone a
revision by the first century A.D. This literalistic revision
has come to be known as the "Kaige".

Barthélemy's study made a double contribution to
attitudes to the Greek text of Ezekiel. Firstly, it added
weight to theories involving revisions, or partial revisions
of a text. Secondly, Barthélemy himself suggested that the b
section of Ezekiel was to be grouped along with the
translations of part of the Psalms and the second book of
Chronicles as attesting a pre-Kaige recensional approach. He
observed that they had in common the non-systematic attempt
characterise the presence of the Hebrew <<gm>> by the Greek
<<kai gar>> (1963: 47). However, he did not develop his
argument.

Yet the issue of whether or not the book could be divided
up at all had not been fully resolved. I. Soisalon-Soininen,
in his study "Die Infinitive in der Septuaginta" (1965), found
the evidence of the infinitive somewhat ambiguous in this
area:

> One could suppose for Ezekiel two or three
> different, yet closely connected, translators, but
> also one can scarcely dismiss the possibility that
> the book has been worked on by a single
> translator. (1965: 175)

P. D. M. Turner, in her unpublished dissertation "The

16

Septuagint Version of Chapters 1-39 of the Book of Ezekiel"
(1970) /9/, found disunity theories about the text
unconvincing. She isolated 4 sections on the basis of language
and translation technique: ch.1-15 + 25-30.19; ch.17-20; ch.16
+ 21-24; and ch.30.20-39. However, these sections did not
represent different translators but rather where different
sections of the Greek Old Testament had predominant influence.
Turner felt that the change in rendering was occasioned by the
need for variation in such a long text.

After a gap of over 30 years, two more significant
portions of the text of 967 were found, one in Madrid, the
other in Cologne. The Madrid Ezekiel papyrus was published by
M. F. Galiano in 1971 /10/, while the Cologne fragments were
published a year later by L. G. Jahn /11/. This has been all
of the codex that has come to light. Chapters 1-11 are still
absent. There is no indication that 36.23c-38 ever was part of
the text of 967.

These more recently published sections showed the same
strong tendency to use a single <<kurios>> wherever other
textual witnesses (including the MT) showed mostly double
forms. At the same time, the witness of the MT to the double
form was reinforced by the strong attestation of <<'dny>> in
many of the Qumran manuscripts of other biblical books.

The result of the apparent extension of evidence on both
sides was a division of opinion on the origins of the double
divine name. Commentators such as Fohrer, Eichrodt, Wevers,
Taylor and Carley saw it as a late insertion, while Baumgärtel
and Lust defended its originality in the MT. Zimmerli remained
undecided (See Chapter III).

The fluctuation of views over the number of translators
continued. T. Muraoka believed Thackeray to be correct /12/,

while E. Tov, on the other hand, suggested that Ez b' and g'
might possibly represent a revised text. Tov had examined the
issue of the divisions in the Greek text of Jeremiah (1976)
and had come to the conclusion that ch.1-28 of the present
text were Old Greek, while ch.29-52 were a revision of the Old
Greek. He believed that there was a close relationship between
the Septuagint of Jeremiah, Ezekiel and the Minor Prophets:

> The similarities between Jer a', Ez and the MP
> [Minor Prophets] are so striking that we postulate
> with Thackeray that the three books were
> translated by one individual or otherwise by one
> group. (1976: 149)

However, it was Ez a' which exhibited the closest affinity
with Jer a'. Hence Tov suggested:

> The considerable agreement of the OG [Old Greek]
> and the MP with only the first part of Ez can
> hardly be coincidental. Hence, it stands to reason
> that Ez a' reflects the OG of Ez, while the other
> two sections contain a different text type,
> possibly a revision. (1976: 150)

No detailed argument was given. Cf. also Tov 1976: 164, 175
note 33.

The transposition of the chapters in 967 and in Codex W
was re-examined in an article by P.-M. Bogaert (1978a). He
agreed with Kase that 36.23c-38 was absent from W but went on
to argue that the order of the chapters in W was probably the
same as in 967 too.

Another grammatical approach, that of R. Sollamo,
"Renderings of Hebrew Semiprepositions in the Septuagint"
(1979), again was inconclusive. The main reason for this was
the scantiness of the semipreposition material (pp. 278-9).

Historical Background

J. Lust (1981a) combined the suggestions of Thackeray, the witness of 967 and W (according to Bogaert), and the general favourable impression of the LXX caused by Qumran to change what had originally been seen as an inner-Greek problem into a more literary-critical one. He argued that the Hebrew text of Ezekiel originally had the chapter order 36-38-39-37-40, with 36.23c-38 being omitted. Lust believed that 36.23c-38 was a late insertion into the Hebrew text, (cf. Irwin above), added as a bridge between 36 and the newly transposed 37. On the other hand, M. V. Spottorno (1981a) felt that the arrangement and omission in 967 could be at least just as easily explained on the grounds of accidental damage to the text at some early stage.

In surveying the history of study of the Greek text of Ezekiel, we can see that several distinct yet interrelated problems have emerged. The initial issue of the major divisions of the book still remains disputed, although not deeply investigated, with respect both to the demarcation of the sections and to their relationship to each other. A second issue, which has an important bearing on the first, is that of the divine names in Ezekiel. Despite the witness of 967 and the Qumran manuscripts, the problem still has not been satisfactorily resolved. A third issue (which will be given only brief consideration here) is that of the small section 36.23c-38 and its relationship to the rest of the book. This originally played a minor part in Thackeray's considerations, but its importance has grown, as it affects our view of how the Greek text came to be in its present form. The primary concern of this study, however, is still the initial problem raised by Thackeray. It is to the question of how best we might investigate this issue that we now turn.

CHAPTER II

METHODOLOGY

The Principles and Practice of Detecting Different
Translations in a Text

The problem of multiple translators has been investigated
by quite a number of scholars and for many LXX books.
Nevertheless, very little consideration seems to have been
given to the exact principles guiding the investigation. This
omission was noted by H. M. Orlinsky:

> the literature on the subject is now considerable,
> and a critical survey of the discussions and
> methodology of "the two-(and even three-)
> translator" theory of a single Book is now very
> much in order. (1975: 90) /1/

In this chapter at least some aspects of that methodology will
be considered.

Translation Criticism

The whole concept of finding different translations in
a book is based on a somewhat intuitive notion of what we
consider a translation to be. We do not expect it to exhibit
total consistency, yet we do expect it to be consistent to a
least a certain extent. If the nature of the translation
changes sufficiently, then we start to suspect that the work
of a different person has taken over.

The idea of isolating differing sections in a translated
text has to be carefully distinguished from other, somewhat

similar concepts. It is not the same as finding 'sources', which are usually visualised as being woven into the fabric of a text by an editor. Nor is it the same as simply observing the broad translation technique /2/ of a passage, although it is obviously closely related to this. Rather, it relies on observations about translation technique as data for its analysis just as source criticism relies on observations about style and vocabulary as data for its analysis. Thus we can speak of 'translation criticism', as distinct from 'translation technique'.

The function of translation criticism would be to map out areas of a translation which seem to be of a different type from others, rather than to evaluate the nature of the translation as such. It could be defined as the procedure by which we find discontinuities in a translation, and hence delimit different sections. In the process of doing so we also learn something about the relationship of each of these sections to the others. Such a type of criticism is concerned with deciding whether a deviation from the 'usual' or expected rendering has any significance, i.e. whether it has its origins in the translator's inconsistency or whether it points to the work of another person (either a revision or a new translation). It presumes that different translators (or revisers) exhibit different styles, despite the nature of the texts they deal with. Translation criticism has to do primarily with the psychology of the translator, rather than with his philosophy of translation (his preconceived notion of what is the right way of translating), or even with the science of translation as such (the descriptive analysis of the transference of a message from one language to another (Cf. E. A. Nida 1964: 3)).

When we begin to examine how a translated text progresses, we can assess several phenomena:

Methodology

a) Rendering of Vocabulary.

This consists of simply noting how nouns, verbs, adjectives, adverbs, roots, phrases, idioms and such like are rendered in the translated text.

b) Rendering of Grammar.

This is concerned with the rendering of certain noun cases, verbal moods and tenses, prepositions and their governing cases, and so on.

c) Rendering of Word Order.

This deals with how the word order of one language is transferred into another language, taking into account how well the receptor language is able to accommodate this.

d) Vocabulary Usage.

This has to do with the translation's range and frequency of vocabulary with respect to a given range of vocabulary in its Vorlage.

Examination of these four groups of translation features should provide us with evidence to make an assessment about the homogeneity of the translation. However, there are several important factors which must be taken into account when making such an evaluation.

Influencing Factors

1. The Vorlage

    The LXX has one feature which differentiates it sharply from many other works of literature. This is the fact that it is a collection mostly of translated works rather than originals. This means that we must make allowances for the

possibility that changes in the Vorlage were carried over int
the translation. The significance of the appearance or absenc
of certain items of vocabulary in a section of translation
must be evaluated in the light of their "hyponyms" — the word
of the Vorlage underlying those items of vocabulary /3/. For
instance, Thackeray gives 36 examples of translation words an
usages common to the a' and g' portions, but absent from the
b' portion. These are intended "to prove the identity of
translators a' and g'" (1903b: 404). Yet fully one quarter of
these have hyponyms which appear only in a' and g', and not i
b':

⟨2.1⟩ και πιπτω επι προσωπον μου (1.28; 3.23; 9.8; 11.13;
      43.3; 44.4)
⟨2.2⟩ κολασις (14.3,4,7; 18.30; 43.11; 44.12)
⟨2.3⟩ εκδυνειν (16.39; 23.26; 26.16; 44.19)
⟨2.4⟩ αιθριον (9.3; 10.4; 10.18; 40.14,15,15,19,19; 47.1)
⟨2.5⟩ οψις (1.13,27; 10.9,9,10; 23.15; 41.21)
⟨2.6⟩ ορασις (1.1,4,5,13,22,26,27,27,27,28,28; 3.23; 7.26;
      8.2,3,4; 11.24,24; 12.22,23,24,27; 13.7; 21.34; 23.16;
      40.2,3; 41.21; 43.3,3,3,3,10)
⟨2.7⟩ συντελειν (4.6,8; 5.13,13; 6.12; 7.8; 13.15;
      20.8,21; 22.31; 42.15; 43.23)
⟨2.8⟩ παραπικραινειν (2.3,3,5,6,7,8,8; 3.9,26,27; 12.2,39,25,
      27; 17.12; 20.21; 24.3,14; 44.6)
⟨2.9⟩ πυλη (8.3,5,14; 9.2; 10.19; 11.1,1; 21.20,27;
      26.10; more than 80 times in 40–48)

(In ⟨2.4⟩ the identification of some of the hyponyms — apart
from ⟨⟨mptn⟩⟩ — in 40–48 is uncertain). These examples are
really arguments from silence. They give us no indication of
their uniqueness and hence no indication of their
significance. Cf. factor 5 below.

Methodology

Again, in order to show the features peculiar to b',
Thackeray presents us with a list of 16 Greek words and
expressions occurring in the b' section but absent in the
others (1903b: 403). Three of these are:

<2.10> γιγας (32.12,21,27,27; 39.18,20)
<2.11> κατεργαζεσθαι (34.4; 36.9)
<2.12> ταρασσειν (30.16; 32.2,13; 34.18,19)

Yet these examples represent Hebrew words which are found
exclusively in ch.28-39 of Ezekiel. Their value as evidence to
distinguish b' from a' and g' must be rated as low.

Another illustration can be seen in the use of <<dioti>>.
N. Turner (1956: 14) adduces as further evidence that a' and
g' were by different translators the fact that the declarative
particle <<dioti>> (used in indirect speech) is frequent in Ez
a' but quite absent from g'. Apart from textual considerations
(see ex. <5.2> in ch.V), there is the crucial matter that
there are no occasions in the Hebrew text of 40-48 where a
declarative clause is used.

It must be remembered too that we do not have the
Septuagint Vorlage. Normally, with frequently recurring terms,
use of the MT as a substitute may be acceptable. However, with
rare or unusual renderings, care must be taken to see that
they do come from a reading identical to that exhibited by the
MT. A possible example of where the translator's Vorlage may
have differed from the MT is found below, where we note the
contrast between the LXX rendering in 43.3 and the renderings
in the other verses /4/:

The Greek Text of Ezekiel

<2.13> שחת (.)/. g/.ה)

5.16	לשחיתכם	< >	διαφθειραι υμας (2-4,6
9.8	המשחית	ει εξαλειφεις	εξαλειψεις (3)/ εις εξαλειψιν (2,6)
16.47	ותשחתי	και υπερκεισαι	–
20.17	משחתם	του εξαλειψαι αυτους	–
20.44	הנשחתות	τα διεφθαρμενα	–
22.30	שחתה	εξαλειψαι αυτην //	–
23.11	ותשחת	και διεφθειρε	διεφθειραν (2)/ εφθειρεν (4)
26.4	ושחתו	και καταβαλουσι	–
28.17	שחת	διεφθαρη	(και) εφθαρη (2,4)
30.11	לשחת	απολεσαι	// αφανισαι (2)
43.3	לשחת	του χρισαι	–

<<khriein>> has almost invariably the verb <<mšḥ>> (to anoint) as its hyponym throughout the LXX. The distinctive use of <<khrisai>> here may then possibly reflect a different Vorlage, perhaps the reading <<lmšḥ>>, rather than a different translation technique.

The effect of the Vorlage is the one factor which, more than any other, places translation criticism of the LXX outside the bounds of many of the more recently developed stylometric methods of text analysis. The emergence of computer-assisted stylistics has created a wide range of authorship identification tests /5/. These tests usually involve a statistical analysis of the text, the results of which are compared with those of a control case, i.e. a text whose author, date, etc., are known definitely. The closeness of both sets of results gives an indication of the probability that the authorship of a disputed work should be ascribed to, say, writer A rather than writer B. However, with the LXX it would be necessary to calculate how many of the characteristics of the original were carried over into the

translation. (See also <2> below). In addition to this
problem, we do not have a wide range of control cases for the
LXX. That is to say, we do not have examples of thoroughly
investigated translation Greek whose statistical stylistic
features are well attested and understood. Furthermore, most
statistical tests operate on discrete units of text, and do
not normally deal with the problem of making the initial
decision of where to separate a single text into separate
blocks /6/.

2. Context

This should be distinguished from the effect of the
Vorlage, although it certainly depends on the text behind the
translation. What was envisaged in the discussion of the
effect of the Vorlage was the change in its content in terms
of vocabulary, grammar and syntax. The effect of context, on
the other hand, is that feature whereby a change in
subject-matter can change the meaning or connotation of
certain words. For example, we find in Ezekiel the following
translation change (cited also by Turner 1956: 15):

<2.14>   כתף

12.6	עַל־כָּתֵף	επ ωμων	−
12.7	עַל־כָּתֵף	επ ωμων	−
12.12	אֶל־כָּתֵף	επ ωμων	−
24.4	וְכָתֵף	και ωμον	αμμον (3)
25.9	אֶת־כָּתֵף	τον ωμον	οικον (2,5)/ νομον (2,3)
29.7	כָּל־כָּתֵף	πασα χειρ	−
29.18	וְכָל־כָּתֵף	και πας ωμος	−
34.21	וּבְכָתֵף	και τοις ωμοις υμων	−
40.18	אֶל־כָּתֵף	κατα νωτου //	και τα νωτα (4)/ κατα νωτον (3,6)
40.40	וְכָתֵף	και κατα νωτου //	−
40.40	וְכָתֵף	και κατα νωτου //	οκτω (4)
40.41	לַכָּתֵף	κατα νωτου //	−

27

40.44	אל-כתף	κατα νωτου //	νοτον // (2)
40.44	אל-כתף	κατα νωτου	νοτον // (2)
41.2	וכתפות	και επωμιδες	αι. επ. (5)
41.26	אל-כתפות	εις τα οροφωματα //	τα οροφωτα (6)/ το οροφωμα (2)
46.19	צל-כתף	κατα νωτου	<> (4)
47.1 מכתף הבית	απο του κλιτους	κλιτου (3)/ α. τ. κλ. του οικου (3,4)
47.2	מן-הכתף	απο του κλιτους	—

The change in translation at 40.18 is quite marked. Yet this example loses its force when the context of the word <<ktp>> is examined. In all the cases before ch.40 the word was used to depict the side or shoulder of a person or being, but from ch.40 onwards it is used to describe part of a building. The LXX has faithfully mirrored this change of context.

Another instance of the influence of context is found in the use of the word <<'p>>:

<2.15> אף

5.13	אפי	ο θυμος μου	—
5.15	באף	//	εν οργη (μου) (2-6)
7.3	אפי	εγω	ε. τον θυμον μου (3,4)/ εκει (6)/ <> (3,5)
7.8	אפי	τον θυμον μου	—
8.17	שלחים את המורה אל-אפם	ως μυκτηριζοντες	μυκτηριζοντος (5)/ ω. μ. με (3,4)
13.13	באפי	εν οργη μου	ε. ο. θυμου (3)
16.12	על-אפך	περι τον μυκτηρα σου	π. των μυκτηρων (2)/ π. τα ωτα (5)
20.8	אפי	οργην μου	—
20.21	אפי	την οργην μου	—
22.20	באפי	// εν οργη μου	—
23.25	אפך	θυμου μυκτηρα σου //	μου (2,5)/ θυμου μου (1-4)/ -ρας (1-5)/ τους -ρας (4)

25.14	באפי	κατα την οργην μου	κ. τ. ο. του θυμου μου (2,3)
35.11	באפך	//	//
38.18	באפי	// <>	εν οργη μου (1-4,6)/ και η οργη μου (4)
43.8	באפי	εν θυμω μου	—

If we leave aside the unusual rendering in 8.17 we find that chapters 16 and 23 seem to agree against the rest of the LXX renderings, which usually denote "anger". However, in both these chapters the sense the context clearly demands of <<'p>> is "nose", not "anger". This the LXX has accurately expressed. Thus the 'deviations' from the norm in this case cannot be taken as pointing to the later insertion of ch.16 or 23 (cf. chapter VII however).

Again, N. Turner provides us with the following ratios of prepositions in Ezekiel:

<2.16>	α	β	γ
απο : εκ	0.8:1	1.7:1	1.8:1

(1956: 14 /7/)

Apart from the problem of evaluating the statistical significance of such figures (see below), the question must be asked as to what exactly they reflect. While it is quite possible that they point to differing translation styles, it is also possible that they mirror a change in the context. Indeed, even if such sections were shown to be the work of different translators, the evidence presented above would still need to be evaluated in the light of what the prepositions actually represented.

Turner assumed that the choice between <<apo>> and <<ek>> was largely a matter of individual style. Hence he saw the

difference between a' and g' as more support for his
hypothesis that the two sections were the work of different
translators. It is true that in most cases both prepositions
have the Hebrew preposition <<mn>> as their hyponym. Yet the
choice of <<apo>> or <<ek>> does not seem arbitrary. In 40-48
there is still a distinct preference for <<apo>> in a
geographical description — "from place A (to place B)". It
happens that ch.47-48 abound with such descriptions, with the
result that <<apo>> appears 41 times and <<ek>> only 7 times
in these two chapters. It is the figures from these last two
chapters which have skewed the ratios given by Turner. If we
assume that 40-46 is a more representative sample, we get the
following ratio:

$$απο : εκ = 30:33 = 0.9:1$$

which is very close to that of a'. However, the point here is
that the context has a strong effect on the choice of <<apo>>
and <<ek>>. Hence the ratios given above may simply reflect
changes in the context in which <<mn>> is used, rather than
indicate agreement or difference in translation technique.

3. Textual Integrity

The issue of how much scribal alteration has distorted
our evidence has been at the heart of arguments over multiple
translators in Ezekiel. The possibility that the translated
text could have been sporadically changed certainly cannot be
ruled out. This means that any collection of data regarding
change in translation must take into account the variation in
textual evidence. Thackeray and Herrmann usually relied on the
witness of B, A and Q. Their work needs to be re-evaluated in
the light of P.967 and the rest of the textual evidence
presented by Ziegler's edition. It must be borne in mind also
that there might have been a substantial degree of

(non-recensional) alteration which could have occurred at such
an early stage that it would have infected our entire
manuscript tradition. In order to detect and minimise the
effect of this, it would be of value to note what type of
lexical form is subject to alteration in the textual witnesses
we have. This might give an indication of what class of forms
would be more susceptible to scribal alteration than others.
These forms would hence be less valuable as witnesses to
translation change. One notable example of this type of
alteration might be transliterations. Thackeray's decision to
delimit his section a' at the end of ch.27 was strongly
influenced by the way the Greek changes from transliterating
to translating the Hebrew word for Tyre (1903b: 400, 406). Yet
if we note the variants for this, as did Kase (1938: 70-72),
we see the following:

<2.17> צר/צור

26.2	צר	σορ	—
26.3	צר	σορ	<> (1)
26.4	צר	σορ	σου (1-4)/ σου σωρ (1)
26.7	צר	σορ	<> (2)
26.15	לצור	τη σορ	χη σορ (5)/ της σωρ (4)/ επι σορ (1,2) επι σοι (2)/ επι σε σορ (1,2)/ <τη σορ> (2)
27.2	על-צר	επι σορ	<> (2)
27.3	לצור	τη σορ	<> (2,4)
27.3	צור	τη σορ	επι σε σορ (1,2)/ επι τη σορ (1,2)/ τη επι σορ (2)
27.8	צור	σορ	—
27.32	כצור	σορ //	τυρου (1)/ σοι (1-3,5)/ σου επι σε (3)/ επι σε (3) //
28.2	צר	τυρου	—
28.12	צור	τυρου	σορ (6)//
29.18	אל-צר	επι τυρον	τυρω (4)/ τυρου (1-3,5,6)
29.18	מצר	επι τυρον	τυρω (4)/ τυρου (4)

The contribution of 967 here was the reading <<turou>> in
27.32. It might be further noted that Tertullian implies the
reading <<sor>> at 28.12. These two readings certainly weaken
the example and raise the possibility that originally the on
rendering for "Tyre" in these chapters was the transliteratio
<<sor>>. The form <<turos>> might have been a later
alteration. If this were so, then the use of this example
would be invalid.

P. 967 affords another instance of the variation between
transliteration and translation:

<2.18> מנחה

42.13	והמנחה	και την θυσιαν	και τας θυσιας (3,6)/ τα τε (δε) δωρα και τ. θ. (4)
44.29	המנחה	και τας θυσιας	−
45.15	המנחה	εις θυσιας	θυσιαν (3,4)
45.17	למנחה	και αι θυσιαι	−
45.17	והמנחה	και την θυσιαν	<> (1,6)
45.24	ומנחה-את	και θυσιαν	−
45.25	ומנחה	και καθως το μαναα	<> (2)/ τα μαναα (2,3,5) μαννα (1,2,4,5)/ αι θυσιαι (1)
46.5	ומנחה	και μαναα	και θυσιαν (1,3)/ μαννα (1−3)
46.5	מנחה	θυσιαν	θυσια (5)/ <> (1,4)
46.7	מנחה	μαναα	μαννα (1−3)/ μανα (2)/ θυσια (1,4)
46.11	המנחה	το μαναα	το μαννα (2,3)/ θυσια (1,4)
46.14	ומנחה	και μαναα	μαννα (2,3)/ θυσιαν (1)
46.14	מנחה	μαναα	μαννα (2,3)/ θυσιαν (1)
46.15	ואת-המנחה	και το μαναα	μαννα (2,3)/ μανα (3) μαα (5)/ την θυσιαν (1)
46.20	את-המנחה	το μαναα	μαννα (1,2,3)

Methodology

In all instances save one (46.20), 967 reads <<thusia>>,
sometimes alone (45.25; 46.14,14,15), sometimes in conjunction
with other MSS (46.5,7,11). Regardless of which reading is to
be preferred, the fact is that we have evidence of variation
in MSS between transliteration and translation. This raises
the possibility that transliterations might well be more
susceptible to scribal alteration than some other forms.
Because of this their testimony in translation criticism is
weakened.

Another type of lexical form which is susceptible to
alteration seems to be certain prepositions. Turner saw the
oscillation between <<peri hamartias>> and <<huper hamartias>>
(and <<peri agnoias>> and <<huper agnoias>> also) as a
striking instance of the different strata within the Greek
translation of Ezekiel:

> One cannot conceive that a single translator would
> deliberately perpetrate such a meaningless
> variety, and the alternatives are within too small
> a space to be lapsus memoriae. This is true of all
> the evidence given above. We have either imperfect
> revision - an attempt here to eliminate <<huper>>
> - or else conflation of two or more earlier
> translations. The later seems more probable ...
> (1956: 23)

Yet if we look at the translations and their variants we find
the following:

<2.19> חטאת

3.20	בחטאתו	και εν ταις αμαρτιαις αυτου	-
16.51	חטאתיך	των αμαρτιων σου	-
16.52	בחטאתיך	εν ταις αμαρτιαις σου	-
18.14	את־כל־חטאת	πασας τας αμαρτιας	-
18.21	מכל־חטאתיו	εκ πασων των ανομιων αυτου	-

18.24	ובחטאתיו	και εν ταις αμαρτιαις αυτου	–
21.29	חטאותיכם	αμαρτιας υμων	τας αμαρ. (3-5)
33.10	וחטאתינו	και αι ανομιαι ημων	
33.14	מחטאתו	απο της αμαρτιας αυτου	ασεβειας (2)/ ανομιας (4)
33.16	כל-חטאתיו	πασαι αι αμαρτιαι αυτου	–
40.39	והחטאת	τα υπερ αμαρτιας	περι (2,5,6)
42.13	החטאת	και τα περι αμαρτιας	υπερ (4,6)
43.19	לחטאת	περι αμαρτιας	–
43.21	החטאת	τον περι αμαρτιας	υπερ (1-6)
43.22	לחטאת	υπερ αμαρτιας	περι (1,6)
43.25	חטאת	υπερ αμαρτιας	περι (3,4,5)
44.27	חטאתו	ιλασμον	(το) περι του ιλ. αυτου (4)
44.29	והחטאת	και τα υπερ αμαρτιας	–
45.17	את-החטאת	τα υπερ αμαρτιας	περι (1)
45.19	החטאת	του εξιλασμου	ιλασμου (3)/ μοσχου (1)
45.22	חטאת	υπερ αμαρτιας	περι (4)
45.23	חטאת	και υπερ αμαρτιας	περι (1)
45.25	כחטאת	καθως τα υπερ της αμαρτιας	⟨τα⟩ (1,3,4)
46.20	את-החטאת	και τα υπερ αμαρτιας	⟨τα⟩ (3)/ υπερ της αμ. (1-6)

The translation change at ch.40 is easily justifiable on the
basis that the context demands the meaning "sin-offering"
rather that just "sin". If we look at the attestation of
<<peri>> and <<huper>>, we find that in many instances there
is strong evidence for either reading, e.g. 40.39; 43.21,22;
45.17,23. It may possibly have been the case that the text ha
a uniform reading at one stage. The degree of variation shoul
make us hesitate to lay much stress on the use of <<peri>> ar
<<huper>> for the origins of our Greek text.

The strength of the witness of the divine names depends
on the factor of textual integrity too. However, because thi
issue turns out to be more complicated than the examples

discussed here, it will be dealt with separately in chapters
III and IV.

4. Distribution and Frequency

When examining a translation it is obviously necessary to
have at least one example in each suspected section in order
that a comparison may be made. It would be even more desirable
to have several examples, as this would strengthen the
evidence. Yet certain distributions (for a given number of
occurrences) are of less value as evidence than others. For
instance, let us consider a distribution such as the following
(cited as a significant example by Herrmann 1923: 16-17):

<2.20> דלת

26.2	דלתות	//	—
38.11	ודלתים	και θυραι	θυρεοι (1)/ θυραιοι (3,5)
41.23	דלתות	θυρωματα	—
41.24	דלתות	θυρωματα	<> (1,4)
41.24	לדלתות	τοις ... θυρωμασι	δε ... θυρωματα (4)
41.24	דלתות	θυρωματα	—
41.24	לדלת	τω ενι	—
41.24	דלתות	θυρωματα	—
41.25	אל-הדלתות	επι τα θυρωματα	—

Despite the fact that there is a reasonable number of
occurrences in all, the evidence from this example is (as it
stands) quite weak. A translator might not have fixed on a
definite rendering of the word <<dlt>>. On encountering it the
first time, he would have selected a suitable Greek
equivalent. By the time he would have come to ch.41, he might
have forgotten his initial choice and have selected a second
equivalent. This he would have retained because the Hebrew
<<dlt>> then appeared quite frequently within the space of a

few verses. The example would have been stronger if there ha
been more occurrences of <<dlt>> in b'.

It would have been stronger still if the occurrences of
<<dlt>> in 40-48 had been more widespread. The close proximi
of several of the same Hebrew terms can have two, almost
opposite effects. These may stem from the translator becomin
more conscious that he is rendering the same term several
times over. On the one hand he may opt to use the same
rendering consistently for that group of occurrences, even
though he might use a different rendering elsewhere. This
would mean that a set of closely grouped renderings may not I
any more significant than a single rendering, even if such
renderings deviate from the norm. On the other hand, the
translator may opt to render closely occurring instances of
the same term each by a different expression, possibly out o
stylistic considerations. The phenomenon of several differine
renderings of the same expression appearing close together h
been noted before by Ziegler (1934: 14-16) and Tov (1976: 27
among others.

If we expect a translator to be inconsistent, then the
more frequently a term occurs in the Vorlage, the more likel
is the possibility that "deviating" translations will occur
too. Hence it is important to take note of the frequency of
occurrence of certain translations. For example, Turner (195
14) cites the translation of <<'kl>> as showing that g' had
different translator from a' and b':

Hebrew	Method in a' and b'	Method in g'
אכל	εσθιω, κατεσθιω, βιβρωσκω,	εσθιω
	αναλισκω, συντελεω, εις	
	καταβρωμα, εις αναλωσιν	

From this it might seem that g' differentiates itself clearl

36

Methodology

from a' and b' by its consistent use of <<esthiein>>. Yet if we look at the distribution and frequency of the terms the distinction fades:

<2.21> אכל

2.8	ואכל	και φαγε	καταφαγε (4)
3.1	אכול אכול	καταφαγε	φαγε καταφαγε (3)
3.3	תכלה	φαγεται	-
3.3	ואכלה	και εφαγον αυτην	-
4.9	תאכלו	φαγεσαι αυτα	(και) φαγεσθαι (4)
4.10	תאכלו	φαγεσαι	φαγεται (4)/ φαγε (3)
4.10	תאכלו	φαγεσαι	-
4.12	תאכלנה	φαγεσαι αυτα	-
4.13	יאכלו	φαγονται	-
4.14	אכלתי	βεβρωκα	εφαγον (4)
4.16	ואכלו	και φαγονται	-
5.10	יאכלו	φαγονται	-
5.10	יאכלו	φαγονται	-
7.15	יאכלו	συντελεσει	τελευτησουσιν (2-5)
12.18	תאכל	φαγεσαι	φαγη (4)/ φαγε (4)
12.19	יאכלו	φαγονται	-
15.4	אכלה	αναλισκει	αναλισκειν (2)/ αφανιζει (4)
15.5	אכלתה	αυτο αναλωση	-
15.7	תאכלם	αυτους κατα-φαγεται	κ. α. (2-4)
16.13	אכלת	εφαγες	-
16.20	לאכול	εις αναλωσις	-
18.2	יאכלו	εφαγον	-
18.6	אכל	φαγεται	εφαγεν (6)
18.11	אכל	εφαγε	-
18.15	אכל	βεβρωκε	βρουση (5)/ εφαγε(ν) (2)
19.3	אכל	εφαγε	-
19.6	אכל	εφαγε	-
19.12	אכלתה	ανηλωσεν αυτην	ανηλωσαν (1)

19.14	אכלה	και κατεφαγεν αυτην	καταφαγεται α. (4)
21.3	ואכלה	και κατεφαγεται	–
22.9	אכלו	ησθοσαν	ησθιοσαν (4)/ εσθωσαν (3) ιστασαι (4)/ ησθιον (1-6)
22.25	אכלו	κατεσθιοντες	κατεσθοντες (1,3)
24.17	תאכל	φαγης	φαγη (4)/ φαγεσε (2)
24.22	תאכלו	φαγεσθε	φαγησθαι (2)/ φαγεσαι (2)
25.4	יאכלו	φαγονται	–
28.18	תאכלן	καταφαγεται σε	–
33.25	תאכלו	< >	φαγεσθε (2-6)
33.27	לאכלו	εις καταβρωμα	καταβρωσιν (3)
34.3	תאכלו	κατεσθιετε	κατεσθετε (1)/ εξεπιετε (1, 2,6)/ κατησθιετε (2,4)
34.28	תאכלם	φαγωσιν αυτους	φαγη α. (4)/ φανωσιν αυτοις (3)/ πτοηση αυτους (2)
36.14	תאכלי	φαγεσαι	καταφαγεσαι (1)/ φαγεσθε (3, 5)
39.17	ואכלתם	και φαγεσθε	–
39.18	תאכלו	φαγεσθε	–
39.19	ואכלתם	φαγεσθε	–
42.13	יאכלו	φαγονται	στανονται (1)
44.3	לאכול	του φαγειν	–
44.29	יאכלום	φαγονται	–
44.31	יאכלו	φαγονται	–

Here we see that <<'kl>> is most frequently rendered
throughout Ezekiel by <<esthien>>, or, to be more exact, by
forms using the <<-phag->> root. The fact that the Hebrew ver
only occurs four times in 40-48 means that we cannot say tha
g' shows any significant deviation from the pattern in the
rest of the book. This example is thus of no value for
distinguishing g' from a' or b'.

A frequently occurring, well distributed word is to be
preferred over a larger phrase as evidence of translation
change. The problem is that while the phrase itself might
occur only a few times, its components might occur frequentl

Methodology

and so have variations in their own rendering. The context of the phrase might not be sufficient to "fix" a particular translation equivalent for each of its components. Danielsmeyer not infrequently uses phrases as translation examples. One of these examples is <<ntn l'klh>>, of which he cites three instances:

15.4   לאש נתן לאכלה = πυρι δεδοται εις αναλωσιν

15.6   אשר-נתתיו לאש לאכלה = ο δεδωκα αυτο τω πυρι εις αναλωσιν

33.27   לחיה נתתיו לאכלו = τοις θηριοις ... δεδοται εις καταβρωμα

Danielsmeyer concludes that the translation techniques of a' and b' were:

α: נתן לאכלה = διδοναι εις αναλωσιν

β: .   .   = διδοναι εις καταβρωμα   (1936: 20)

Yet if the word <<'klh> is examined on its own a different picture emerges:

<2.22> אכלה

15.4	לאכלה	εις αναλωσιν	—
15.6	לאכלה	εις αναλωσιν	—
21.27	לאכלה	καταβρωμα	—
23.37	לאכלה	δι εμπυρων	δια εμπυρω (2)/ δι εμπυρωσεως (4)/ δια πυρωσεως (5)/ εν πυρι (1)/ δια πυρος (3-6)
29.5	לאכלה	εις καταβρωμα	ε. βρωσιν (2)/ ε. βρωμα (5)
34.5	לאכלה	εις καταβρωμα	—
34.8	לאכלה	εις καταβρωμα	ε. καταβρωσιν (3)
34.10	לאכלה	εις καταβρωμα	ε. κατακριμα (3)
35.12	לאכלה	εις καταβρωμα	ε. κατασχεσιν (2,4)
39.4	לאכלה	εις καταβρωμα	ε. καταβρωσιν (4)/ καταβρωθηναι (1-6)/ ε. κ. καταβρωθηναι (2)/ ε. κ. καταστρωθηναι (5)

(Cf. the rendering of 33.27 in ex. <2.21> above). The
difference between a' and b' is diminished by the appearance
of <<katabròma>> in 21.37. This is further reduced when we
find that <<'klh>> is used here in a similar sense — "fuel"
for fire — to that in 15.4,6 and 33.27.

This case does not show that the use of phrases to
indicate difference of translation technique is invalid. But
it does demonstrate that components of a phrase should be
examined individually as well.

5. The Translator's Vocabulary

Consideration must be given to the lexical stock of the
receptor language and to how it is linked to the lexical stoc
of the source language. The translator's vocabulary is
dictated not only by the material on which he works, but also
by the conventions and resources of the language into which I
translates. Certain agreements and disagreements in the
renderings of a given term can have less significance than
others. For example, the fact that in both of two suspected
sections <<byt>> is translated by <<oikos>> is very little
support for seeing the work of the same person in both
sections. This is because the rendering of <<byt>> by
<<oikos>> is common throughout the LXX (Camilo dos Santos
1973: 25). Words which have a stereotyped rendering in the L
are of little value here.

If we expect different translations to differ at times
their rendering of a given word or phrase, then we should al
expect (because of the limitations of the size and range of
the translators' lexical stock) that sometimes a term sharec
by the translations will have different hyponyms. In this ca
the seemingly uniform use of a term may mask a change in the
hyponyms. For example:

Methodology

<2.23> διασπειρειν

1.17	ויצפום	διεσπειρα αυτους	διεσκορπισα (4)
2.14	אזרה	διασπερω	–
2.15	והריתי	και διασπερω	διασπειραι (2,3,5)
7.21	ישרפו	διασπερω	–
2.15	והריתיך	και διασπερω σε	–
9.12	והצפתי	και διασπερω	–
0.23	והפיצותי	διασπερω	–
0.26	והפיצותי	διασπερω	διασκορπιω (4)
2.15	בהכתי	οταν διασπειρω	διασπερω (3-5)
4.5	ותצפינה	και διεσπαρη	διεσπαρησαν (2,4)
4.6	ותצפינה	και διεσπαρη	διεσπαρησαν (2)
4.6	נצפו	διεσπαρη	–
4.12	נצפו	διεσπαρησαν	–
6.19	ואפיץ	και διεσπειρα	διεσκορπισα (4)

The pattern of uniformity suggested by the occurrence of <diaspeirein>> in both a' and b' sections becomes less clear when we see that <<diaspeirein>> sometimes has the hyponym <zrh>> in a' but not in b', even though <<zrh>> appears in b' too. The significance of this change, however, needs to be evaluated in the light of (among other things) the translation of the Hebrew synonyms for "to scatter" before any strong inference can be drawn. (Cf. also the translations of <<zrh>> and the "sin" vocabulary in chapter V).

The occurrence of a supposedly "unusual" phrase or word shared by two different sections of translation must also be treated carefully. Some of the vocabulary Thackeray had listed to prove the identity of the translators of a' and g' is of this type. A few examples are:

<2.24> κομη :

       (24.23) και αι κομαι υμων — ופארכם

       (44.20) και τας κομας αυτων — ופרע

<2.25> ξιπλασιαζειν :

       (21.19) και ξιπλασιασον ρομφαιαν — ותכפל חרב

       (43.2)   ως φωνη ξιπλασιαζοντων   — כקול מים

<2.26> παρεξ :

  (15.14)   παρεξ πυρι — הנה לאש

  (42.19) ουκ εισελευσονται εκει παρεξ των ιερων — מ֞ הכהנים

(All the occurrences of the Greek words are given). It may b
the case here that one translator was relying on his stock
words and phrases, using them even when the hyponyms differe
However, it is equally plausible to suggest that two differ
translators happened by coincidence to choose the same few
words when confronted with quite different expressions. A f
instances out of the several hundred translation examples
which could be found in even a short text would not be
improbable.

Again, the occurrence of an "unusual" form in each of
sections, even with the same hyponyms, may have other
explanations. If someone uses an expression which seems
unusual, but was nevertheless extant in a language for a
period, then it would not be surprising to find a contempor
using it as well. Indeed, if contemporaneous translators
discussed some of the more difficult constructions in a tex
then we might expect to find some agreement in renderings.

When it comes to illustrating differences between
sections, a 'mistranslation' has to be evaluated carefully.
must ask what exactly the translator wanted his Greek
rendering to mean. There exists the possibility that he mean

omething quite different from its New Testament or classical
ense. It may even be that he was simply using a term as a
filler" for a Hebrew word which was obscure.

. Progression of Translation

'Progression of translation' is the concept of how a
ranslator develops and alters his approach to a text as he
rogresses in his translation of it. The question asked here
s how, if at all, we might expect a translator to differ in
is rendering of two near identical passages, say, thirty
hapters apart. It might well be argued that a translator does
ot change his style or vocabulary essentially in the course
f translation, or that, if he does, the change is so small or
o random or so subtle as to be valueless as a factor to be
onsidered. It would be easy also to postulate complications
uch as the translator's own revision of his work or the
ossibility that he did not start at the beginning of the
ext. Nevertheless, it is still legitimate to ask if any such
hanges can be detected. After all, it seems acceptable to say
hat translators, being human, are inconsistent to some
egree. (This applies even to Aquila). It is a simple
xtension from this statement to consider the manner in which
hey are inconsistent, and to ask is there is any discernible
rend or consistency in their inconsistency.

Sometimes it is possible to see where a translator seems
o change his mind about a particular translation equivalent.
he translation of <<tw'bh>> in the first half of Ezekiel
ppears to be one such example:

<2.27> תועבה

5.9	כל-תועבתיך	παντα τα βδελυγματα σου	—
5.11	ובכל-תועבתיך	εν πασι τοις βδελυγ-μασι σου	—
6.9	לכל תועבתיהם	εν πασι τοις βδελυγ-μασιν αυτων	—
6.11	כל-תועבות	πασι τοις βδελυγ-μασιν	—
7.3	את כל-תועבתיך	παντα τα βδελυγματα σου	—
7.4	ותועבותיך	και τα βδελυγματα σου	—
7.8	תא כל-תועבותיך	παντα τα βδελυγματα σου	—
7.9	ותועבותיך	και τα βδελυγματα σου	—
7.20	תועבתם	των βδελυγματων αυτων	—
8.6	תועבות	ανομιας	—
8.6	תועבות	ανομιας	αμαρτιας (2)
8.9	את-התועבות	τας ανομιας	—
8.13	תועבות	ανομιας	—
8.15	תועבות	επιτηδευματα	—
8.17	את-התועבות	τας ανομιας	συν τας ανομιας (3)
9.4	על כל-התועבות	επι πασαις ταις ανομιαις	επι πασας τα ανομιας (4)
11.18	ואת-כל-תועבותיה	και πασας τας ανομιας αυτης	ασεβειας (4)
11.21	ותועבותיהם	και των ανομιων αυτων	—

	Hebrew	Greek	Variants
12.16	את-כל-תועבותיהם	πασας τας ανομιας αυτων	–
14.6	כל-תועבתיכם	πασων των ασεβειων υμων	αδικιων (3,5)
16.2	את-תועבתיה	τας ανομιας αυτης	αμαρτιας (6)
16.22	כל-תועבתיך	<>	και τα βδελυγ-ματα σου (1-6)
16.36	תועבותיך	των ανομιων σου	–
16.43	על כל-תועבתיך	επι πασαις ταις ανομιαις σου	–
16.47	ובתועבותיהן	κατα τας ανομιας αυτων	–
16.50	תועבה	ανομηματα	ανομημα (1,2)/ ανομα (2)
16.51	את-תועבותיך	τας ανομιας σου	αμαρτιας (1-3, 5)/ ασεβειας
16.51	בכל-תועבותיך	εν πασαις ταις ανομιαις σου	αμαρτιαις (4)
16.58	ואת-תועבותיך	και τας ανομιας σου	ταις ανομιαις σου (2,3,5)/ ταις ασεβειαις (5)
18.12	תועבה	ανομιαν	–
18.13	את כל-התועבות	πασας τας ανομιας	–
18.24	ככל התועבות	κατα πασας τας ανομιας	κ. π. τας αδικιας (2-5)
20.4	תועבת	τας ανομιας	αμαρτιας (2-6)
22.2	כל-תועבותיה	πασας τας ανομιας αυτης	αμαρτιας (2, 4-6)
22.11	עשה תועבה	ηνομουσαν	ηνομουν (1,3,4) / ηνομησαν (4)
23.36	תועבותיהן	τας ανομιας αυτων	–

33.26	תועבה	<>	βδελυγμα (2-6 βδελυγματα (2 5)
33.29	על כל-תועבתם	δια παντα τα βδελυγ- ματα αυτων	—
36.31	ועל תועבותיכם	και εν τοις βδελυγ- μασιν αυτων	επι τ. β. (1, / περι τ. β. (4)/ περι τοι βδελλυριων (4
43.8	בתועבותם	εν ταις ανομιαις αυτων	—
44.6	מכל-תועבותיכם	απο πασων των ανομιων υμων	—
44.7	אל כל-תועבתיכם	εν πασαις ταις ανομιαις υμων	—
44.13	ותועבותם	εν τη πλανησει //	και τα βδελυγ ματα εαυτων (

From ch.5 to ch.7 <<bdelugma>> was preferred. Then <<anomia>>
is used for the next 16 or so chapters. This change does not
seem to be paralleled by any other translation change at the
same point and appears to be a case of where the translator
changed his mind.

Another type of example, which perhaps appears slightly
more frequently, is that of a gradual swing in preference to
one out of several options. This can be seen in the case of
<<glwl>>:

גלול   <2.28>

6.4	גלוליכם	των ειδωλων υμων	—
6.5	גלוליהם	<>	των ειδωλων αυτ (2-6)
6.6	גלוליכם	τα ειδωλα υμων	—
6.9	גלוליהם	των επιτηδευματων	ειδωλων (3)

6.13	גלוליהם	των ειδωλων υμων	-
6.13	גלוליהם	τοις ειδωλοις υμων	-
8.10	גלולי	τα ειδωλα	-
14.3	גלוליהם	τα διανοηματα αυτων	-
14.4	את-גלוליו	τα διανοηματα αυτου	νοηματα (4)
14.4	גלוליו	η διανοια αυτου	-
14.5	בגלוליהם	εν τοις ενθυμημασιν	επιθυμ. (3,5)
14.6	גלוליכם	των επιτηδευματων υμων	-
14.7	גלוליו	τα ενθυμηματα αυτου	διανοηματα (3)
16.36	כל-גלולי	παντα τα ενθυμηματα	επιθυμ. (4,5)
18.6	אל-גלולי	προς τα ενθυμηματα	επιθυμ. (4)/ ειδωλα (1,3-6)
18.12	ואל-הגלולים	και εις τα ειδωλα	-
18.15	אל-גלולי	εις τα ενθυμηματα	επιθυμ. (5)
20.7	ובגלולי	και εν τοις ενθυμηματα	-
20.8	ואת-גלולי	και τα επιτηδευματα	βδελυγματα (5)
20.18	ובגלוליהם	και εν τοις επιτηδευμασιν αυτων	-
20.24	גלולי	των ενθυμηματων	επιθυμ. (2)/ επιθυμιων (5)
20.31	לכל-גלוליכם	εν πασι τοις ενθυμημασιν υμων	επιτηδευμασιν (3)
20.39	גלוליו	τα επιτηδευματα	-
20.39	ובגלוליכם	και εν τοις επιτηδευμασιν υμων	-
22.3	גלולים	ενθυμηματα	-
22.4	ובגלוליך	και εν τοις ενθυμημασι σου	-
23.7	בכל-גלוליה	εν πασι τοις ενθυμημασιν αυτης	επιθυμ. (4,5)/ επιτηδευμασιν (1)
23.30	בגלוליה	εν τοις ενθυμημασιν αυτων	επιθυμ. (2)
23.37	ואת-גלוליהן	τα ενθυμηματα αυτων	εν τοις ενθυμημα- σιν αυτων (1,3,4)
23.39	לגלוליהם	τοις ειδωλοις αυτων	-
23.49	גלוליכן	των ενθυμηματων υμων	επιθυμ. (4)/ επιτηδευματων (5)
30.13	גלולים	<>	βδελυγματα (2-6)
33.25	גלוליכם	<>	ειδωλα υμων (2-6)

36.18	ובגלוליה	<>	και εν τοις ειδωλ- οις αυτων (2-6)
36.25	ומכל-גלוליכם	και απο παντων των ειδωλων υμων	–
37.23	בגלוליהם	εν τοις ειδωλοις αυτων	–
44.10	גלוליהם	των ενθυμηματων αυτων	ειδωλων (4)
44.12	גלוליהם	των ειδωλων αυτων	–

Here we see that <<enthumèma>>, comparatively unused in the first 15 chapters, occurs much more often in ch.16-23. Some other examples, such as <<oti/dioti>> show this too, but must be treated with care as they seem subject to textual variation.

These six factors are not necessarily independent of each other. For example, the context is obviously related to the Vorlage, and certain textual variants may have been generated by the frequency or distribution of a word. It may be the case too that certain renderings are affected by a combination of several factors, rather than just one.

Our investigation of what should be taken into consideration when evaluating the homogeneity of a translation has revealed weaknesses in at least some of the examples cited in studies on the Ezekiel text. It should be noted, however, that not all the instances of translation change in Ezekiel have been invalidated. Indeed there still are grounds for believing that the text of Ezekiel is not homogeneous. Our aim up to this stage has been only to elucidate and illustrate those features which can affect the validity of examples used. It is the case, nevertheless, that those same features have distorted past arguments.

Methodology

Procedure

The procedure used here represents an attempt to
overcome some of the difficulties mentioned above. We have
noted that at least six influencing factors had to be borne in
mind in the evaluation of a translation: 1) the Vorlage, 2)
the context, 3) the integrity of the text, 4) the distribution
and frequency of terms, 5) the vocabulary of the translator,
and 6) the progression of the translation. As we have seen,
one or more of these factors may be responsible for what would
seem to be a deviation from the "normal" rendering of a given
term. If we wish to show that the deviation is significant, we
must use a method which takes the effect of those factors into
account.

In order to deal with this effect a two-fold approach is
used here. The two parts of this approach consist of
filtration and correlation. An initial assumption will be that
the text is the work of one translator. To show that the text
is not homogeneous, we shall have to prove this assumption
wrong. In order to do this we must provide sufficient examples
of translation change which are as free as possible from the
effect of the six factors mentioned above. Hence we need to
filter out those cases of translation change which might be
brought about by the above factors.

This method can be applied in a reasonably
straightforward way for the first five factors. However, the
effects of the progression of translation (and some aspects of
distribution and frequency) require a different treatment.
Even if we manage to filter out the distortion which the first
five factors produce, we still are left with the fact that a
translator may change his mind without any apparent reason.
However, even if any one case of translation change might be
explained in terms of a translator's arbitrariness, this

explanation becomes less likely when several other cases show a translation change in the same part of the text. Hence it is necessary to correlate examples of translation change. It is only when there is significant correlation of (filtered) examples that the case against the homogeneity of a text becomes strong.

There is the problem of how the evidence should be presented for evaluation. There are two main desiderata: 1) that the effect of the six factors should somehow be catered for, and 2) that the exact location of divisions in the text (if found) should be made clear. Earlier works proposing multiple translator theories concerning Ezekiel (and other books as well) have differed little from each other in their general pattern of presentation. A table or list would give first the Hebrew word and then its translation in one of the proposed sections, followed by its translation in another section, and so on. The number and references of the occurrences of the Hebrew word may or may not be given. Sometimes only the Greek term is noted, the Hebrew underneath being ignored.

This type of presentation has the obvious disadvantage that it is difficult to assess each example given in the light of the factors mentioned above. Not all of these can be easil displayed in tabular form, but inclusion of data about some c them is desirable. A second disadvantage is that suggestions about the exact location of boundaries or discontinuities are difficult to assess. With Ezekiel, for example, there is disagreement as to whether a break should be made after ch.2! or after ch.27. Yet it is not easy to tell from the tables of either viewpoint which is the stronger case. It may well be impossible to be exact about the location of a dividing-line but it would be of help to see clearly the evidence used to ascertain it.

Methodology

A third disadvantage is that the existence of small sub-sections different in nature from their enclosing section of text can go unnoticed /8/. A block of translation need not necessarily split into two or three roughly equal homogeneous units. It may simply contain one or more than one small section of differing text. Alternatively, a translation may split into two or more main sections, and each of those may contain subsections. It would be of value to use a procedure which catered for such possibilities.

A second type of presentation and evaluation must be considered here also. It has been noted earlier that the statistical authorship identification tests which have recently been developed could not be used in translation criticism. This restriction was primarily because of the distorting effect of the Vorlage, although other factors were involved too. Nevertheless, it does not mean that all forms of numerical analysis are barred from this area. Indeed, there is one type of approach which already treats differences in translation technique in a more numerical manner. This approach, which was nascent in Turner's article on Ezekiel (1956), has been used extensively by I. Soisalon-Soininen in his grammatical studies, and has been adopted by his students, R. Sollamo and A. Aejmelaeus. In it the occurrences of a given translation feature are expressed either a) as a ratio, i.e. as the ratio of actual occurrences to potential occurrences or of actual occurrences to occurrences of a near-synonymous feature, or b) as a percentage, i.e. they are given as the percentage of the number of total possible occurrences.

This approach admittedly takes into account the effect of the Vorlage, but it too fails to overcome the other disadvantages suffered by the first method. The influence of the other factors apart from the Vorlage, the location of boundaries between sections, and the existence of small sections are all problems which are not resolved by this method.

However, there are further difficulties here. At first sight the use of figures, for all of their weaknesses, might seem to give at least a more objective picture of what is happening than before. Yet this is not the case. For example in her work "Parataxis in the Septuagint" (1982a), Aejmelaeus gives us the following table showing the number of times <<kai>> has been used to translate waw in ordinary paratactic clauses:

Gen	1919 / 3053	62.9 %	
Ex	1373 / 1906	72.0 %	
Lev	1112 / 1232	90.3 %	
Num	1489 / 1660	89.7 %	
Deut	1068 / 1273	83.9 %	
Total	6961 / 9124	76.3 %	(1982a: 1

The percentages have been calculated from the total of translated waw clauses (i.e. the second column of numbers). Let us assume that the disadvantages mentioned above do not apply in the case of the Pentateuchal books. Aejmelaeus note that:

> The above percentages also demonstrate the
> differences between the books of the Pentateuch. A
> divergence from 63 % to 90 % must be considered
> significant. (1982a: 13)

The first problem here arises from the term "significant". I may well be precise to say that <<kai>> appears 90 % of the time in one book and only 63 % of the time in another book. Yet there is nothing inherent in the divergence of 27 % to tell us whether this is "significant" or not. We have no criteria to tell us what is the permissible range of variation. The 27 % difference is meaningless unless measured against results from control cases, which are lacking in the LXX /9/.

There is another problem with the use of figures to characterise a section of text. This characterisation depends on the assumption that, given a sufficiently large section of text, the variations caused by subject-matter, context, etc., will balance out, and a representative "average" will be attained. This assumption might well be valid in the case of frequently occurring phenomena in a large amount of material, as in the example above, but it does become questionable when only a small section of text is involved, or when the phenomena are comparatively rare. Although 1 out of 3 occurrences and 100 out of 300 occurrences can both be represented by the figure 33 % approximately, the former ratio is much more sensitive to the effects of slight alteration. A useful numerical approach must be capable of giving some estimate of how representative certain ratios or percentages are. This estimate would not be easy to supply in the case of the LXX.

It should be noted that these two problems are not the same as the difficulties involved in assessing the effects of the Vorlage and context on certain values /10/. These problems – the "significance" of a figure and the need for a representative section – are statistical issues and do not lend themselves easily to intuitive interpretation /11/. It is true that we cannot avoid using numbers when comparing certain translation differences between sections. However, the point here is that the use of a number to characterise the translation technique of a section of text is by itself inadequate. We need criteria by which to evaluate the number, and those criteria are lacking at present. The quantitative form of presentation is thus best avoided for the time being.

It may be possible to use it when we have sufficiently increased our knowledge of the statistical features of language in general and of translation Greek in particular.

The approach used here is illustrated by the format in which the translation examples are given. Each case contains a listing of all the occurrences of a given Hebrew term, together with the corresponding Greek translation and the relevant variants. This should reduce the possibility of an example of translation change being the result of the influence of the Vorlage and textual variation, and also show clearly the frequency and distribution of the term. Some degree of uncertainty cannot be ruled out. In using the MT as our Hebrew text we are assuming that the Greek Vorlage was quite similar to it. It is also the case that we do not have all the evidence about inner-Greek textual variation.

With this format a more objective display of evidence is achieved too, in that no initial division of supposed section needs to be indicated. Such a form of display should ease re-assessment of the data as well.

However, this form of listing cannot show information about the influence of the context and the nature of the translator's vocabulary. These still have to be investigated case by case.

Consideration of the effect of the above factors should give us some indication of the cases that would be most important as evidence for translation change. Renderings which are frequent, well distributed, textually sound, and relatively independent of context are of high value. Unusual renderings are not necessarily so (cf. Muraoka 1972a: 91-2). Differing sets of inconsistent renderings could be significant too. In practice, though, it may be difficult to obtain many

of the most desirable examples. The lexical stock shared by
the Vorlagen of two suspected sections may be insufficient to
provide decisive evidence either way.

Examples of translation change will differ in their
degree of cogency. Here they will be listed, where possible,
in their approximate order of strength. Those which are
significant in their own right will be given first, those
which are merely corroborative later.

Conclusions regarding the exact location of the
dividing-line between sections generally have not rested
solely on the evidence of translation change. It may seldom be
the case that good instances of translation change occur very
close to the boundaries of disputed sections. Usually the line
of demarcation is placed where a new theme or topic is taken
up, the assumption being that translators or revisors would be
more likely to start at the beginning of an oracle or
narrative passage than in the middle of it. This seems
reasonable, as long as it is borne in mind that accidental
change of text-type in the course of transmission might occur
too.

Although Thackeray, Herrmann, Danielsmeyer and N. Turner
had cited many cases which have been shown to be invalid, they
did nevertheless uncover some which do seem to be sound. A
number of those valid examples will be listed in this study
too, on account of the fact that a different form of
presentation is taken here.

As noted before, it will be an initial assumption here
that the text is the work of one translator, who may have been
inconsistent. In order to disprove this, we must first provide
sufficient counter-examples which agree in pointing to a
discontinuity in the Greek text of Ezekiel as we now have it.

CHAPTER III

DIVINE NAMES - I

The Problem of the Nomina Sacra in Ezekiel

As we have seen, the divine names in Ezekiel have played a
significant part in the discussion concerning the number of
translators of the book. It is therefore desirable to make an
accurate appraisal of the weight of the evidence presented by
these forms. However, the issue of the nomina sacra in Ezekiel
is more complex than at first appears. Not only is there
uncertainty as to what the Old Greek rendering was, but there
is also disagreement as to what exactly lay in the Hebrew
Vorlage. Indeed, questions about the original form of the
divine names were raised some time before the translator
issue. In order to examine the problem more closely, we shall
first of all trace the development of the debate.

History of Research on the Divine Names in Ezekiel

1. Cornill, Dalman and Redpath

The first person to have dealt specifically with the
divine names in Ezekiel seems to have been C. H. Cornill, who
included in his commentary a short appendix entitled "Der
Gottesname bei Ezechiel" (1886: 172-175). He observed that
<<'dny yhwh>> occurred 228 times, while single <<yhwh>>
occurred 218 times /1/. However, he could find no grounds for
distinguishing between the two forms, and inferred that the
picture that the MT presented had been distorted by scribal
error. Ezekiel himself had used <<'dny yhwh>> "in a limited
way", but in the course of time this use had been extended

randomly by scribes (p.173). Cornill's examination of the LXX manuscripts led him to believe that B was nearest to the original text in this matter, seeing that it was almost free of the hexaplaric <<adònai>>, a Greek transliteration of the Hebrew word. He noted that in the majority of cases B gave a single <<kurios>> where the MT had <<'dny yhwh>>. In ch.1-39 the MT showed the double form (i.e. <<'dny yhwh>>) 201 times, while B had <<kurios kurios>> only 58 times /2/. These 58 occurrences Cornill took as indicating the original text.

However, in ch.40-48 B had not <<kurios kurios>> but <<kurios (o) theos>>. Cornill understood the latter form as being a translation of <<yhwh 'lhym>>, which must have been in the text of the "Alexandrian recension" of Ezekiel. Two factors were suggested to explain this:
1) In the first section of the book (ch.1-39) the relationship between God and Israel was essentially a legal one, where God was the master or "Lord". But in ch.40-48 the relationship was that of grace, whence the use of <<'lhym>>.
2) Apart from Ezekiel, <<yhwh 'lhym>> is also a characteristic name of God in Genesis 2 and 3 - the "Paradise" story. Apparently Ezekiel wished to set his vision of the new Jerusalem in parallel with the Paradise account.

Having given this explanation, Cornill felt free to follow B almost throughout when it came to deciding which form of the divine names was correct.

Whereas Cornill had raised the issue of the divine names in the context of his commentary on Ezekiel, G. H. Dalman approached the problem from consideration of the history and meaning of the Hebrew word <<'dny>>. In his book, "Der Gottesname Adonaj und seine Geschichte" (1889), Dalman argued that the suffix of <<'dny>> implied a personal relationship of the speaker to God. This was particularly so in the Prophets

who related a personal commissioning from God. Accordingly,
the passages where the word <<'dny>> appears in plain
narrative or in the mouth of God were seen to be later
additions. For Ezekiel this meant 13.9; 23.49; 24.24; 28.24
/3/. Dalman dismissed the witness of the Greek manuscripts
because of their lack of uniformity (p.28) and did not seem to
be aware of Cornill's view.

However, it was Cornill's, and not Dalman's, argument
that seemed to influence subsequent commentators. Both
Bertholet (1897: 14) and Kraetzschmar (1900: 24) accepted
Cornill's conclusion that the scribes had greatly distorted
the original distribution of the divine names. Toy (1899), on
the other hand, retains the MT forms without apparent comment.

Cornill had implicitly assumed the uniformity of the
Greek text, but this assumption was called into question when
Thackeray put forward his two translator-hypothesis. With
respect to the divine names he commented that:
> The B text is certainly nearest to the original,
> and the result ... is to show that b' rendered the
> double name by <<ks ks>>, g' by <<ks (o) ths>>,
> while a', in so far as his Hebrew contained the
> double name at all, agreed rather with b' than
> with g' in his rendering of it. (1903b: 405).

Initially Thackeray dismissed this discrepancy between a' and
g' by accepting Cornill's argument that ch.40-48 originally
read <<yhwh 'lhym>> instead of <<'dny yhwh>>.

A little later, another solution to the origin of the
double name in the Hebrew text was put forward by H. A.
Redpath in his commentary on Ezekiel. He suggested that:
> The form of the title may be due to the fact that
> when, in later times, the Name Jehovah was
> declared unutterable, the word Adonai may have at

first been placed in the margin as its substitute,
and then afterwards incorporated into the text.
(1907: 9)
This view has proved attractive to many.

2. Divine names and multiple translator theories

In 1909 J. Schäfers suggested in a short article that the
Greek text of Ezekiel was the work of three translators and
not two (1909: 289-291). He seems to have been unaware of
Thackeray's work. His theory was based on the differing
renderings of the divine name in B and ran as follows:
1) Ch.1-11 were the work of one translator. It could not be
accidental that almost all the double forms in the MT of these
chapters are rendered by a simple <<kurios>>, while in
ch.12-39 the <<kurios kurios>> forms correspond with <<'dny
yhwh>> at least 51 times. In ch.1-11 <<kurios>> must have
rendered <<'dny yhwh>>.
2) Ch.12-39 were therefore by another translator, who rendered
<<'dny yhwh>> by <<kurios kurios>>.
3) In ch.40-48 <<kurios (o) theos>> represents not <<yhwh
'lhym>> but simply a third translator's rendering of <<'dny
yhwh>>.
Schäfers did not examine the translation of any other
words.

An important contribution to the divine names issue was
made in J. Herrmann's article, "Die Gottesnamen im
Ezechieltexte" (1913). Here he re-examined the use of <<'dny
yhwh>> in Ezekiel amd came to the conclusion that its
distribution was definitely not random, a fact which suggests
its originality. The double name appeared almost always in on
of three categories. Of the 217 occurrences of <<'dny yhwh>>,
122 were to be found in the proclamatory form <<kh 'mr 'dny
yhwh>>, 81 in the form <<n'm 'dny yhwh>> and 5 in address to
God. On the other hand, the 218 /1/ occurrences of single

Divine Names: The Problem

<<yhwh>> could also be easily categorised. There were 87 cases of divine self-reference, <<'ny yhwh>>, 94 cases where <<yhwh>> appeared at the end of a construct chain, and 37 other cases where <<yhwh>> appeared as either subject or object. The number of counterexamples was seen as too small to be of consequence (4 instances of <<kh 'mr yhwh>>, 4 of <<n'm yhwh>>, 5 instances of <<'ny 'dny yhwh>>, and 4 where <<'dny yhwh>> appears in a construct chain). There were also 4 instances of single <<'dny>>.

Herrmann explained the differentiation by reasserting the view of G. A. Daechsel /4/ that <<'dny>> implied Yahweh's kingship and authority. The prophetic proclamations were analogous to royal edicts. The 5 cases of address to God fitted well with Ezekiel's theology, as for him God was Lord above all.

Herrmann then examined the LXX text in the light of his findings. Being aware of Thackeray's and Schäfer's theories, he suggested a fusion of the two, though he did not call it such. He said that the LXX could be divided up into three: 1-27; 28-39; 40-48 - Thackeray's divisions. But he believed that each of those sections was the work of a different translator. He did not attempt to go further than refer to the rendering of the divine names. The task of substantiating his hypothesis would wait for several years.

Herrmann did not convince Thackeray, who repeated some of his earlier views in the 1920 Schweich Lectures (published as "The Septuagint and Jewish Worship" in 1921). Thackeray reaffirmed that a' and g' were "undoubtedly the work of a single translator" (1921: 38). However, as noted in chapter I, he did show a change of mind over the problem of the divine names. He now suggested that:

> Translator a' in i-xxvii wrote <<kurios>>, finding

The Greek Text of Ezekiel

<<yhwh>> only in his text; in xl–xlviii he found
<<'dny yhwh>> which he rendered by <<kurios (o)
theos>>. The inconsistency of practice lies not in
the translation but in the original Hebrew. (1921:
122)

Thackeray shared Cornill's view that Ezekiel's occasional use
of <<'dny yhwh>> was widely extended by copyists.

As if in reply to this, although only Thackeray's initial
work is mentioned, Herrmann produced his article reaffirming
the three-translator view (1923). He maintained his views too
on the significance of <<'dny yhwh>>, noting in his commentary
(1924):

This formula [i.e. <<kh 'mr 'dny yhwh>>] may be
modelled on the opening formula of the royal edict
<<kh 'mr hmlk>> ... The prophet is thus the one
who has to proclaim the edict of the royal Lord
Yahweh. (1924: 20)

In a companion article to Herrmann's, F. Baumgärtel
(1923a: 81–95) examined the attestation of Codex A to the
<<'dny yhwh>> of Ezekiel and the relation of A to the Arabic
translation (Arab) and to Codex Marchalianus (Q). He concluded
that, with respect to the divine names, Arab had transmitted a
more original form of A (p. 83) which in turn originally had
shown a very strong similarity with Q (p. 90).

The next relevant study to appear was the extensive
four-volume opus of W. W. Baudissin, entitled "Kyrios als
Gottesname im Judentum und seine Stelle in der
Religionsgeschichte" (1929). This work was written at least
partly as a response to Dalman's earlier study (1889, see
above). It made a powerful impact, at least on views
concerning the authenticity of <<'dny>> in the MT in general
and in Ezekiel in particular.

Divine Names: The Problem

3. Baudissin and contemporaries

Baudissin's main contention was that the word <<'dny>> had originally only occurred in the Hebrew text in forms of address, all other instances being later additions. It was the use of the Greek <<kurios>> which was the model for the later <<'dny>> forms. Indeed, <<'dny>> was not used as a substitute for <<yhwh>> until the first century B.C.

In the case of Ezekiel, Baudissin proposes quite a complicated history underlying the various phenomena:

1) Originally there was, apart from the vocative, only a single <<yhwh>> form in the Hebrew of Ezekiel.
2) When ch.1-39 were translated they originally had just a single <<kurios>>. Two translators were involved at this stage. The dividing line between their work would seem to lie round the beginning of ch.21, though the end of ch.27 was not totally to be ruled out. The intervening chapters had suffered from scribes mixing up the vocabulary from the two parts.
3) <<'dny>> was added to the Hebrew text by an editor.
4) Ch.21/28-39 in the LXX suffered the work of a reviser, who added another <<kurios>> on the basis of the revised Hebrew text.
5) Later, the <<kurios kurios>> forms penetrated the first section.
6) Later still, the Lucianic <<adònai kurios>> came into passages where <<kurios kurios>> had not been.
7) The section containing ch.40-48 (with <<'dny>>) was translated separately from and probably later than the other two sections. Both the Greek and Hebrew texts of these last chapters had existed separately from the rest of the book for a while.

Baudissin bases this outline on several arguments. Firstly, he notes that in ch.1-39 B represents only 54 of the

200 of the MT's <<'dny yhwh>> by <<kurios kurios>>. 140 are
rendered by simple <<kurios>> /2/. A and Q have a large number
of <<adònai kurios>> forms — 84 in A and 99 in Q. But these
are seen as later additions on the basis of a Hebrew text,
since they almost always correspond to an <<'dny yhwh>> in the
MT. Hence we see that only the relatively few double forms in
B have manuscript support. On the other hand, A, B and Q all
agree in reading <<kurios (o) theos>> in ch.40-48.

According to Baudissin, Jacob of Edessa noted in a
scholion (to a work written in 701) that the 'Seventy' did
"not at all translate" the tetragram "nor alter the Hebrew
characters with which it was written". However, "the others"
replaced it by <<adònai>> in the text and "Lord" in the
margin. Jacob apparently went on to say of Lucian that "when
he saw the word <<adònai>> in the text and "Lord" in the
margin, he linked the two together and set them together" (vol
1, p. 531). Although he does not think that Jacob was
entirely correct, Baudissin infers that "the others" refers to
a group of manuscripts of Ezekiel which had only <<yhwh>> in
their text. This group had not yet suffered any revision of
the divine names.

Again, the witness of the Old Latin texts, where extant,
showed that they read a single <<Dominus>> even where B read
<<kurios kurios>>. This also would indicate that B too had
been revised and that originally its text of ch.1-39 had read
only <<kurios>>.

With respect to ch.40-48, the reading <<kurios (o)
theos>> was certainly prehexaplaric, as the Old Latin supports
it. But it was not original, according to Baudissin, as the
Lucianic manuscripts have <<adònai kurios>> here as well,
indicating an expansion from a single <<yhwh>> form. Because
the Greek of ch.40-48 uses a quite different rendering of

<<'dny yhwh>>, it is quite possible that this section was translated later than the rest of the book.

Baudissin thought it unlikely that a divine name would be shortened by translators. It is more often the case that the divine name is lengthened or doubled (vol 1, p. 559). Again, the "principle by which <<'dny yhwh>> and simple <<yhwh>> are used differently is not hard to discover": <<'dny>> implies the sense of being "Lord of all" (vol 1, p. 576). The regularity of usage need not lead to the assumption that <<'dny yhwh>> is original. It might be due to "a stylistic preference or some manner of religio-aesthetic feeling of the presumed redactors, which stood firmly in opposition to that of the author" (vol 1, p. 587).

Baudissin's work was reviewed in detail by L. Cerfaux in two articles: "Le nom divin <<Kyrios>> dans la bible grecque" (1931a) and "Adonai et Kyrios" (1931b). He disagreed with the fundamental thesis of Baudissin, namely, that the Hebrew text of the Old Testament had originally <<'dny>> only in forms of address. Although he did not construct a complete counter-scheme, Cerfaux did point out what he felt were important weaknesses in Baudissin's arguments. He suggested that the Greek translators might have rendered an original double divine name by <<kurios kurios>>, which then was gradually replaced by a single <<kurios>>. "If we admit that <<kurios kurios>> is the more difficult reading, it is only normal that we see its gradual elimination in the manuscript tradition." (1931a: 44). With respect to the Old Latin, Cerfaux suggested that the translator of ch.1-39 had shortened the double form of the Greek, producing the more sensible single <<Dominus>>.

He observed too that <<'dny yhwh>> in address suffered exactly the same treatment in the Greek manuscripts as <<'dny

yhwh>> in any other context. This weakened Baudissin's
contention that the vocative use of <<'dny>> was original.
Again, he argued that, because B was more reliable than A or
Q, its reading should be preferred when it read <<kurios
kurios>> and A or Q read just single <<kurios>>. One should
not always prefer the shorter reading.

Cerfaux dismisses other arguments somewhat summarily.
With respect to Jacob of Edessa he says, "We maintain all the
same that the value of the Massoretic Text has not been
affected by a conjecture resting on the strange, to say the
least, scholion of Jacob of Edessa." (1931a: 46). The
suggestion of a revision of ch.21/28-39 to expand single
<<kurios>> forms to <<kurios kurios>> is treated similarly:
"We think that the complexity of this system carries its
condemnation" (1931a: 47).

Cerfaux's comments seem to have been overlooked or
ignored at that time, whereas Baudissin's view was further
promulgated by J. B. Harford in his "Studies in the Book of
Ezekiel", especially pp. 67-69 and 102-162 (1935). Harford
arrives at conclusions very similar to those of Baudissin.
Indeed, it would seem safer to say that his treatment of the
topic has a strong dependence on Baudissin rather to say that
he had come to a similar view independently. He does refer to
Baudissin occasionally. However, Harford treats the issue
specifically from the point of view of the book of Ezekiel and
offers more detailed statistics than Baudissin on the
distribution and use of the divine name in the MT and LXX
manuscripts of Ezekiel.

Harford's and Baudissin's arguments seem to have been
overlooked by G.A. Cooke, who suggested in his commentary on
Ezekiel that:

'Adonai Jahveh' may be a sort of a scribal
direction to pronounce 'Adonai' where 'Jahveh'
stands in the text ... But when the text of
Ezekiel assumed its present form the rule had not
yet become rigid; neither the Hebr. copyists nor
the Gk. translators felt at liberty to enforce it
at every instance (1936: 33).

With regard to the evidence of the LXX, he says:

This variation in the rendering shews, beyond
doubt, that the Gk. translation was made by
several hands..." (1936: 33).

Cooke felt that it was possible that the prophet himself had
used the double name "now and again" (1936: 34).

4. Papyrus 967 and the double divine name

The discovery and publication of parts of Papyrus 967 in
the nineteen thirties appeared to give strong support to
Baudissin's contention that the original Greek of ch.1-39 had
only a single <<kurios>>. Johnson declared that, "Perhaps the
most striking characteristic of the Scheide text is the use of
the single <<ks>> in designating the nomen sacrum ..."
(Johnson, Gehman, Kase 1938: 19). In addition, all four of the
main Old Latin witnesses attested a single <<Dominus>>
usually, thus agreeing with 967's single <<kurios>>. (There
were a few instances where 967 read <<kurios (o) theos>> /5/).

As regards the present witness of the Greek and Hebrew
texts, Kase believed that:

The frequent substitution in B of <<kurios
kurios>> for an original <<kurios>>, and the
occasional occurrence of <<kurios (o) theos>> in
the Scheide codex, can be attributed to sporadic
revision of the Septuagint based on a Hebrew text
in which the original reading <<yhwh>> had been
systematically expanded to <<'dny yhwh>>, the

67

reading of the present Massoretic text. (1938:
51)

However, Kase did not follow Baudissin in assigning a separate
fate for ch.40-48. He believed that the best way to explain
the variants to <<kurios (o) theos>> in this section was to
regard all of them as subsequent revisions of a single
<<kurios>>. He felt that it would be unlikely for <<kurios
kurios>> or << adònai kurios>> to replace <<kurios (o)
theos>>, which sometimes did occur, e.g. in the Lucianic
manuscripts. In order to explain the distribution of variants
he even suggested that the section containing ch.40-48 was
bisected (for reasons of ease of use). Kase deduced that
it was evident that:

> the variant forms of the nomen sacrum occurring in
> the different manuscripts cannot be accepted as
> criteria in an attempt to establish the
> translation of xl-xlviii either as the work of a
> different, though contemporary, hand, or as being
> of late origin. (1938: 62)

Therefore the three-translator hypothesis should be abandoned
Kase then went on to attack the views that suggest even a
two-translator approach, eventually postulating a
one-translator, one-reviser theory /6/.

Essentially, Ziegler accepted Kase's arguments concerning
the number of translators. He believed the differing rendering
of the divine names was the main pillar ("Hauptpfeiler") of
the multiple-translator theories (Ziegler 1946: 93). Once the
pillar had fallen the rest of the edifice would collapse. And
now 967 seemed to provide conclusive proof that the LXX
originally had just a single <<kurios>>. With the amount of
material discovered at that time, Ziegler could say, "Now
Papyrus 967 shows the astounding fact that it has <<kurios>>
76 times and <<kurios (o) theos>> only 6 times." (Ziegler
1946: 93).

Divine Names: The Problem

Ziegler put his conclusions into practice when he edited the Göttingen Septuagint edition of Ezekiel (1952). Out of 217 instances where the text of BHS has <<'dny yhwh>>, Ziegler's Greek text only once has a double <<kurios>> form: <<kurie kurie>> in 21.5 (20.49). This contrasts with the text of his predecessor, Rahlfs, which attests a <<kurios kurios>> form at least 66 times, presumably on the basis of B.

Perhaps it was due to Ziegler's text that Elliger in the BHS edition of Ezekiel (1967) felt constrained to indicate the spuriousness of the <<'dny>> in every instance of <<'dny yhwh>> in the book. This he usually did by noting ">G*, add", though for some reason he used ">G*, dl" in most of ch.25-29.

5. Present views

The line taken by Baudissin, Kase and Ziegler with respect to the divine name in Ezekiel seems to have won wide acceptance, at least among German scholarship. Commentators Fohrer (1955: 15) and Eichrodt (1970: 12) both consider <<'dny>> secondary and added by a late redactor, as does Quell (in TDNT III: <<kurios>>, (1966: 1059-61)) with some reservations. Eissfeldt (in TDOT I : <<Adhon>>) accepts that it was possible that after c. 300 B.C. <<'dny>> "was added to biblical passages which already contained statements showing the majesty of God, as the introductory and concluding formulas in the prophets, koh 'amar and ne'um." (Eissfeldt 1974: 72).

It is of note, however, that English-speaking commentators tend to the "gradual accretion" theory proposed by Redpath and later Cooke. Wevers (1969: 52), Taylor (1969: 48) and Carley (1974: 22) do this. For example, Wevers comments at ch.2.4 that, "Apparently 'Lord' as the perpetual Qere for 'Yahweh' crept into the text, and only 'Yahweh' should be read throughout Ezekiel." (1969: 52).

The Greek Text of Ezekiel

An interesting attitude is that of W. Zimmerli. In the text of his commentary he brackets off the words "the Lord" in his translation of Ez 2.4 (1979: 90 /7/), which is the first verse to attest the double name, and refers the reader to excursus 1. In the commentary to the same verse he omits the word again (1979: 133), obviously regarding it as secondary. However, more than thirteen years separate the writing of the first parts of the book and the completion of the excursuses, as Zimmerli himself tells us in his foreword (1979: xiii). He advises:

> The long duration of the task of exposition has occasioned that here and there the view of the commentator was slightly changed. ... In the excursus on the divine names something quite different finally emerged than in the exposition of the detailed text. The reader is therefore asked to refer to the excursus for the passages which use the double name of God. (1979: xiii)

However, the excursus itself reflects the indecision of the author. After examining some specific usages, Zimmerli summarises the arguments of Cornill, Herrmann, Baudissin, Harford and Baumgärtel, adding the views expressed through private communication by H. Stegemann to the effect that <<'dny yhwh>> might be understood "as a Yahwistic expansion ... of an initially single <<'dny>>." (1969: 1257). He also notes Stegemann's suggestion that at an early stage Jewish Greek manuscripts would have retained <<yhwh>> in Hebrew characters and so Ezekiel texts would have read <<kurios yhwh>>. The Greek double forms of the divine name would be the result of later expansion /8/. Yet Zimmerli offers no detailed analysis himself, and concludes by saying:

> we must reckon with the possibility that the <<'dny yhwh>> in these formulaic groups — the plaintive invocation of Yahweh, the introduction of the message of judgment from Yahweh, and the

Divine Names: The Problem

decree from God — could originally have been
resident in the word of the prophet, whatever we
might decide about the origin of the double
designation. (1969: 1258).

The matter does not quite end there, as Zimmerli adds a
short supplement to his excursus. The reason for this was that
he had just received J. Lust's article on the divine names
(see below). Zimmerli remains doubtful but ends by saying that
Lust's hypothesis requires further careful investigation
(1969: 1265).

There were a few who disagreed with the consensus that
<<'dny>> was mostly a late addition to the Ezekiel text. After
a period of almost forty years F. Baumgärtel published an
article "Zu den Gottesnamen in den Büchern Jeremia und
Ezekiel" (1961b). In this he observed that <<'dny yhwh>> in
Ezekiel and <<yhwh ṣb'wt>> in Jeremiah often occurred in the
same expression — <<kh 'mr ...>>. He inferred that the manner
of usage of <<'dny yhwh>> in the MT was the same as that of
<<yhwh ṣb'wt>>. Regarding the LXX he suggested that the
translators had rendered <<yhwh ṣb'wt>> in Jeremiah and <<'dny
yhwh>> in Ezekiel a' by a single <<kurios>>. The reason for
this was that the LXX was made for the needs of synagogue
reading and hence must supply a reading that made sense to its
hearers, something which, say, <<kurios kurios>> would not do.
Double forms in the Greek witnesses were due to later
revisions.

This suggestion was attacked strongly by Janzen in his
"Studies in the Text of Jeremiah" (1973). Janzen's criticisms
have primarily a textual basis. Of Baumgärtel's work he says:

it may be stated categorically that both his
methods and his conclusions are totally
unacceptable. His exclusive reliance upon the
uncial codices of the Greek text tradition (to the

> neglect of the cursive and other witnesses), and
> the resultant lack of any attempt to reconstruct
> critically the old Greek text, let alone his
> failure to make any use of the Göttingen critical
> edition of the Septuagint in the Prophets, already
> gives some notion to both the vintage and the
> caliber of his textual methods. (1973: 168-9)

Janzen did not accept that the readings of the MT were
necessarily original in this instance.

A different approach to the meaning and use of <<'dny
yhwh>> was suggested in an article by J. Lust (1968). (It was
Lust's article which prompted Zimmerli to supplement his
excursus, even though he was not convinced by it). Lust
revived the arguments used by L. Cerfaux in his reviews of
Baudissin's work (Cerfaux 1931a, 1931b), accepting the
authenticity of the double name in the MT, but adding that we
should read "Adoni Yahweh" instead of "Adonai Yahweh". This
repointing of <<'dny>> was intended to imply that the meaning
of the double name was "my lord Yahweh". The prophet was
saying "Yahweh is my master", implying too that he was a true
servant of Yahweh. This would tie in with the fact that all
the double forms of the divine name appear in address, not in
narrative. (Lust regarded the few exceptions to this as
secondary). Ezekiel was emphasising his links with the true
God and the gulf of separation that lay between apostate
Israel and his God.

The discovery of early scrolls in the Dead Sea area added
much written evidence of the use of the divine name at a time
about which scholars in the earlier part of this century could
only make conjectures. In his investigation, "The Divine Name
at Qumran, in the Masada Scroll, and in the Septuagint"
(1980), P. W. Skehan observed that "before 100 B.C., to judge
by the Hodayot and 1QIsa/a, Adonay was both a name that might

be used in prayer by any Israelite, and the name regularly spoken as the substitute for Yhwh in reading the Scriptures." (1980: 36). This fact certainly puts paid to one part of Baudissin's thesis, namely that <<'dny>> was not employed as a spoken or written substitute for <<yhwh>> until the first century B.C.

In examining the LXX Ezekiel Skehan counted 15 occurrences of <<kurios (o) theos>> in the whole of papyrus 967. He saw them as evidence of a Jewish source that judged the best rendering of <<'dny yhwh>> to be that of the Palestinian qere "Adonai Elohim". This was consistent with a large part of the LXX prophetic corpus (apart from Jeremiah), which showed a tendency to use <<kurios (o) theos>> for <<'dny yhwh>> at an early stage and also to use a single <<kurios>> for multiple forms of the double name (1980: 36-38). Skehan does not attempt to give reasons for the situation he describes, but he does observe that "a new look at the divine names in papyrus 967 of LXX Ezechiel seems called for." (1980: 35).

6. Summary

A brief overview of the situation would highlight two main points. Firstly, we could note the dominance of the theories suggesting the spuriousness of the word <<'dny>> in Ezekiel. These fall into two categories: those suggesting that <<'dny>> was gradually introduced as a qere for <<yhwh>> (Redpath, Cooke, Wevers, etc.), and those suggesting that <<'dny>> was added by a later redactor (Baudissin, Harford, Fohrer, etc.). It should be added that these theories do not have total support. Zimmerli, Lust and Skehan show varying degrees of reluctance to expel <<'dny>> from the Hebrew text. Secondly, we observe the seemimgly strong support for the view that the Greek text of Ezekiel originally read only <<kurios>> in passages where the MT now has <<'dny yhwh>> (Kase,

Ziegler). It follows from this second point that the double
readings for the divine name in the Greek manuscripts are the
result of later revisions of the Greek towards the MT and
consequently those readings are invalid as criteria for
distinguishing the work of different translators in the Greek
text.

It is to a re-evaluation of these points that we now
turn.

CHAPTER IV

DIVINE NAMES - II

A Proposed Solution to the Problem

It might seem that the situation regarding the nomina sacra in Ezekiel is satisfactorily described by the two points noted at the conclusion of the preceding chapter. However, an attempt will be made here to offer a different explanation of the problems raised. It will be maintained here that:

1) <<'dny yhwh>> occurred in the original Ezekiel text in a distribution similar to that of the present MT.

2) The LXX translator(s) met the <<'dny yhwh>> form in the Vorlage, but rendered it by a form which has been almost totally lost.

3) The present distribution of the nomina sacra in the Greek witnesses is not due to fully recensional treatment but is the result of early scribal activity.

Originality of <<'dny yhwh>>.

Several observations must be made in support of the first part. Firstly, we now know that the word <<'dny>> is to be found in biblical manuscripts which date from very near the time that the LXX translation was made, i.e. the third to second centuries B.C. The first Isaiah scroll at Qumran (1QIsa/a) is dated in the second century B.C. and exhibits a considerable number of <<'dny yhwh>> forms /1/. The scroll even exhibits indications that <<'dny>> was pronounced when

<<yhwh>> was read in the text. This can be inferred from the occasional alterations of <<'dny>> to <<yhwh>> and vice versa (examples of both types of alteration can be seen in the scroll at Is 3.16-20).

Indeed, it seems that <<'dny>> already had gained some of the status attributed to a proper name of God. In the Damascus Document, which is dated around the beginning of the first century B.C., we read, "(he shall not) swear, even by the Aleph and Lamedh [i.e. Elohim], nor by the Aleph and Daleth [i.e. Adonay] but with the oath..." /2/. It might be inferred that the Qumran community was already long familiar with the use of the word <<'dny>> in biblical texts. There is no reason to suppose that this familiarity was restricted to Qumran Jews.

Unfortunately, we do not possess much manuscript evidence from the Dead Sea area of the text of Ezekiel. The largest fragment published is given in Appendix C. It can be seen that no passage where <<'dny yhwh>> would be expected has been preserved. Yet at least some corroboration may be gained from this fragment, which contains part of Ez 10.17-11.10. If we count the length of the lines of the section 11.2-10, (assuming a text similar to our MT), we get the following results:

Line	Number of letters	
11.2-3	41	
11.3-5a	42	
11.5a-5b	43	
11.5b-6	42	
11.6-7a	40	(36)

11.7a–8	38	
11.8–9	41	(37)
11.9–10	38	

The average number of letters per line is 40.55. The two figures given in brackets represent the line lengths if the <<'dny>> forms found there are omitted. It can be seen that these two figures are lower than any other, which would make them less likely to be correct. This would give at least a little more support to the view that <<'dny>> was already in the Ezekiel text by the time that the book was translated into Greek.

Furthermore, it must be stressed that the work of J. Herrmann ("Die Gottesnamen im Ezechieltexte", 1913) has not been invalidated. Re-examination of the context and use of the divine names in Ezekiel indicates that there is a distinct difference in this respect between the forms <<'dny yhwh>> and <<yhwh>>. Appendix A contains tables showing the results of this re-examination. Most of the tables reiterate the findings of Herrmann, but there have been corrections and extensions. Table A.6 summarises these findings. It is striking to note that out of a total of 125 occurrences of the KM phrase and 85 occurrences of the NE phrase only 3 of the KM phrases and 4 of the NE phrases used a single <<yhwh>>. The rest (122 KM phrases and 81 NE phrases) used <<'dny yhwh>>. Again, we find 93 instances of <<yhwh>> being used in the CC category but only 4 instances of <<'dny yhwh>> used in the same way. This is most definitely a non-random distribution and should lay to rest a view that ought to have died years ago, namely, that <<'dny>> was added gradually here and there as a reminder to pronounce <<yhwh>> as "Adonay". If this view were true, we should expect a random distribution of <<'dny yhwh>>. The distribution is not random, so the premise is wrong.

The alternative explanation, that <<'dny>> was added by a redactor to the Hebrew text some time after Ezekiel was translated into Greek, also has difficulties. A major problem with this is the question why this revision took place at all. It is only in the book of Ezekiel that this type of use of <<'dny>> is found so extensively /3/. Yet it is not very clear what the exact intention of such a revision was. The end result does not change the message of the text substantially. Baudissin suggested that the revision might have been occasioned by "a stylistic preference or some manner of religio-aesthetic feeling of the presumed redactors" (1929: vol 1, 587). It must have been quite a strong feeling for someone to pick carefully through over 400 occurrences of <<yhwh>> and add <<'dny>> to half of them. Yet the procedure does not seem to have been extended to the rest of the Old Testament.

There is too the problem of why the word <<'dny>> was used. If the revision took place after the translation of Ezekiel into Greek, then we would expect to find some similar use of the word in the Qumran manuscripts. Instead, we note that it already seems to be pronounced in place of <<yhwh>> i reading biblical text, and that otherwise it is scarcely used at all, as a glance at Kuhn's concordance shows.

It might be argued that the revision was done much earlier, and that the LXX translators happened to work on a text that had escaped the revision. Nevertheless, it must be noted that the initial objection still holds. Furthermore, it could be added that this 'formulaic' usage is in keeping with the style of the book. The single <<yhwh>> form appears in the CC category 93 times. Yet three-fifths of these occurrences are taken up by just one phrase — "the hand of Yahweh" (57 times; see Table A.2). The expression "... know that I am Yahweh" appears 62 times. So over one half of the total occurrences of <<yhwh>> without <<'dny>>, i.e. 119 out of 217 instances, are taken up by just two expressions. Cf. Tables A.2 and A.6.

It would seem that the only strong support for the revision hypothesis has been the witness of the Greek. Indeed, the conclusion that the LXX text of Ezekiel originally had only the single <<kurios>> form throughout (or at least throughout ch.1-39) and the view that <<'dny>> was added late to the Hebrew text support one another. Sufficient doubt has been cast on the latter to merit re-investigation of the former and to ask whether the Old Greek really had just the single <<kurios>> form throughout.

Divine Names in the Greek Texts.

Firstly, however, we must examine the witness of the LXX manuscripts to the divine names in Ezekiel. Table B.1 shows the readings of the Greek texts (and their daughter translations) at the 434 passages where BHS records a <<yhwh>> or <<'dny yhwh>>. Several features may be noted:

1) Non-random distribution

There is a wide variety of readings in places in the text which correspond with those in the MT where <<'dny yhwh>> appears. At the same time, this profusion of readings very seldom spills over onto those places corresponding with the Hebrew reading of a single <<yhwh>>. Only 9 out of 208 single <<yhwh>> readings have corresponding LXX renderings with a significant number of double forms: 4.13; 11.5b; 20.38; 21.8; 25.5; 30.6a; 35.15; 37.14b; 43.5.

These in themselves are interesting. Three of them — 11.5b; 21.8; 30.6a — make up the entire group of KM phrases which lacked <<'dny>> in the text of B19a, cf. Table A.1. One of them — 37.14b — is from the NE group which also lacked <<'dny>>. (Of the three remaining instances in this NE group (13.6a; 13.7; 16.58; cf. Table A.1 again) two might be exceptional in that the phrase "declares Yahweh" comes from the mouths of the false prophets (13.6a; 13.7). At 16.58 the Vulgate has "ait dominus deus", and Jerome reports that Aquila's version reads the same while Theodotion gives "dicit adonai dominus". Cf. Ziegler's text and apparatus.)

Three more of the nine exceptions — 4.13; 20.38; 35.15 — have strong support for a <<kurios (o) theos>> reading. This might indicate a rendering of <<yhwh 'lhm>> instead of <<'dny yhwh>>, though 4.13 could have been influenced by 4.14. The remaining exceptions — 25.5; 43.5 — do not have major support and might be due to random error.

Thus it does seem that in general the Greek witnesses, whether revised or not, show very little sign whatever of having double divine names outside the pattern set by the MT. It is of note that, out of the four instances where the MT has <<'dny yhwh>> in the CC, two of them (i.e. 25.3a and 36.4a) show at least reduced Greek manuscript support. That is to say, many of the Greek witnesses which normally exhibit double renderings at other references have only a single <<kurios>> in these two instances.

2) Most frequent forms.

The most frequent corresponding Greek forms for <<'dny yhwh>> are <<adònai kurios>>, <<kurios kurios>>, <<kurios (theos>> and also single <<kurios>>. Few manuscripts exhibit

only one of these forms. Most have at least three and some
have in addition what seem to be conflations — <<kurios kurios
(o) theos>>, <<adònai kurios (o) theos>>, <<adònai kurios
kurios>>, etc.

3) Variation within groups.

The variation of readings is even quite pronounced within
manuscript groups. The manuscripts in the A and B groups show
considerable differences among themselves in this respect. For
example, A and 106 differ 108 out 217 times in their
renderings of <<'dny yhwh>>. The manuscripts of the Lucianic
and Catena groups show more uniformity within their respective
groups because of their close textual relationships. Ziegler
describes the subgroups 22-36-48-51-96-231-763 and V-46-449 as
"closed" (1952/77: 46). Regarding the Catena manuscripts, he
believes that the subgroup 87-91-490 come from an archetype,
as do 130-233-534. The subgroup 49-90-764 are seen as a
development of 87-91-490 (1952/77: 58).

4) Three-fold division.

Despite the amount of variation, there is a discernible
three-fold division in the distribution of the double divine
name readings. This division can be detected in many
manuscripts, though the boundaries are hard to define
precisely.
The three sections are :
     a.   ch.1 to mid-ch.20
     b.   mid-ch.20 to ch.40/42
     c.   ch.40/42 to ch.48
Section (a) is characterized by the dominance of the <<adònai
kurios>> form and a relative uniformity. Section (b) has the

most variety of readings, with the <<kurios kurios>> form
occurring most frequently. Section (c) exhibits a
preponderance of <<kurios (o) theos>> readings.

Although general characterizations can be made, it would be
wrong to take these as norms for any one section. It would be
truer to say that in any given section witnesses can be found
to the forms characterized by the other two sections. The
differences between two sections in one manuscript may not be
the same as the differences between the same two sections in
another manuscript. This will become more apparent if we
consider some examples.

Section (a) was characterized as having mostly the <<adônai
kurios>> form. If we examine the A group, we find them
conforming to this description. Occasionally some <<kurios
kurios>> and some single <<kurios>> forms appear also. The
Catena and Q-88-Syh groups follow this pattern too, though
there is a tendency for <<adônai kurios>> instead of single
<<kurios>> to occur. The Lucianic group shows most consistenc
in rendering <<'dny yhwh>> by <<adônai kurios>>, and indeed i
almost unique in continuing to do so for nearly the whole
book. B, on the other hand, shows no <<adônai kurios>>
readings at all, giving mostly single <<kurios>> and a few
<<kurios kurios>>. 967 gives mostly single <<kurios>> too, bu
also has 7 <<kurios (o) theos>> forms (or 8, if one considers
the reading in 16.62 to be misplaced). Unfortunately, 967 is
missing for about the first half of this section.

The <<kurios kurios>> and <<kurios (o) theos>> readings in B
and 967 should not be dismissed lightly. 967 has been taken
strong evidence that originally only <<kurios>> was in the O
Greek text. However, these 7 <<kurios (o) theos>> forms
testify to an awareness of the double divine name. If these
are the result of revision, then the question arises as to w

the revision was so sporadic, when the Hebrew text must have attested a distribution of forms close to that of the MT. The <<kurios kurios>> and <<adônai kurios>> readings might have been contracted somehow. (Later scribes might have seen them as "dittographies" and omitted one of the two words.) But <<kurios (o) theos>> is more stable.

<<kurios (o) theos>> appears 26 times in the whole of 967 (14.23; 16.8; 16.19; 16.43; 16.62; 17.9; 17.16; 17.19; 20.7; 20.12; 20.19; 20.20; 24.3; 24.9; 28.26; 34.17; 34.30a; 35.15; 37.3; 37.5; 37.9; 39.5; 39.22; 39.28; 39.29; 44.2b) in passages where some form of <<yhwh>> is present in the MT. Yet out of these 26, 9 must be taken as rendering <<yhwh 'lhym>> (20.7; 20.19; 20.20; 28.26; 34.30a; 35.15; 39.22; 39.28; 44.2b) /4/. A further 5 instances must be viewed as possible scribal errors due to the influence of other nearby clusters of <<kurios (o) theos>> readings. These instances would include 20.12 (due to 20.7,19,20), 39.29 (due to 39.22,28) and 37.3,5,9 (also due to 39.22,28, because in 967 ch.37 follows ch.39). This leaves us with 12 instances of <<kurios (o) theos>>, 8 of which have appeared in section (a). The remaining 4 instances are 24.3,9; 34.17; 39,5. So it does appear that section (a) has the strongest attestation of <<kurios (o) theos>> in 967.

If we consider section (b), we find quite a difference from the data in section (a). The A group show the most variety of readings — <<kurios kurios>>, <<adônai kurios>>, <<kurios (o) theos>>, <<kurios>> and <<kurios kurios (o) theos>>. It is significant that the Hexaplaric manuscripts, Q-88-Syh, also show a change, but only to exhibiting a preponderance of <<kurios kurios>> readings, together with some instances of <<adônai kurios>>. The Catena group do likewise. Manuscript 62 exhibits Aquila readings, according to Ziegler, whereas Q-88-Syh follow Theodotion. Hence 62 goes its own way here, and continues to attest mostly <<adònai kurios>>. However, its readings differ from those in section (a) in that <<adònai kurios>> occurs much less frequently, single <<kurios>> appearing instead.

The readings in B show a change in frequency too, <<kurios kurios>> now appearing more frequently. Bo starts to exhibit a great variety of renderings, though it still often has a single <<kurios>> where others have a doubled form of some sort.

The Lucianic manuscripts continue their attestation of <<adònai kurios>>, (which might be an example of where Lucian followed Aquila's revision). Some of the manuscripts attest only a single <<kurios>> in ch.22 to ch.27. This is because they follow a non-Lucianic text-type in these chapters.

It might be said that the double readings in the A manuscripts point to the possible existence of a manuscript which, like 967 in section (a), attested at least some <<kurios (o) theos>> readings. There are 25 instances of <<kurios kurios (o) theos>> in section B of manuscript A, and these most probably are the result of conflation of <<kurios kurios>> an <<kurios (o) theos>> forms found in separate witnesses.

In section (c) <<kurios (o) theos>> is by far the dominant rendering. Yet the Hexaplaric group retains witness to <<kurios kurios>> in several instances. It is of note that even 62 attests <<kurios (o) theos>> at least 5 times at places where <<adònai kurios>> would be expected, though <<adònai kurios>> is still frequent. The Old Latin witnesses, which usually have a single "Dominus", conform here as well and occasionally show "Dominus Deus". Only 967 consistently renders <<'dny yhwh>> by <<kurios>>.

Divine Names: A Solution

It is difficult here to say where the exact dividing line
between the two sections is, owing to the lack of <<'dny
yhwh>> forms in ch.40-42 and to the fact that the textual
witnesses disagree as to where the <<kurios (o) theos>> forms
begin, cf. the readings at 43.18; 44.6 and 44.9.

It has been argued that the witness of 967, the Old Latin
and B, which attest the earliest ascertainable stages of the
text, leads to the conclusion that originally the Old Greek
had a single <<kurios>> throughout. Accordingly, all double
forms now present in the manuscripts must be the result of
revisions. It must be admitted that certain revisions did take
place, as the Hexaplaric and Lucianic manuscripts show. Yet
even if we ignore those, we still find a large variety of
renderings which imply <<'dny yhwh>>. They are not random in
that they follow the pattern of the MT, and hence must be
based, directly or indirectly, on the readings of a Hebrew
text. However, it seems a little unusual that such revisions
were so careful to get the place right, and yet only
sporadically altered the renderings of the double names. The
wide variety of names would point to several revisions too, at
least three in each section. This is not impossible, but does
not seem very likely. It is even less likely that such
revisions were then applied just to sections of the book.

The Early Form of The Divine Name in Greek Texts.

There is another interpretation which may explain the
variety and distribution of readings more satisfactorily.
Recently, it has become fairly clear that in many of the early
Greek MSS the divine name Yahweh was written in Hebrew letters
(either in the old or in the square script) within the Greek
text. The evidence /5/ for this may be summarised as follows:

The Greek Text of Ezekiel

1. Origen comments that, "in the most accurate of texts the
    [tetragrammaton] is found in Hebrew characters, not in the
    present Hebrew characters, but in the very ancient ones."
    (Commentary on the Psalms. Ps 2.2. PG 12, col 1104).

2. Jerome tells us that, "Even today we find in some Greek
    manuscripts the tetragrammaton name of God written in the
    old characters." (Preface to the Books of Samuel and
    Kings. PL 28, col 550). He also relates that, "the ninth
    [name of God] is the 'tetragram', which they consider
    'anekphoneton', i.e. ineffable, and which is written in
    the letters Iod, He, Waw, He. Some who were not acquainted
    with the word used to read PIPI on account of the
    similarity of the characters, when they met it in the
    Greek books." (Letter to Marcellus. Concerning the Names
    of God. PL 22, col 429).

3. Jacob of Edessa observes that, "... some do not translate
    it [the divine name] at all and do not even alter the
    Hebrew characters with which it was written ..." (taken
    from the German translation in the article by E. Nestle,
    "Jakob von Edessa über den Schem hammephorasch und
    andere Gottesnamen", 1878: 498).

4. The Hexaplaric Syriac uses "pipi" freely for <<kurios>> i
    its Septuagint text.

5. Fragments of Aquila published by Burkitt (1897) and Taylc
    (1900) showed the divine name written in palaeo-Hebrew
    characters in parts of the books of Kings and Psalms.

6. The Ambrosian Palimpsest, discovered around the turn of
    the century and published by G. Mercati in 1958, contain
    parts of the Hexapla of the book of Psalms. In all the
    columns the name <<yhwh>> was left untranslated, being

written in square Hebrew characters.

7. Oxyrhynchus Papyrus 1007 (vol 7, 1910), dated late third
    century, contained fragments of Genesis which represented
    <<kurios>> by two barred z's. These are taken to represent
    doubled yodhs.

8. Papyrus Fouad Inv. 266, of which further fragments have
    recently been published, (cf. Aly and Koenen, "Three Rolls
    of the Early Septuagint: Genesis and Deuteronomy", 1980),
    showed a Greek text of Deuteronomy which contained
    <<yhwh>> written in square Hebrew characters. The papyrus
    dates from the first century B.C. and is thus one of the
    earliest witnesses to this phenomenon.

9. The scroll of the Minor Prophets which Barthélemy
    published in his book "Les Devanciers d'Aquila" (1963) had
    a Greek text which contained <<yhwh>> written in
    palaeo-Hebrew. The scroll is dated around A.D. 50.

10. Some translations or transliterations of <<yhwh>> were
    also noted by ancient writers, and others have been found
    in Oxyrhynchus and Qumran material. These usually take the
    form <<iao>> or <<iae>>. Cf. Skehan 1980: 28-31.

        So it is quite possible, even probable, that <<yhwh>>
appeared in Hebrew letters of some sort in the Greek texts of
Ezekiel /6/. Indeed, a few Hexaplaric readings attest <<PIPI>>
in some versions, cf. Ziegler's apparatus at 2.4; 12.23; 13.7;
18.23; 21.18; 30.6a; 33.1; 36.23a. Let us assume that the
translator(s) did render <<'dny>> by <<kurios>>. This is quite
possible as it was frequently rendered thus when not applied
to God. It cannot quite be ruled out that a transliteration
<<adònai>> was used, but it affects our argument little. There
is much less evidence for an early use of <<adònai>>.

Our text would thus contain a mixture of <<yhwh>> and <<kurios yhwh>> readings. At some stage the <<yhwh>> form was changed to <<kurios>>. This procedure was straightforward until a <<kurios yhwh>> was met, and here we find the key to our problem. Certainly, the scribe had a number of options before him, including <<adònai kurios>>, <<kurios kurios>> and <<kurios (o) theos>>. But there was also the possibility that he assumed the <<kurios>> in the text already stood for <<yhwh>> and so he would just have written a single <<kurios>> in his copy instead of the double form.

This hypothesis about the reduction of the divine name has some support from manuscripts containing certain early forms of nomina sacra. Oxyrhynchus Papyrus 656 (Grenfell, Hunt 1904 <vol 4>: 28-36), which contains fragments of Genesis, drew the comment from its editors that:

> A peculiar feature is the tendency to omit the
> word <<kurios>> when applied to the Deity;
> this occurs in no fewer than four passages
> (11.17,122,155,166), in three of which
> (11.17,122,166) the omission has been made
> good by the second hand. (1904: 30).

In all of them the <<kurios>> left out rendered the word <<yhwh>> in the Hebrew, whereas instances of <<kurios>> which meant "master" are retained. In two of the four the MT has a double divine name, and indeed in one case (11.17 - i.e. 15.8) this is <<'dny yhwh>>. In this verse most MSS read <<despota kurie>>, but the Papyrus 656 text retains only the first word, the second having been inserted by another hand.

The Hexapla fragments edited by Mercati (1958) also contain an indication why <<kurios yhwh>> might simply have been copied as <<kurios>> at some stage. In these fragments of the Psalms the word <<yhwh>> is attested by

Divine Names: A Solution

the Greek witnesses at 42 locations in the text.
Unfortunately there are no occurrences of <<'dny yhwh>>
extant. An examination of the Ziegler edition of the
Psalms shows a uniform attestation of single <<kurios>>
forms. Yet the striking fact is that in 20 out of these 42
instances the LXX column gives a doubled form:

References in MT (LXX) of Psalms	LXX column in Hexapla fragments	Reading in LXX (Ziegler text)	Reading in MT
18.42 (17.42)	κν יה>הו<לי	κυριον	יהוה
28.7 (27.7)	κϛ יהוה	κυριοϛ	יהוה
28.8 (27.8)	וחזי κϛ יהוה	κυριοϛ	יהוה
29.3 (28.3)	κυ יהוה	κυριου	יהוה
29.3 (28.3)	κϛ יהוה	κυριοϛ	יהוה
30.3 (29.3)	יהוה κε	κυριε	יהוה
30.5 (29.5)	יהוה κωι τωι	τω κυριω	ליהוה
30.8 (29.8)	יהוה κε	κυριε	יהוה
30.11 (29.11)	יהוה κϛ	κυριοϛ	יהוה
30.13 (29.13)	יהוה κε	κυριε	יהוה
31.2 (30.2)	κε יהוה	κυριε	יהוה
31.10 (30.10)	κε יהוה	κυριε	יהוה
31.22 (30.22)	κϛ יהוה	κυριοϛ	יהוה
31.24 (30.24)	κϛ יהוה	κυριοϛ	יהוה
32.10 (31.10)	κν יהוה επι	επι κυριον	ביהוה
35.1 (34.1)	κε יהוה	κυριε	יהוה
35.22 (34.22)	יהוה ,κε	κυριε	יהוה
35.24 (34.24)	κε יהוה	κυριε	יהוה
35.27 (34.27)	κϛ ο יהוה	ο κυριοϛ	יהוה
36.1 (35.1)	κυ יהוה	κυριου	יהוה

There are also 6 occurrences of <<'dny>>, which the Greek
columns render variously. Some translate it by <<kurios>>,
which is indistinguishable from the <<kurios>> in the

double readings. Neither it nor the several other names of
God which appear are ever retained in Hebrew letters in
the Greek columns.

It seems from this case that there was a tendency at
a later stage of the Greek text for the <<kurios>> form to
creep in, probably because <<yhwh>> was pronounced that
way by Greek readers /7/. Scribes who were aware of this
might have assumed that every instance of <<kurios yhwh>>
was the result of a "kethiv" and "qere" written together
and so have retained only <<kurios>> when replacing the
<<yhwh>> forms.

If this deduction is applied to the Greek text of
Ezekiel, then we can see immediately why the distribution
of divine names has so much variety and yet retains a
certain accuracy. At one stage in the history of the text
it was deemed desirable or necessary to replace the Hebrew
name <<yhwh>> with a Greek equivalent. Scribes did not
need to check a Hebrew manuscript to find the double
names. They were already in the text. However, each scribe
had several options for replacing these double forms —
<<adònai kurios>>, <<kurios kurios>>, <<kurios (o) theos>>
and also just <<kurios>> by itself. Thus we have a variety
of readings. In some instances here and there the doubled
form might first have already been written beside the word
<<yhwh>>.

The Three Sections.

The three-fold division of the names is probably
best explained by assuming that the Greek text of Ezekiel
circulated for a while in scrolls. It might have been that
the most convenient size of scroll contained around 20

chapters of text at a time. Sections (a) and (b) are
approximately the same length, while section (c) is
smaller. Although papyrus rolls could and did vary greatly
in dimensions, there were standard sizes. E. G. Turner
comments, "The sheets were immediately pasted together to
form rolls, a common number (Pliny wrongly says it was
never exceeded) being twenty sheets to a roll" (1968: 4).
Interestingly, Aly and Koenen (1980: 6) conjecture that
Papyrus 848 might have been one of two rolls containing
the text of Deuteronomy, ch.1-16 being in one roll and
ch.17-33 in the other. A very rough guide to the
comparative sizes may be had by counting the number of
pages of the respective sections in the Rahlfs Septuagint:

Section	No. of Pages
Ez 1.1 - 20.34	32
Ez 20.34 - 40.4	39
Ez 40.4 - end	20
Deut 1 -16	36
Deut 17 - 33	33

The divisions may have varied a little. It might be
due to an overlap that the Catena group have so many
conflated readings in 20.39 - 22.3. The break between
scrolls may even have contributed indirectly to the change
in text-type of certain of the Lucianic manuscripts at
22.12.

Summary of the Transmission of the Nomen Sacrum.

The history of the divine name in the Greek
manuscripts of Ezekiel may be summarised thus:

The Greek Text of Ezekiel

First, the translator(s) of the LXX, finding <<'dny yhwh>> in the Vorlage, rendered it by <<kurios yhwh>>.

Second, there came a stage when the Hebrew word <<yhwh>> was to be replaced by a Greek equivalent. This caused particular problems in Ezekiel, as <<kurios>> was already beside <<yhwh>>. Several solutions were possible, including <<adònai kurios>>, <<kurios kurios>>, <<kurios (o) theos>> and single <<kurios>>. These were applied by scribes. The text circulated in three rolls.

Third, several recensions of the text were made. These included the work of Aquila, Symmachus, Theodotion, Origen and Lucian. Some relied on the witness of earlier texts for their renderings of the divine names. Others translated directly from the Hebrew.

Fourth, the process of textual transmission continued, with the effects of the revisions spreading to other manuscripts as well, resulting in further complication of the picture.

Implications for the Homogeneity Issue.

Several conclusions may be drawn.

1. The present distribution of the divine names in the Greek manuscripts represents a stage subsequent to that of the translation and cannot be taken as evidence by itself for or against multiple-translator hypotheses.

2. The distribution of variants cannot be taken on its own as support for an early (fully recensional) revision of some part of the text. The early stage of transmission of the word <<yhwh>> was a unique, scribal phenomenon.

Divine Names: A Solution

3. There does seem to have been a stage when the text existed
    in three independent sections. It could be expected that
    each of these sections might exhibit a different textual
    tradition from the others. There may exist minor scribal
    idiosyncrasies which would further distinguish the
    sections one from another.

CHAPTER V

SECTIONS OF THE TEXT — I

The Division of Chapters 1-39

Up to this point our findings concerning the Greek text
of Ezekiel have been somewhat negative. In chapter II we had
seen that many of the examples previously cited to support
division of the text were invalid. In chapters III and IV we
found that the most notable case, that of the divine names,
could not be used either. However, the demonstration of the
invalidity of some examples does not imply the invalidity of
all of them.

In the next three chapters we shall see that there are
still grounds for believing that the Greek text of Ezekiel is
not homogeneous. It will be argued here that the evidence
still points to a three-fold division of the text, the
sections consisting of 1-25, 26-39, and 40-48. This is in
agreement with N. Turner, and differs from the (normally
accepted) division made by Thackeray, Herrmann and
Danielsmeyer: 1-27, 28-39, and 40-48. In order to prevent
confusion by redefining the limits of a' and b', the sections
are named here in the following way:

S1 = 1-25; S2 = 26-39; S3 = 40-48.

In this chapter we shall concentrate on 1-39 and shall
attempt to show that it divides into 1-25 (S1) and 26-39 (S2).
Here it will be maintained that the evidence supports the view
that the difference between S1 and S2 indicates different
translators, rather than a translator and a reviser. This
conclusion against revision concurs with the views of

Thackeray, Herrmann and Turner, rather than Ziegler, Kase and Tov.

In general the LXX translation of Ezekiel follows the Hebrew word order as closely as possible, regardless of how the individual words are rendered. This feature has a two-fold effect. Firstly, it excludes the possibility of examining significant stylistic variation in Greek word order for signs of change in translation technique. Secondly, and more helpfully, it means that we can be fairly certain in most cases which word in Greek corresponds to what we have in the Hebrew. Most of the translation examples cited below deal with individual words. The few phrases which are examined are given because they help to fix the context in which their components occur.

There may be some instances where the translation displays elements of a more interpretative nature, e.g. in ch.40-42. However, these are not widespread and are difficult to compare, and so have usually been omitted here, (but cf. <6.40>).

We shall first list the examples of translation change (in approximate order of strength) and then discuss the overall picture they present.

As mentioned before, a number of examples previously cited by Thackeray, Herrmann or Turner will be presented here too, along with references to their previous citation(s). In most instances these had simply been noted in lists and had not been discussed. References to previous citations of such cases are given here at the beginning of the comments following each example. Other cases are discussed in the comments.

Sections of the Text: Chapters 1-39

Translation Examples

```
                    <5.1-3>  (יהוה) אני כי ידע
              <5.1> ידע  <5.2> כי  <5.3> (יהוה) אני
```

2.5	וידעו	και γνωσονται	
5.13	וידעו	και επιγνωση	-ονται (4)/ -εσθαι (2)
	כי-אני	διοτι εγω	οτι (2)
6.7	וידעים	και επιγνωσεσθε	<επι> (5)
	כי-אני	οτι εγω	εγω ειμι (4)
6.10	וידעו	και επιγνωσονται	-εσθαι (2)/ <επι> (3)
	כי-אני	διοτι εγω	οτι (2-5)
6.13	וידעתם	και γνωσεσθε	επι- (3)/ -ονται (2,5)
	כי-אני	διοτι εγω	οτι (2-6)
6.14	וידעו	και επιγνωσεσθε	-ονται (4)/ <επι> (3)
	כי-אני	οτι εγω	
7.4	וידעתם	και επιγνωση	<επι> (2-6)
	כי-אני	διοτι εγω	οτι (2,3,5)
7.9	וידעתם	και επιγνωση	
	כי אני	διοτι εγω ειμι	<ειμι> (2,4)
7.27	וידעו	και γνωσονται	–
	כי-אני	οτι εγω	
10.20	ואדע	και εγνων	–
11.5	ידעתיה	επισταμαι	–
11.10	וידעתם	και επιγνωσεσθε	<επι> (4)
	כי-אני	οτι εγω	διοτι (6)
11.12	וידעתם	και επιγνωσεσθε	
	כי-אני	διοτι εγω	οτι (2,5)
12.15	וידעו	και γνωσονται	επι- (6)
	כי-אני	διοτι εγω	οτι (2,3)
12.16	וידעו	και γνωσονται	–
	כי-אני	οτι εγω	
12.20	וידעתם	και επιγνωσεσθε	-σονται (2)
	כי-אני	διοτι εγω	οτι (4,5)
13.9	וידעתם	και γνωσονται	-εσθε (6)
//	כי אני	διοτι εγω	οτι (2,4,5)/ δε οτι (5)
13.14	וידעתם	και επιγνωσεσθε	
	כי-אני	διοτι εγω	οτι (1,2)
13.21	וידעתן	και επιγνωσεσθε	
	כי-אני	διοτι εγω	οτι (1,2,4,5)
13.23	וידעתן	και γνωσεσθε	επι- (2-5)
	כי-אני	οτι εγω	διοτι (2-5)
14.8	וידעתם	και επιγνωσεσθε	-σθησεσθε (6)
	כי-אני	οτι εγω	
14.23	וידעתם	και επιγνωσεσθε	<επι> (6)

The Greek Text of Ezekiel

15.7	וידעתם כי אני	και επιγνωσονται οτι εγω	-εσθαι (2)/ ‹επι› (2-6) διοτι (2)/ εγω ειμι (6)
16.62	וידעת כי-אני	και επιγνωση οτι εγω	γνωση (5)
17.12	הידעתם	επιστασθε	επιστασαι (6)
17.21	וידעתם כי אני	και επιγνωσεσθε διοτι εγω	‹επι› (3,5) οτι (1,2)
17.24	וידעו (... כי א)	και γνωσονται (... διοτι εγω)	-ται (4,5)/ επι- (4) οτι (2,4,6)
19.7	וידע	και ενεμετο	-
20.12	לדעת כי אני	του γνωναι αυτους διοτι εγω	οτι (1,2,4,5,6)
20.20	לדעת כי אני	του γινωσκειν διοτι εγω	οτι (1,2,4,5,6)
20.26	// וידעו	‹›	γνωσιν (2-6)
20.38	וידעתם כי-אני	και επιγνωσεσθε διοτι εγω	οτι (2,4,5)
20.42	וידעתם כי-אני	και επιγνωσεσθε διοτι εγω	οτι (1,2,4)
20.44	וידעתם כי-אני	και επιγνωσεσθε διοτι εγω	οτι (1,4)
21.10	וידעו (... כי א)	και επιγνωσεται (διοτι εγω)	-ονται (3)/ -εσθε (2,5; οτι (1-4)
22.16	וידעת כי-אני	και γνωσεσθε διοτι εγω	γνωση (1,2) οτι (1-4)/ ειμι (2,6)
22.22	וידעתם כי-אני	και επιγνωσεσθε διοτι εγω	οτι (4)
23.49	וידעתם // כי אני	και γνωσεσθε διοτι εγω	οτι (1,4)
24.24	וידעתם // כי-אני	και επιγνωσεσθε διοτι εγω	‹επι› (1,2) οτι (1,2,4)
24.27	וידעו כי-אני	και επιγνωσονται διοτι εγω	‹επι› (1,4)/ -εσθαι (2 οτι (1,3,4)
25.5	וידעתם כי-אני	και επιγνωσεσθε διοτι εγω	‹επι› (1) οτι (1-4)
25.7	וידעת כי-אני	και επιγνωση διοτι εγω	-εσθε (2,3)/γνωση (1,2 οτι (1,4)
25.11	וידעו כי-אני	και επιγνωσονται διοτι εγω	-εσθε (2,6)/‹επι› (1,4 οτι (1,4)
25.14	וידעו	και επιγνωσονται	-εται (5)/ ‹επι› (1)
25.17	וידעו כי-אני	και επιγνωσονται διοτι εγω	‹επι› (1) οτι (4)
26.6	וידעו כי-אני	και γνωσονται οτι εγω	επι- (3) διοτι (3,5)/ ειμι (1,
28.19	ידעיך	οι επισταμενοι σε	-

Sections of the Text: Chapters 1-39

	Hebrew	Greek	Notes
28.22	וידעו / כי-אני	και γνωση / οτι εγω ειμι	γνωσονται (3) / διοτι (2,6)/ <ειμι> (5)
28.23	וידעו / כי-אני	και γνωσονται / οτι εγω ειμι	επι- (4)/ γνωση (2) / διοτι (1)/ <ειμι> (4,5)
28.24	וידעו // כי אני	και γνωσονται / οτι εγω ειμι	<ειμι> (4,5)
28.26	וידעו / כי אני	και γνωσονται / οτι εγω ειμι	<ειμι> (5)
29.6	וידעו / ... כי א...	και γνωσονται / ... οτι εγω ειμι	<ειμι> (2)
29.9	וידעו / כי-אני	και γνωσονται / οτι εγω ειμι	επι- (4) / <ειμι> (3,5,6)
29.16	וידעו // כי אני	και γνωσονται / οτι εγω ειμι	<ειμι> (3,6)
29.21	וידעו / כי-אני	και γνωσονται / οτι εγω ειμι	<ειμι> (3,4,5)
30.8	וידעו / כי-אני	και γνωσονται / οτι εγω ειμι	διοτι (3)/ <ειμι> (2-4)
30.19	וידעו / כי-אני	και γνωσονται / οτι εγω ειμι	<ειμι> (5)
30.25	וידעו / כי-אני	και γνωσονται / οτι εγω ειμι	-
30.26	וידעו / כי-אני	και γνωσονται ... / οτι εγω ειμι	επι- (2)
32.9	ידעתם	εγνως	-
32.15	וידעו / כי-אני	και γνωσονται / οτι εγω ειμι	-εσθε (4)
33.29	וידעו / כי-אני	και γνωσονται / οτι εγω ειμι	- / <ειμι> (4,5)
33.33	וידעו	και γνωσονται	-
34.27	וידעו / כי-אני	και γνωσονται / οτι εγω ειμι	<ειμι> (1,2)
34.30	וידעו / כי אני	και γνωσονται / οτι εγω ειμι	-εσθε (6) / <ειμι> (1)
35.4	וידעת / כי-אני	και γνωση / οτι εγω ειμι	<ειμι> (4)
35.9	וידעתם / כי-אני	και γνωση / οτι εγω ειμι	-ονται (1,5,6)
35.12	וידעת / כי-אני	και γνωση / οτι εγω ειμι	-
35.15	וידעו / כי-אני	και γνωση / οτι εγω ειμι	-ονται (1-6)
36.11	וידעתם / כי-אני	και γνωσεσθε / οτι εγω ειμι	-ονται (6) / διοτι (2,3)/ <ειμι> (3)
36.23	וידעו / ... כי-אני ...	και γνωσονται / ... οτι εγω ειμι	-εται (1,4) / <ειμι> (3,5,6)

36.36	וידעו (... כי אני)	και γνωσονται (... οτι εγω //)	-εται (4) ειμι (1,2,3)
36.38	וידעו כי-אני	και γνωσονται οτι εγω	ειμι (2,4,5)
37.3	ידעת	συ επιστη ταυτα	επιστασαι (1-6)
37.6	וידעתם כי-אני	και γνωσεσθε οτι εγω ειμι	διοτι (2)/ <ειμι> (6)
37.13	וידעתם כי-אני	και γνωσεσθε οτι εγω ειμι	<ειμι> (1,6)
37.14	וידעתם כי-אני	και γνωσεσθε οτι εγω	διοτι (3)/ ειμι (1,4-6)
37.28	וידעו (... כי אני)	και γνωσονται (... οτι εγω ειμι)	-εται (4) <ειμι> (1,6)
38.14	תדע	<>	γνωση (4)
38.16	דעת	γνωσι	γνω με (4)/ γνωμεν (4)
38.23	וידעו כי-אני	και γνωσονται οτι εγω ειμι	-
39.6	וידעו כי-אני	και γνωσονται οτι εγω ειμι	<ειμι> (3)
39.7	וידעו ... כי-אני	και γνωσονται ... οτι εγω ειμι	-εται (4)
39.22	וידעו ... כי אני	και γνωσονται ... οτι εγω ειμι	-εται- (4)
39.23	וידעו	και γνωσονται	-εται (4)
39.28	וידעו כי אני	και γνωσονται οτι εγω ειμι	<ειμι> (3,6)

This example sets the pattern. (For the sake of completeness
all instances of <<yd'>> have been included.) A quite clear
distinction can be seen between S1 and S2:

S1	S2
(επι-)γινωσκειν	γινωσκειν
διοτι/ οτι	οτι
εγω	εγω ειμι

It must be admitted that the textual variation for
<<oti>>/<<dioti>> and the prefix <<epi>> does put doubt on
their validity in some instances. The evidence for the
omission or addition of <<eimi>> is stronger.

Sections of the Text: Chapters 1-39

S2 shows more consistency and hence deviations are more noticeable. The omission of <<eimi>> in 37.14 is possibly incorrect. (P. 967 attests its use here). However, the omission of the same word in 36.36,38 points to the unusual character of 36.23c-38 (see later).

This example had been adduced by Thackeray, who took the dividing-line to be between 26.6 and 28.23 (1903b: 400). He relied on the witness of B, which omits <<eimi>> in 26.6, as does the Ziegler text. However, neither Thackeray nor Ziegler had 967 for this part, and both 967 and the A manuscripts contain <<eimi>> at 26.6. The testimony of 967 in particular greatly reinforces the external support for retaining <<eimi>>, and thus links 26.6 with ch.27-39. The strength of manuscript attestation against retaining the prefix <<epi->> and the form <<dioti>> also allies 26.6 with the chapters following it.

It is at 26.6 that a somewhat circular relationship between translation criticism and textual criticism can be seen. Conclusions concerning which reading to adopt affect the decision about where to locate the dividing-line between sections. Conversely, the decision about the location of the dividing-line can reduce or increase support for a particular textual reading.

<5.4> חרב

5.1	חרב	ρομφαιαν	—
5.2	בחרב	εν ρομφαια	<εν> (6)
5.2	וחרב	και μαχαιραν	—
5.12	בחרב יפלו	εν ρομφαια πεσουνται	—
5.12	וחרב	και μαχαιραν	—
5.17	וחרב	και ρομφαιαν	—
5.3	חרב	ρομφαιαν	—

6.8	חרב	εκ ρομφαιας	μαχαιρας (3)
6.11	בחרב...יפלו	εν ρομφαια...πεσουνται	–
6.12	בחרב יפול	εν ρομφαια πεσειται	–
7.15	החרב	εν ρομφαια	και η ρομ. (1,4,5) / εν τη ρομ. (2)
7.15	בחרב ימות	εν ρομφαια τελευτησει	–
11.8	חרב	ρομφαιαν	–
11.8	וחרב	και ρομφαιαν	–
11.10	בחרב תפלו	εν ρομφαια πεσεισθε	–
12.14	וחרב	και ρομφαιαν	–
12.16	מחרב	εκ ρομφαιας	–
14.17	חרב	ρομφαιαν	–
14.17	חרב	ρομφαια	–
14.21	חרב	ρομφαιαν	–
16.40	בחרבותם	εν τοις ξιφεσιν αυτων	–
17.21	בחרב יפלו	εν ρομφαια πεσουνται	–
21.8	חרבי	το εγχειριδιον μου	χειριδιον (4)
21.9	חרבי	το εγχειριδιον μου	–
21.10	חרבי	το εγχειριδιον μου	–
21.14	חרב חרב	ρομφαια ρομφαια	<ρομφαια> (1,2,4)
21.16	חרב	ρομφαια	η ρομφαια (1,4)
21.17	אל-חרב	επι ρομφαια	ρομφαιαν (1-5)
21.19	חרב	ρομφαιαν	–
21.19	חרב	ρομφαια	–
21.19	חרב	ρομφαια	<> (1)
21.20	חרב	ρομφαιας	–
21.24	חרב	ρομφαιαν	-ας (6)/ -α (6)
21.25	חרב	ρομφαιαν	–
21.33	חרב חרב	ρομφαια ρομφαια	<ρομφαια> (3)
23.10	בחרב	εν ρομφαια	–
23.25	בחרב תפול	εν ρομφαια καταβαλουσιν	βαλουσιν (5) αποκτενουσιν (2)
23.47	בחרבותם	εν τοις ξιφεσιν αυτων	–
24.21	בחרב יפלו	εν ρομφαια πεσουνται	–
25.13	בחרב יפלו	εν ρομφαια πεσουνται	–
26.6	בחרב	μαχαιρα	–

26.8	בחרב	μαχαιρα	< > (5)
26.9	בחרבותיו	εν ταις μαχαιραις αυτου	εν τοις οπλοις αυτου (4,6)
26.11	בחרב	μαχαιρα	εν μαχαιρα (2,6)
28.7	חרבותם	τας μαχαιρας αυτων	—
28.23	בחרב	εν μαχαιραις	(εν) μαχαιρα (1,5, 6)/ <εν> (1,4)
29.8	חרב	ρομφαιαν	εν ρομφεα (2)
30.4	חרב	μαχαιρα	η μαχαιρα (2,5,6)
30.5	בחרב יפלו	μαχαιρα πεσουνται	—
30.6	בחרב יפלו	μαχαιρα πεσουνται	—
30.11	חרבותם	τας μαχαιρας αυτων	—
30.17	בחרב יפלו	εν μαχαιρα πεσουνται	<εν> (1-6)
30.21	לתפש בחרב	επιλαβεσθαι μαχαιρας	—
30.22	החרב	την μαχαιραν αυτου	—
30.24	חרבי	την ρομφαιαν μου	<μου> (1)
30.25	חרבי	την ρομφαιαν μου	<μου> (1)
31.17	חרב	απο μαχαιρας	εν ταις -ραις (3)/ <απο> (2,4)/ < > (2)
31.18	חרב	μαχαιρας	μαχαιρα (2)
32.10	חרבי	την ρομφαιαν μου	—
32.11	חרב	ρομφαια	—
32.12	בחרבות	εν μαχαιραις	-ρα (2,4)/ ρομφαια (4)
32.20	חרב	μαχαιρας	μαχαιρα (2,3,5,6)
32.20	חרב	< >	—
32.21	חרב	μαχαιρας	—
32.22	הנפלים בחרב	οι πεπτωκοτες μαχαιρα	—
32.23	נפלים בחרב	< > //	πιπτοντες μαχαιρα (2-6)/ π. εν μαχ. (4)
32.24	הנפלים בחרב	οι πεπτωκοτες μαχαιρα	—
32.25	חרב	< >	μαχαιρα/-ας (3,4)
32.26	חרב	απο μαχαιρας	—
32.27	חרבותם	τας μαχαιρας αυτων	—
32.28	חרב	μαχαιρα	μαχαιρας (2)

32.29	חרב	μαχαιρας	−
32.30	חרב	μαχαιρας	μαχαιρα (6)
32.31	חרב	< >	μαχαιρα/ −ας (2−6)
32.32	חרב	μαχαιρας	−
33.2	חרב	ρομφαιαν	κριμα αιματος (2)
33.3	החרב	την ρομφαιαν	−
33.4	חרב	η ρομφαια	−
33.6	החרב	την ρομφαιαν	−
33.6	חרב	η ρομφαια	−
33.26	חרבכם	< >	ρομφαια(−ν/−ς) (2−6)/ μαχαιρας (3)
33.27	יפלו בחרב	μαχαιρα πεσουνται	μαχαιραις (1,3)
35.5	חרב	μαχαιρα	−ας (2,4,5)
35.8	חרב	μαχαιρα	−
38.4	חרבות	και μαχαιραι	−ας (4)
38.8	מחרב	απο μαχαιρας	−
38.21	חרב ירי	φοβον	φοβον μαχαιρας (1−6)
38.21	חרב	μαχαιρα	−αι (3)
39.23	ויפלו בחרב	και επεσεν παντες μαχαιρα	<μαχαιρα> (2)

Thackeray does refer to the use of <<makhaira>> but contrasts it with the term <<xiphos>> rather than with <<romphaia>> (1903b: 403; cf. Herrmann 1923: 9). According to his observations <<makhaira>> occurs "33 times from xxviii 7 to xxxix 23" (1903b: 403). Yet it is clear from the list above that the break occurs well before 28.7. The predominant use <<romphaia>> ends at 25.13, while that of <<makhaira>> begins at 26.6. Textual variation has little effect on the evidence in this case.

In addition we can note how the phrase "to fall by the sword" is rendered differently in each section. S1 selects the use of <<en>> + <<romphaia>> (5.12; 6.11,12; 11.10; 17.21; 23.25; 24.21; 25.13), while S2 prefers the dative of <<makhaira>> (30.5,6; 32.22,24; 33.27). The retention of

<<en>> at 30.17 in the Ziegler text may be incorrect. Papyrus
67 and the A MSS omit it.

There does not seem to be any appreciable change of
context to merit such a marked change in the rendering. In by
far the majority of instances in both S1 and S2 the term
"sword" is used in a synecdochic way to express the violent
manner of retribution which will befall the subjects of the
prophecies. For example, in 6.11 we read:

Thus says my Lord Yahweh:

Clap your hands and stamp your feet

and cry "Alas" because of all

the evil abominations of the house of Israel.

They will fall by the sword, famine and plague.

Either section is totally consistent. When Yahweh refers to
"my sword", S1 employs <<egkheiridion>> (21.8,9,10 = LXX
1.3,4,5) and S2 uses <<romphaia>>. The rendering <<xiphos>>
occurs only in 16.40 and 23.47. In these two cases, and
nowhere else in Ezekiel, the context is that of a crowd
stoning adulterous women and then hacking them to pieces with
their swords. Again, it is only in these two locations in S1
that the Hebrew term appears in the plural.

Although the terms <<romphaia>> and <<makhaira>> were not
synonymous in Classical Greek, it seems that the translators
of the LXX found difficulty in deciding which was more
suitable as a rendering. Both terms are commonly found in the
LXX. Apparently the Kaige used <<romphaia>>, while Aquila and
Symmachus used <<makhaira>>, cf. O'Connell (1972: 288) and
Bodine (1980: 26).

<5.5> אמר אל/ל (פ.)

2.1   ויאמר אלי   και ειπε προς με   <> (3)/
                                             κ. ε. μοι (4)

2.3   ויאמר אלי   και ειπε προς με   <> (2,3,5)/
                                             <προς με> (3,5)

2.4	ואמרת אליהם	και ειπε προς αυτους	–
3.1	ויאמר אלי	και ειπε προς με	–
3.3	ויאמר אלי	και ειπε προς με	κ. ε. μοι (3)
3.4	ויאמר אלי	και ειπε προς με	–
3.10	ויאמר אלי	και ειπε προς με	–
3.11	ואמרת אליהם	και ερεις προς αυτους	<> (2,4)
3.18	באמרי לרש	εν τω λεγειν με τω ανομω	... εν τω ανομω
3.22	ויאמר אלי	και ειπε προς με	κ. ε. εις με (5)
3.24	ויאמר אלי	και ειπε μοι	–
3.27	ואמרת אליהם	και ερεις προς αυτους	–
4.15	ויאמר אלי	και ειπε προς με	–
4.16	ויאמר אלי	και ειπε προς με	<> (3,6)
6.3	כה-אמר ... להרים	ταδε λεγει ... τοις ορεσι	–
6.11	ואמר-אח אל כל-תועבות	και ειπον ευγε ευγε επι πασι τοις βδελυγμασιν	κ. ειπε ... (4)/ εν πασι ... (6)
7.2	כה-אמר ... לאדמת	ταδε λεγει ... τη γη	–
8.5	ויאמר אלי	και ειπε προς με	κ. ε. επι με (3)
8.6	ויאמר אלי	και ειπε προς με	–
8.8	ויאמר אלי	και ειπε προς με	–
8.9	ויאמר אלי	και ειπε προς με	–
8.12	ויאמר אלי	και ειπε προς με	–
8.13	ויאמר אלי	και ειπε προς με	–
8.15	ויאמר אלי	και ειπε προς με	–
8.17	ויאמר אלי	και ειπε προς με	–
9.4	ויאמר יהוה אל	και ειπε προς αυτον	κ. ε. κυριος π. (2-6)
9.5	ולאלה אמר	και τουτοις ειπεν	κ. αυτοις ε. (4)
9.7	ויאמר אליהם	και ειπε προς αυτους	–
9.9	ויאמר אלי	και ειπε προς με	–
10.2	ויאמר אל-האיש	και ειπε προς τον ανδρα	–
11.2	ויאמר אלי	και ειπε κυριος προς με	κ. ε. π. μ. κυρι (2,3,5)/ <κυριος> (2)
11.5	ויאמר אלי	και ειπε προς με	–

11.15	אמרו להם	ειπαν αυτοις	ειπον α. (3,4)
12.9	אמרו אליך	ειπαν προς σε	ειπον π. σ. (2-4,6) / ειπε π. σ. (4)
12.10	אמר אליהם	ειπον προς αυτους	ειπε ... (4)/ ειπον ... (4)
12.19	ואמרת אל-עם	και ερεις προς τον λαον	—
12.19	כה-אמר ... לי ושבי	ταδε λεγει ... τοις κατοικουσιν	—
12.23	אמר אליהם	ειπον προς αυτους	ειπε ... (4)
12.28	אמר אליהם	ειπον προς αυτους	ειπε ... (4)
13.2	ואמרת לנביאי	και ερεις προς αυτους	—
13.11	אמר אל-טחי	ειπον προς τους αλειφοντας	ειπε ... (4)
13.15	ואמר לכם	και ειπα προς υμας	κ. ειπον ... (3,4)
14.4	ואמרת אליהם	και ερεις προς αυτους	κ. ε. αυτοις (1,3)
14.6	אמר אל-בית	ειπον προς τον οικον	ειπε ... (4)
16.3	כה-אמר ... לירושלם	ταδε λεγει ... τη ιερουσαλημ	—
17.12	אמר-נא לבית	ειπον &η προς τον οικον	ειπε ... (4)/ <&η> (1-4,6)
20.3	ואמרת אלהם	και ερεις προς αυτους	κ. ε. αυτοις (3)
20.5	ואמרת אליהם	και ειπε προς με	
20.30	אמר אל-בית	ειπον προς τον οικον	ειπε ... (4)
21.3	ואמרת ליער	και ερεις τω &ρυμω	<> (2)
21.5	אמרים לי	λεγουσι προς με	—
21.8	ואמרת לאדמת	και ερεις προς την γην	—
21.12	יאמרו אליך	ειπωσι προς σε	—
21.12	ואמרת אל-שמועה	και ερεις επι τη αγγελια	κ. ε. προς αυτους (συ) επι ... (1,4)/ ... επαγγελια (3,5)
21.33	כה אמר ... אל-בני	ταδε λεγει ... προς τους υιους	—
22.24	אמר-לה	ειπον αυτη	ειπε α. (4)
23.36	ויאמר יהוה אלי	και ειπε κυριος προς με	<κυριος> (1)
24.3	ואמרת אליהם	και ερεις προς αυτους	—
24.21	אמר לבית	ειπον προς τον οικον	ειπε ... (4)
25.3	ואמרת לבני	και ερεις τοις υιοις	—

26.15	... כה אמר לצור	ταδε λεγει ... τη σορ	τ. λ. γη σορ (5)/ ... της σωρ (4)/ ... επι σορ (1,2)/ ... επι σοι (2)/ ... επι σε σορ (1, 2)/ <τη σορ> (2)
26.17	ואמרו לך	και ερουσι	κ. ε. σοι (1-4)
27.3	ואמרת לצור	και ερεις τη σορ	<> (2)/ <τη> (1)/ <τη σορ> (4)
28.2	אמר לנגיד	ειπον τω αρχοντι	ειπε ... (1,4)
28.12	ואמרת לו	και ειπον αυτω	κ. ειπε α. (2,4)
31.2	אמר אל-פרעה	ειπον προς φαραω	ειπε ... (4)/ ε. αυτον (3)/ <φαραω> (1)
32.2	ואמרת אליו	και ερεις αυτω	—
33.2	ואמרת אליהם	και ερεις αυτω	—
33.10	אמר אל-בית	ειπον τω οικω	ειπε ... (4)
33.11	אמר אליהם	ειπον αυτοις	ειπε ... (4)
33.12	אמר אל-בני	ειπον προς τους υιους	ειπε ... (4)
33.13	באמרי לצדיק	εν τω ειπειν με τω δικαιω	εν τω ειπαι ... (1, 6)
33.14	ובאמרי לרשע	και εν τω ειπειν με τω ασεβει	... ειπαι ... (1,6)
33.25	אמר אליהם	ειπον αυτοις	ειπεν α. (2,3)/ ειπε α. (2-6)/ ε. προς αυτους (2-5)
33.27	כה-תאמר אלהם	<>	//
34.2	ואמרת אליהם לרעים	και ειπον τοις ποιμεσι	κ. ειπε ... (4)/ κ ερεις ... (3)/ κ. ε. αυτοις (2)/ κ. ε. προς αυτους τ. π. (3)
34.20	... כה אמר אליהם	ταδε λεγει ... <>	... προς αυτους (3 //
35.3	ואמרת לו	και ειπον αυτω	κ. ειπε α. (4)/ <αυτω> (1)
36.4	... כה-אמר להרים	ταδε λεγει ... τοις ορεσι	—
36.6	ואמרת להרים	και ειπον τοις ορεσι	κ. ειπε ... (4)
36.13	אמרים לכם	ειπαν σοι	<> (4)/ ειπον σ. (4)
36.20	באמר להם	εν τω λεγεσθαι αυτους	... αυτοις (4)
36.22	אמר לבית	ειπον τω οικω	ειπε ... (4)
37.3	ויאמר אלי	και ειπε προς με	—
37.4	ויאמר אלי	και ειπε προς με	—

Sections of the Text: Chapters 1-39

37.4	ואמרת אליהם	και ερεις αυτοις	κ. ε. προς αυτα (4, 6)/ <αυτοις> (6)
37.5	כה אמר ... לעצמות	ταδε λεγει ... τοις οστεοις	-
37.9	ויאמר אלי	και ειπε προς με	-
37.9	ואמרת אל-הרוח	και ειπον τω πνευματι	-
37.11	ויאמר אלי	και ελαλησε κυριος προς με	-
37.12	ואמרת אליהם	και ειπον	κ. ειπε (4)/ <> (6) /κ. ερεις (5)/ κ. ε. προς αυτους (2-6)
37.18	יאמרו אליך	λεγωσι προς με	λεγουσι ... (5)/ ειπωσι(ν) ... (4)
38.13	יאמרו לך	ερουσιν σοι	-
38.14	ואמרת לגוג	και ειπον τω γωγ	κ. ειπε ... (3,4)/ κ. ε. αυτω γ. (2)
39.17	אמר לצפור	ειπον παντι ορνεω	<ειπον> (5)/ ειπε ... (4)
41.4	ויאמר אלי	και ειπε	κ. ε. προς με (2-4, 6)
42.13	ויאמר אלי	και ειπε προς με	-
43.7	ויאמר אלי	και ειπε προς με	κ. ειπον ... (5)
43.18	ויאמר אלי	και ειπε προς με	-
44.2	ויאמר אלי	και ειπε ... προς με	<...> (1-6)
44.5	ויאמר אלי	και ειπε ... προς με	-
44.6	ואמרת אל-מרי	και ερεις προς τον οικον	-
46.20	ויאמר אלי	και ειπε προς με	-
46.24	ויאמר אלי	και ειπε προς με	-
47.6	ויאמר אלי	και ειπε προς με	-
47.8	ויאמר אלי	και ειπε προς με	-

Here S1 shows a definite preference for the use of <<pros>>
after a verb of speaking (a similar distribution is found with
<<dbr>> too), while S2 favours the dative. The change comes
after 24.21. However, it is difficult to see the location of
the dividing-line in this example because even S1 prefers to
translate the preposition <<l>> by a dative rather than by a
preposition. Neither section is totally consistent.

It seems to be the case that <<pros>> was used with the

first person pronoun in all three sections. We note that S2
always has <<pros me>> where <<moi>> might be expected:
37.3,4,9,11,18. If this is typical of the translation
technique of S2, then this example provides only weak evidence
for seeing a distinction between S2 and S3.

<5.6>   הנבא (...) ואמרת

6.2	...והנבא	και προφητευσον...	−
-3	ואמרת	και ερεις	−
13.2	...הנבא	προφητευσον...	//
	ואמרת	και ερεις	−
13.17	...והנבא	και προφητευσον...	−
-18	ואמרת	και ερεις	−
21.2	...והנבא	και προφητευσον...	−
-3	ואמרת	και ερεις	−
21.7	...והנבא	και προφητευσεις...	προφητευσον (1-4) /.
-8	ואמרת	και ερεις	<> (1,2,4,5)
21.14	הנבא	προφητευσον	−
	ואמרת	και ερεις	−
21.33	הנבא	προφητευσον	−
	ואמרת	και ερεις	−
25.2	...והנבא	και προφητευσον...	−
-3	ואמרת	και ερεις	−
28.21	...והנבא	και προφητευσον...	−
-22	ואמרת	και ειπον	ειπε (4)/
			ερεις (4,5)
29.2	...והנבא	και προφητευσον...	−
-3	ואמרת	και ειπον	ειπε (4)
30.2	הנבא	προφητευσον	−
	ואמרת	και ειπον	ειπε (4)
34.2	הנבא	προφητευσον	−
	ואמרת	και ειπον	ειπε (4)/ ερεις (3)
35.2	...והנבא	και προφητευσον...	−
-3	ואמרת	και ειπον	ειπε (4)
36.1	...הנבא	προφητευσον...	−
	ואמרת	και ειπον	ειπε (4)
36.3	הנבא	προφητευσον	−
	ואמרת	και ειπον	ειπε (4)
36.6	...הנבא	προφητευσον...	−
	ואמרת	και ειπον	ειπε (4)
37.4	...הנבא	προφητευσον...	−
	ואמרת	και ερεις	−

37.9	...הנבא	προφητευσον...	—
	ואמרת	και ειπον	ειπε (4)
37.12	הנבא	προφητευσον	—
	ואמרת	και ειπον	ειπε (4)/
			ερεις (5)/ <> (6)
38.2	...והנבא	και προφητευσον...	προφητευε (5)
-3	ואמרת	και ειπον	ειπε (4)
38.14	...הנבא	προφητευσον...	—
	ואמרת	και ειπον	ειπε (3,4)
39.1	...הנבא	προφητευσον...	—
	ואמרת	και ειπον	ειπε (4)/ ερεις (6)

Again, textual variation does not distort the overall picture. S1 uses a simple future after the imperative, while S2 prefers a second imperative.

Thackeray also cited 27.3, where <<ereis>> is used, as another example of this particular phrase. He took this as another case which supported his view that the text should be split after ch.27 (1903b: 400). However, the opening verses of ch.27 contain no <<whnb'>> to precede the <<w'mrt>>, and so this instance cannot be used here. Indeed, S2 does occasionally use <<ereis>> after other verbs in the imperative, e.g. 32.2; 33.2; cf. 37.4 above.

<5.7> עון

3.18	בעונו	τη αδικια αυτου	(εν) τη ανομια
			(2-6)
3.19	בעונו	εν τη αδικια αυτου	εν τη ανομια
			(2-6)
4.4	את-עון	τας αδικιας	—
4.4	את-עונם	τας αδικιας αυτου	—
4.5	את-שני עונם	τας δυο αδικιας αυτων	διαθηκας (5)
4.5	עון	τας αδικιας	αμαρτιας (5)
4.6	את-עון	τας αδικιας	—
4.17	בעונם	εν ταις αδικιαις αυτων	—
7.13	בעונו	εν οφθαλμω	εν οφθαλμοις
			(1-6)
7.16	בעונו	εν ταις αδικιαις αυτου	—

111

7.19	צונם	των αδικιων αυτων	–
9.9	צון	αδικια	αδικιαι (1,5,6)
14.3	צונם	των αδικιων αυτων	–
14.4	צונו	της αδικιας αυτου	–
14.7	צונו	της αδικιας αυτου	–
14.10	צונם	την αδικιαν αυτων	–
14.10	כעונ	κατα το αδικημα	επερωτημα (3)
14.10	כעונ	κατα το αδικημα	κατα τα αδικηματα ταυτα (2)
16.49	צון	το ανομημα	ανομια (3)
18.17	כעונ	εν αδικιαις	αδικια (3,6)
18.18	כעונו	εν τη αδικια αυτου	ταις αδικιαις (5)
18.19	כעונ	την αδικιαν	αδικιας (2)
18.20	כעונ	την αδικιαν	την αμαρτιαν (6)/ τας αδικιας (1)
18.20	כעונ	την αδικιαν	–
18.30	צון	αδικιας	–
21.28	צון	αδικιας	αδικιαν (1,3,4)/ ανομιαν (4,6)
21.29	צונם	τας αδικιας υμων	–
21.30	צון	αδικιας	–
21.34	צון	αδικιας	–
24.23	כעונתכם	εν ταις αδικιας υμων	ανομιαις (5)/ καρδιαις (3,4)
28.18	צונך	των αμαρτιων σου	ανομιων (4,6)
29.16	צון	ανομιαν	αμαρτιαν/ –ας (2
32.27	צונתם	αι ανομιαι αυτων	–
33.6	כעונו	δια την αυτης ανομιαν	αμαρτιαν (4)
33.8	כעונו	τη ανομια αυτου	τη ασεβεια (6)/ τη αμαρτια (1)
33.9	כעונו	τη ασεβεια αυτου	ανομια (2,4,6)
35.5	צון	αδικιας	α. αυτων (6)
36.31	על צונתכם	εν ταις ανομιαις υμων	περι των ανομιων ασεβειων (4)
36.33	צונתכם	των ανομιων υμων	⟨των ανομιων⟩ (6
39.23	צונם	δια τας αμαρτιας αυτου	–
43.10	מעונתהם	απο των αμαρτιων αυτου	–
44.10	צונם	αδικιαν αυτων	ατιμιαν (4)

44.12	צור	αδικιας	ανομιας (4)
44.12	צודם	<>	την ανομιαν (2-6)/ την ατιμιαν (2,3)

S1 seems reasonably consistent here in its use of <<adikia>> and related nouns. The "deviating" rendering in 16.49 will be discussed in chapter VII. S2, in contrast, is quite inconsistent. The LXX in general has no stereotyped rendering of <<'wn>>, the terms <<hamartia>>, <<anomia>> and <<adikia>> all being commonly used.

The differences in the rendering of the "sin" vocabulary in Ezekiel are by themselves illustrative of the differences in translation technique found between the two sections. Cf. examples <2.9; 2.27; 5.13; 5.22>.

<5.8> עם

3.5	אל-עם	προς λαον	—
3.6	אל-עמים רבים	προς λαους πολλους	—
3.11	עמך	του λαου σου	—
7.27	עם הארץ	του λαου της γης	—
11.1	העם	του λαου	—
11.17	מן-העמים	εκ των εθνων	—
11.20	לעם	εις λαον	—
12.19	אל-עם הארץ	προς τον λαον της γης	—
13.9	עמי	του λαου μου	—
13.10	את-עמי	τον λαον μου	—
13.17	עמך	του λαου σου	—
13.18	לעמי	του λαου μου	—
13.19	אל-עמי	προς τον λαον μου	—
13.19	לעמי	λαω	—
13.21	את-עמי	τον λαον μου	—
13.23	את-עמי	τον λαον μου	—
14.8	עמי	του λαου μου	—
14.9	עמי	του λαου μου	<μου> (6)

113

14.11	לעמי	εις λαον	–
17.9	בעם־רב	εν λαω πολλω	–
17.15	ועם־רב	και λαον πολυν	–
20.34	מן־העמים	εκ των λαων	–
20.35	העמים	των λαων	–
20.41	מן־העמים	εκ των λαων	–
21.17	בעמי	εν τω λαω μου	εκ του λαου (2)/ ⟨εν⟩ (3,6)
21.17	את־עמי	εν τω λαω μου	συν (4,6)
22.29	עם הארץ	λαον της γης	λαος (2,3,5)/ τον λαον (2-4)
23.24	עמים	λαων	–
24.18	אל־העם	προς τον λαον	–
24.19	העם	ο λαος	ο λ. μου (4)
25.7	מן־העמים	εκ των λαων	–
25.14	עמי	λαου μου	–
26.2	העמים	τα εθνη //	–
26.7	ועם־רב	εθνων πολλων σφοδρα	πολλης (2,5)/ πολυς (5)
26.11	עמך	τον λαον σου	
26.20	אל־עם	προς λαον	λακκον (3)
27.3	העמים	των λαων	–
27.33	עמים רבים	εθνη	–
27.36	בעמים	απο εθνων	α. των ε. (4)
28.19	בעמים	εν τοις εθνεσι	–
28.25	מן־העמים	εκ των εθνων	ε. τ. χωρων (2)
29.13	מן־העמים	απο των εθνων	–
30.11	ועמו	και του λαου αυτου	–
31.12	כל־עמי הארץ	παντες οι λαοι των εθνων	π. ο. λ. της γης (4,5)
32.3	עמים	λαων πολλων	⟨λαων⟩ (5)
32.9	לב עמים	λαων πολλων	⟨λαων⟩ (3)
32.10	עמים רבים	εθνη πολλα	πολλοι (2)/ ⟨πολλα⟩ (2)
33.2	עמך	του λαου σου	–
33.2	עם הארץ	ο λαος της γης	–
33.3	את־העם	τω λαω	–
33.6	והעם	και ο λαος	–

114

33.12	עמך	του λαου σου	–
33.17	עמך	του λαου σου	–
33.30	עמך	του λαου σου	–
33.31	עם	λαος	ο λαος (3)
33.31	עמי	< >	ο λαος μου (2-6)
34.13	מן-העמים	εκ των εθνων	–
34.30	עמי	λαος μου	–
36.3	ודבת-עם	και εις ονειδισμα εθνεσι	εθνων (1)
36.8	לעמי	ο λαος μου	–
36.12	את-עמי	τον λαον μου	–
36.15	עמים	λαων	εθνων (2)
36.20	עם-יהוה	λαος κυριου	–
36.28	לעם	εις λαον	–
37.12	עמי	< >	λαος μου (4)
37.13	עמי	τον λαον μου	λαος (2,3,5,6)
37.18	עמך	του λαου σου	–
37.23	לעם	εις λαον	–
37.27	לעם	λαος	εις λαον (2,3,5,6)
38.6	עמים	εθνη πολλα	–
38.8	מעמים רבים	απο εθνων πολλων	α. λαων π. (4)
38.8	מעמים	εξ εθνων	εκ των εθνων (2)
38.9	ועמים רבים	και εθνη πολλα	–
38.12	ואל-עם	και επι εθνος	–
38.14	עמי	τον λαον μου	–
38.15	ועמים רבים	και εθνη πολλα	–
38.16	על-עמי	επι τον λαον μου	–
38.22	על-עמים רבים	και επι εθνη πολλα	–
39.4	ועמים	και τα εθνη	εθνη πολλα (1)/ πολλα ε. (1)
39.7	עמי	λαου μου	λαων (1)/ < > (3)
39.13	כל-עם הארץ	πας ο λαος της γης	οικος ισραηλ (5)
39.27	מן-העמים	εκ των εθνων	–
42.14	לעם	του λαου	–
44.11	לעם	τω λαω	–
44.19	אל-העם	προς τον λαον	–

44.19	את-העם	τον λαον	—
44.23	ואת-עמי	και τον λαον μου	—
45.8	את-עמי	τον λαον μου	<> (1,6)
45.9	מעל-עמי	απο του λαου μου	—
45.16	כל העם הארץ	και πας ο λαος	ισραηλ (1)/ κ. π. ο λ. της γης (3)
45.22	כל-עם הארץ	παντες του λαου της γης	—
46.3	עם-הארץ	ο λαος της γης	—
46.9	עם הארץ	ο λαος της γης	<της γης> (2)
46.18	העם	του λαου	τ. υιοι (2)
46.18	עמי	ο λαος μου	—
46.20	את-העם	τον λαον	—
46.24	העם	του λαου	των λαων (1)

Cf. Turner (1956: 16). S2 distinguishes itself from S1 by the much more frequent use of <<ethnos>> to render <<'m>>. It should be noted, however, that this use of <<ethnos>> is not entirely random. S2 uses it only, but not always, in contexts where there is a strong sense of foreignness. Hence "my people" and "your people" are still rendered by <<laos>> in S2. The occurrence of <<laos>> alone in 42-46 is thus of no value in showing the difference between S2 and S3, as all occurrences of <<'m>> in S3 refer to the people of Israel.

<5.9> קהל

16.40	קהל	οχλους	—
17.17	ובקהל	εν οχλω	—
23.24	ובקהל	μετ' οχλου	οχλων (3)
23.46	קהל	οχλον	πληθη (4)
23.47	קהל	οχλων	οπλων (4,5)
26.7	וקהל	συναγωγης	—
27.27	קהלך	η συναγωγη σου	<η> (1,5)/ -γωγην (3)
27.34	קהלך	η συναγωγη σου	<η> (1,5)

Sections of the Text: Chapters 1-39

32.3	בקהל	< >	εν εκκλησια (2-6)
32.22	קהלה	η συναγωγη αυτου	-
32.23	קהלה	η συναγωγη αυτου	-
38.4	קהל	συναγωγη	συναγωγην (2,5)
38.7	קהלך	η συναγωγη σου	την συναγωγην (5)/ <η> (3)
38.13	קהלך	συναγωγην σου	-χης (5)/ τον λαον (4)
38.15	קהל	συναγωγη	-

Cf. Herrmann (1923: 11) and Turner (1956: 17). Here the distinction is clear. Again, ch.26 aligns itself with S2, rather than S1. In this case the two Greek terms used could hardly be termed synonymous. Yet the contexts of <<qhl>> throughout the book of Ezekiel show no significant difference. In every instance a great horde of people is envisaged. In every case except possibly two (27.27,34) their destructive intent is implied, and the Hebrew is often rendered in English translations by "army", "mob" or "throng". Thus <<okhlos>> appears to be a more appropriate rendering here. <<sunagògè>> would seem to be more suited to a religious assembly. It is found only in S2.

Again, the dividing line can be seen to come before 26.7.

<5.10> זרה (פ./ל./ק.)

5.2	תזרה	διασκορπιεις	διασκορπισεις (1,3)/ κατακοψεις (2)
5.10	וזריתי	και διασκορπιω	διασπερω (4)
5.12	אזרה	διασκορπιω αυτους	σκορπιω (1,3,4,6)/ διασπερω (2,3,5)/ διασκορπισθησεται (6)
6.5	וזריתי	και διασκορπιω	-
6.8	בהזרותיכם	και εν τω διασκορπισμω υμων	διασκορπισθηναι υμας (1)/ διασκορπησαι με υμας (5)/ διασκορπιω υμων (3)
12.14	אזרה	διασπερω	-

12.15	וזריתי	και διασπερω	διασπειραι (2,3,5)
20.23	ולזרות	διασπειραι	διασκορπισαι (2,4)
22.15	וזריתיך	και διασπερω σε	–
29.12	וזריתים	και λικμησω αυτους	–
30.23	וזריתם	και λικμησω αυτους	–
30.26	וזריתי	και λικμησω	–
36.19	ויזרו	και ελικμησα αυτους	–

Cf. Thackeray (1903b: 402) and Herrmann (1923: 9). Despite
textual variation in S1, this example remains valid. In all
except two instances, 5.2 and 6.5, the context is that of
scattering people to far-off places. In six cases – 12.15;
20.23; 22.15; 29.12; 30.23,26 – <<zrh>> occurs in parallel
with a synonym, the renderings of which are given in the next
example. <<likman>> occurs only in S2, five times in all.
<<diaskorpizein>> and <<diaspeirein>> are found in both
sections.

<5.11> פוץ (.ה)

11.16	הפיצותים	διασκορπιω αυτους	διασκορπισω (4)
12.15	בהפיצי	εν τω διασκορπισαι με	–
20.23	להפיץ	του διασκορπισαι	διασπειραι (4)
22.15	והפיצותי	διασκορπιω σε	διεσκορπισω (2,3, 5)
29.12	והפצתי	και διασπερω	–
30.23	והפצתי	διασπερω	–
30.26	והפצתי	διασπερω	διασκορπιω (4)
34.21	הפיצותם	//	//
36.19	ואפיץ	και διεσπειρα	διεσκορπισα (4)

Cf. Herrmann (1923: 10). In the translation of the Hiphil we
again find a difference between S1 and S2. However, the
renderings of the Qal and Niphal forms show no consistency:

Sections of the Text: Chapters 1-39

פוץ (.פ/.)

11.17	(נפצתם	διεσπειρα αυτους	διεσκορπισα (4)
20.34	(נפצתם	διεσκορπισθητε	–
20.41	(נפצתם	διεσκορπισθητε	διεσπαρισθητε (5)
28.25	(פצי	διεσκορπισθησαν	διεσπειρα αυτους (5)
29.13	(פצי	διεσκορπισθησαν	–πισαν (3)/ διεσπαρησαν (5)
34.5	ותפוצינה	και διεσπαρη	διεσπαρησαν (2,4)
34.5	ותפוצינה	και διεσπαρη	διεσπαρησαν (2)
34.6	(פצי	διεσπαρη	–
34.12	(פצי	διεσπαρησαν	–
46.18	יפצי	διασκορπιζηται	–

The differentiation found with the renderings of the Hiphil
contrasts with the mixing found with those of the Qal and
Niphal. Cf. example <5.10>. S2 seems to be more consistent in
its translation of terms for "scatter".

<5.12> שממה

6.14	שממה	εις αφανισμον	–
12.20	שממה	εις αφανισμον	–
14.15	שממה	εις αφανισμον	–
14.16	שממה	εις ολεθρον	–
15.8	שממה	εις αφανισμον	–
23.33	ושממה	αφανισμου	αφαν(ε)ιας // (1,4)/ αφ. αφαν(ε)ιας (3,6)/ <> (1,2)
29.9	לשממה	απωλεια	εις απωλειαν (3,4)
29.10	שממה	και απωλειαν	και εις απ. (3,4)/ και ηφανισμενην (4)
29.12	שממה	απωλειαν	εις απ. (1-5)
29.12	שממה	<>	αφανισμος (2-5)
32.15	שממה	εις απωλειαν	ως απ. (2)
33.28	שממה	ερημον	εις ερ. (3,4)

119

33.29	שממה	ερημον	εις ερ. (1)
35.3	שממה	ερημον	εις ερ. (1-3)
35.4	שממה	ερημος	-ον (3)/ εις ερημον (2,4
35.7	לשממה	εις ερημον	-
35.7	ושממה	και ηρημωμενον	-
35.9	שממות	ερημιαν	ερημον (3,4)
35.14	שממה	ερημον	-
35.15	שממה	ερημον	-μος (2,3,5)/ εις ερ. (4
36.34	שממה	ηφανισμενη	-

Cf. Thackeray (1903b: 402) and Herrmann (1923: 11, 12). S2
changes from using <<apòleia>> to <<erèmos>> after ch.32.
<<aphanismos>> is only found in S1 (but cf. the variant
readings to 29.12). The rendering in 36.34 points to the
unusual nature of 36.23c-38. The Hebrew term here is employe
in Ezekiel usually in prophecies announcing that the land wi
be made "desolate" because of the sins of the people. The on
exception to this type of context is possibly 23.33, where t
cup of "desolation" is promised to the adulterous Jerusalem.
The distribution of <<erèmos>> in this example should be
contrasted with that in ex. <5.24>.

<5.13> רשע

3.18	לרשע	τω ανομω	-
3.18	רשע	τω ανομω	-
3.18	הרשעה	< >	-
3.18	רשע	ο ανομος	-
3.19	רשע	τω ανομω	-
3.19	הרשעה	ο ανομος	-
7.21	ולרשעי	και τοις λοιμοις	λοιποις (3,5)
13.22	רשע	ανομου	ανομων (3,5)/ ανθρωπου (2)
18.20	רשע	ανομου	ανομω (1)
18.21	הרשע	ο ανομος	-

Sections of the Text: Chapters 1-39

18.23	רשע	του ανομου	του αμαρτωλου (1,3-6)
18.24	הרשע	ο ανομος	-
18.27	רשע	ανομον	-
21.8	ורשע	και ανομον	αδικον (6) //
21.9	ורשע	και ανομον	<> (1,2,4,5)
21.30	רשע	ανομε	βεβηλε (1,2)
21.34	רשעים	ανομων	ανομιων (3)
33.8	לרשע	τω αμαρτωλω	-λον (5)/ ανομω (2)
33.8	רשע	<>	αμαρτωλε (3,4)
33.8	רשע	τον ασεβη	ανομον (2,6)
33.8	הוא רשע	αυτος ο ανομος	-
33.9	רשע	τω ασεβει	ανομω (4,6)
33.11	הרשע	του ασεβους	αμαρτωλου (2,5,6)
33.11	רשע	τον ασεβη	αυτον (4,6)
33.12	הרשע	ασεβους	ανομου (2-6)
33.14	לרשע	τω ασεβει	-
33.15	רשע	<>	ανομος (4) //
33.19	רשע	τον αμαρτωλον	ανομον (4,6)

Cf. Herrmann (1923: 11). The strength of this example is reduced somewhat by the fact that all the instances in S2 are confined to part of one chapter. On the other hand, the text of 3.18-19 is very similar to 33.8-9, thus enabling a close comparison to be made. Cf. also <5.7> for other examples of "sin" vocabulary.

<5.14> זהר (.ו/.ה)

3.17	והזהרת	και διαπειληση	διαπελησεις (2)/ απειληση (2,3,5)
3.18	והזהרתו	και ου διεστειλω αυτω	και εαν μη διαστειλη α. (4)
3.18	להזהיר	του διαστειλασθαι	-
3.19	הזהרת	διαστειλη	-
3.20	והזהרתו	διεστειλω αυτω	-
3.21	והזהרתו	διαστειλη	-

3.21	ונהר	διεστειλω αυτω	—
33.3	והיהיר	και σημανη	σημανει (3)/ σημαινει (4)/ σημανανη (4)
33.4	ונהר	φυλαξηται	—
33.5	ונהר	εφυλαξατο	εφυλαξε(ν) (5)
33.5	ונהר	εφυλαξατο	εφυλαξεν (3)
33.6	ונהר	φυλαξηται	//
33.7	והזהרת	< >	και προφυλαξεις (3,4,6)/ και διαφυλαξεις (3,4)
33.8	להזהירו	του φυλαξασθαι	-ξαι (5)/ αποστηναι (2,6)/ διαστειλαι (4)/ διαστειλη (4) //
33.9	הזהרת	προαπαγγειλης	-γγελης (5)/ προαναγγ. (3, 4)/ προπαραγγ. (1)/ παραγγ. (3)/ απαγγ. (5)/ προαγγιλης (3)/ διαστειλη (4)

Cf. Herrmann (1923: 9). As with <5.13>, the strength of this
example would seem to be reduced by the fact that the
occurrences of <<zhr>> are closely grouped in each of only two
chapters. Again, however, the contexts of both groups are very
similar.

<5.15> נצל (.ה/.נ/.פ)

3.19	הצלת	ρυση	ερυσω (2,3)
3.21	הצלת	ρυση	—
7.19	להציλם	< >	εξελεσθαι (2-6)
13.21	והצלתי	και ρυσομαι	—
13.23	והצלתי	και ρυσομαι	—
14.14	ינצלו	σωθησονται	σωσουσιν (4)
14.16	יצילו	σωθησονται	—
14.16	ינצלו	σωθησονται	—
14.18	יצילו	ρυσωνται	—
14.18	ינצלו	σωθησονται	—
14.20	יצילו	υπολειφθωσιν	εξελωται (2,4)/ υπολειφθησονται (3)
14.20	יצילו	ρυσονται	φεισονται (2)

Sections of the Text: Chapters 1-39

33.9	הצלת	εξηρησαι	εξαιρηση (3)/ εξερησαι (3,6)/ ερ(ρ)υσω (2,4)/ ρυση (1)
33.12	תצילנו	εξεληται αυτον	εξελειται (5,6)
34.10	והצלתי	και εξελουμαι	ρυσομαι (4)
34.12	והצלתי	και απελασω	συναξω (2,3,5,6)/ ρυσομαι (1,3,4)/ αποστρεψω (6)
34.27	והצלתים	και εξελουμαι αυτους	—

<<ruesthai>> occurs in 37.23, as well as in a number of variants to examples in S2. <<exairein>> does not appear in S1 (except in variant readings). In this instance the Hebrew term occurs in varying contexts. However, the variation in context does not correspond with the translation change. For example, men save themselves from retribution (3.19,21; 14.14,20; 33.9), men save other people from retribution (14.16,18,20), and God saves his people from their enemies (13.21,23; 34.10,27).

<5.16> כרת (.ה)

14.8	והכרתי	και εξαρω αυτον	—
14.13	והכרתי	και εξαρω	εξολεθρευσω (4)
14.17	והכרתי	και εξαρω	—
14.19	להכרית	του εξολεθρευσαι	—
14.21	להכרית	του εξολεθρευσαι	—
17.17	להכרית	του εξαραι	—
21.8	והכרתי	και εξολεθρευσω	—
21.9	והכרתי	εξολεθρευσω	εξολεθρευσα (3)
25.7	והכרתיך	και εξολεθρευσω σε	—
25.13	והכרתי	και εξολεθρευσω	—
25.16	והכרתי	και εξολεθρευσω	—
29.8	והכרתי	και απολω	απολεσω (4)
30.15	והכרתי	και απολω	απολειται (6)
35.7	והכרתי	και απολω	—

In S1 <<apolluein>> is also used to translate forms of

<<'bd>>, while in S2 it renders various forms apart from
<<krt>>. <<exolethreuein>> is found in S2 as well (31.12, cf.
35.15), where it renders the Qal of <<krt>>. <<exairein>> is
not found in S2. The contexts vary slightly, but again the
translation change does not correlate with the change in
context. In all instances except one (17.17) Yahweh is the
subject of the verb.

<5.17> זב/בזז (ק.)

7.21	בזז	του διαρπασαι αυτα	διαφθειραι (2)/ παραδοσαι (4)
23.46	ולבז	και διαρπαγην	αρπαγην (4)
(25.7)	לבז	εις διαρπαγην	αρπαγην (5)
26.5	בזז	εις προνομην	νομην (5)
26.12	ובזזו	και σκυλευσει	//
29.19 בזה ובזזו	και σκυλευσει τα σκυλα	//
34.8	לבז	εις προνομην	–
34.22	לבז	εις προνομην	–
34.28	בז	εν προνομη	εις προνομην (2,4,5)
36.4	לבז	εις προνομην	–
36.5	לבז	εν προνομη	εις προνομην (3-5)
38.12 בז ולבז	και σκυλευσαι σκυλα αυτων	και προνομευσαι προνομην (4)/ σκυλευσον (2)
38.13 בז הלבז	και σκυλευσα σκυλα	–
39.10 ובזזו את-בזזיהם	και σκυλευσουσι τους σκυλευσαντος αυτους	και προνομευσουσι τους προνομευσαντος αυτους (4)/ <> (1,5)

Cf. Thackeray (1903b: 402), Herrmann (1923: 8) and Turner
(1956: 16). The LXX seems to have read <<lbz>> (the qere) and
not <<lbg>> (the kethiv) at 25.7. S2 appears to have been
constrained to use <<skuleuein/ skulon>> for <<bz>> by the
proximity of synonyms, cf. the next example.

    S2 does not use any forms of <<diarpazein>> or its
corresponding noun.

Sections of the Text: Chapters 1-39

<5.18> שלל/שלל (ק.)

7.21	לשלל	εις σκυλα	ε. σκυβαλα (3)
26.12	ושללו	και προνομευσει	κ. προνομευσουσι (3)
29.19	ושלל שללה	και προνομευσει την προνομην αυτης	//
38.12	לשלל שלל	προνομευσει προνομην	του σκυλευσα σκυλα (4)/ προνομευσον (2)/ προνομευσω (3)
38.13	הלשלל שלל	ει προνομην του προνομευσαι	ε. π. εις προνομην (1,2)
38.13	לשלל שלל	του σκυλευσαι σκυλα	τ. σκυλευσασθαι σκ. (5)
39.10	ושללו את-שלליהם	και προνομευσουσι τους προνομευσαντας αυτους	και σκυλευσουσι τους σκυλευσαντας αυτους (4)

Cf. Thackeray (1903b: 402). This example is placed here not because of its strength but because it goes closely with the preceding case. In S2 all the examples occur in the same verses as <<bz/ bzz>>. Apart from 30.24, <<pronomeuein>> and its noun form, as well as <<skuleuein>>, are only found here in S2, and do not appear in S1.

<5.19> חזק (התה./ה./ס./ק.)

3.14	חזקה	εγενετο ... κραταια	—
7.13	יתחזקו	κρατησει	—
13.22	ולחזק	και του κατισχυσαι	—
16.49	החזיקה	αντελαμβανοντο	αντελαβοντο (2)/ κατελαμβ. (4,5)
22.14	אם-תתחזקנה	ει κρατησουσιν	κρατησουσιν (4)
27.9	מחזיקי	ενισχυον	—
27.27	מחזיקי בדקך	και οι συμβουλοι σου	<> (1)/ και οι (συν) επιμιχνυντες την επιμιξιαν σου (4)
30.21	לחזקה	ισχυν //	και κατισχυσαι αυτον (4)
30.24	וחזקתי	και κατισχυσω	—

30.25	יהחזקתי	και ενισχυσω	-
34.4	חזקתם	ενισχυσατε	-
34.16	אחזק	ενισχυσω	-

Cf. Thackeray (1903b: 403) and Herrmann (1923: 9). S1 shows a tendency to use forms based on <<krataios>>, while S2 prefers words showing the root <<iskhus>>, cf. example <5.20>. The variety of context here does weaken this case, as exact comparison is difficult to make. The rendering in 16.49, which deviates from what might be expected in S1, is yet another indication of the unusual nature of this chapter. The problem of ch.16 will be discussed in chapter VII.

<5.20> חזק

2.4	חזקי-לב	<>	στερεοκαρδιοι (1-6)/ σκληροκαρδιοι (6)/ θρασυκαρδιοι (4,6)
3.7	חזקי-מצח	φιλονεικοι	-
3.8	חזקים	δυνατον	-
3.8	חזק	κατισχυσω //	-
3.9	חזק ממצר	κραταιοτεραν πετρας	κρατερον (2)/ στερεωτερον (4)
20.33	חזקה	κραταια	-
20.34	חזקה	κραταια	-
26.17	חזקה	<>	ισχυρα (2-6)
30.22	את-החזקה	τους ισχυρους	-
34.16	ואת-החזקה	και το ισχυρον	-

The translations of this adjective corroborate the testimony of the previous example. The adjective is applied to a variety of objects throughout the book. <<krataios>> occurs only in S1, whereas <<iskhuros>> occurs only in S2.

<5.21> גאון

.20	לגאון	εις υπερηφανιαν	—	
7.24	גאון	το φρυαγμα	—	
6.49	גאון	υπερηφανια	—	
6.56	גאונך	υπερηφανιας σου	της υ. (4)	
24.21	גאון	φρυαγμα	—	
30.6	גאון	η υβρις	<> (2)	
30.18	גאון	η υβρις	—	
32.12	את־גאון	την υβριν	—	
33.28	גאון	η υβρις	—	

Cf. Thackeray (1903b: 403) and Herrmann (1923: 8). In 7.24;
24.21; 30.6; 30.18 and 33.28 <<g'wn>> occurs in the phrase
"the pride of her strength". <<hubris>> appears also in 7.10
as a rendering of <<zdwn>>, while <<phruagma>> and
<<huperèphania>> appear only in S1 and only in the instances
given above.

<5.22> פשע

14.11	בכל־פשעיהם	εν πασι τοις παραπτω- μασιν αυτων	—
18.22	כל־פשעיו	παντα τα παραπτωματα αυτου	πασαι αι αδικιαι αυτου (1,2,5,6)
18.30	מכל־פשעיכם	εκ πασων των ασεβειων υμων	... ανομιων υ. (5,6)
18.31	את־כל־פשעיכם	πασας τας ασεβειας υμων	—
21.29	פשעיכם	τας ασεβειας υμων	τ. αδικιας υ. (3)
33.10	פשעינו	αι πλαναι ημων	α. π. μεν η. (4)
33.12	פשעו ביום	εν η αν ημερα πλανηθη	—
37.23	פשעיהם	<>	ταις ασεβειας αυτων (1-6)/ ανομιαις (3)/ βασιλειαις (2)
39.24	וכפשעיהם	και κατα τα ανομηματα αυτων	κ. κ. το ανομημα α. (5)/ κ. κ τας ανομιας α. (4)

The Greek Text of Ezekiel

Cf. Herrmann (1923: 11). The LXX varies in its rendering of this item of "sin" vocabulary, the most common translations being <<hamartia>>, <<asebeia>> and <<anomia>>. Cf. ex. <5.7 <<paraptòma>> occurs only in S1.

<5.23> מורשה

11.15	למורשה	εις κληρονομιαν	. −
25.4	למורשה	εις κληρονομιαν	εις κατακληρονομιαν (3-5)
25.10	למורשה	εις κληρονομιαν	ε. κ. και δωσω αυτην εις εξαρσιν (3,4)
33.24	למורשה	εις κατασχεσιν	−
36.2	למורשה	εις κατασχεσιν	−
36.3	מורשה	εις κατασχεσιν	−
36.5	למורשה	εις κατασχεσιν	κληρονομιαν (4)

Cf. Herrmann (1923: 10). <<kataskhesis>> occurs only in S2 and S3. <<klèronomia>> is absent in S2 entirely. The context is either that of territory given as a possession by Yahweh (11.15; 33.24), or territory taken by people (36.2,3), or people given as a possession by Yahweh (25.4,10). Again, context change does not correspond with translation change.

<5.24> חרבה

5.14	לחרבה	εις ερημον	<εις> (3,5)
13.4	בחרבות	εν ταις ερημοις	−
25.13	חרבה	ερημον	−
26.20	כחרבות	ερημον	−
29.9	וחרבה	και ερημος	και ερημωσιν (4)
29.10	לחרבות	εις ερημον	−
33.24	החרבות	τας ηρημωμενας	−

Sections of the Text: Chapters 1-39

33.27	בחרבות	εν ταις ηρημωμεναις	-
35.4	חרבה	ερημιαν	-
36.4	ולחרבות	και τοις εξηρημωμενοις	τοις ηρημωμενοις (5)/ ταις (εξ)ηρημωμενας (2,4)/ ταις (εξ)ερημωμεναις (2,4)
36.10	והחרבות	και η ηρημωμενη	ηρημωμεναι (2-6)/ ερημοι (3,4)
36.33	החרבות	αι ερημοι	-
38.8	לחרבה	ερημος	-
38.12	על-חרבות	εις την ηρημωμενην	-

Cf. also Thackeray (1903b: 402) and Herrmann (1923: 9). S2 uses <<erèmos>> more frequently than S1, cf. ex. <5.12>. However, it is only in ch.26-38 that the verb <<erèmoun>> is to be found, either in its perfect participle form or otherwise. The word appears mostly in one of three different contexts:

a) a country will be made a "ruin" (25.13; 29.9,10),

b) a town will be made a "ruin" (5.14; 35.4),

c) "ruins" (deserts ?) which already exist (13.4; 26.20; 33.24,27; 36.4,10,33; 38.12).

Again, context does not seem to be the factor causing translation change.

<5.25> דלית

17.6	דליותיו	τα κληματα αυτης	-
17.7	ודליותיו	και τα κληματα αυτης	-
17.23	דליותיו	και τα κληματα αυτου	των κλαδων (4)/ των δενδρων (6)
19.11	דליתיו	κληματων αυτης	-
31.7	דליותיו	των κλαδων αυτου	-
31.9	דליותיו	των κλαδων αυτου	-
31.12	דליותיו	οι κλαδοι αυτου	-

Cf. Thackeray (1903b: 402) and Herrmann (1923: 8). The term
<<dlyt>> occurs only once outside Ezekiel and denotes here
"branches" of cedars (17.23; 31.7,9,12) or vines (17.6,7;
19.11). In Ezekiel the word <<klèma>> is used only in S1,
where it appears in 15.2 also. Conversely, <<klados>> is found
only in S2, and occurs in 36.5,6,8 as well as in the above
references.

Summary of Examples

Although further examples will be considered in other
chapters, it can be seen from those already given that (a) the
text of 1-39 does fall into two sections, and (b) the division
comes around the end of ch.25, and not ch.27 as Thackeray,
Herrmann and Danielsmeyer had argued. This two-fold division
is not substantially affected by the textual variation
exhibited by the MSS available. The witness of 967, as we saw
earlier, did nevertheless undermine the case for using the
rendering of "Tyre" to locate the exact division of the text.

The table overleaf shows the distribution of some of the
examples.

    x = the majority rendering in S1.

    o = the majority rendering in S2.

    (x is not the same rendering as o).

    . = a rendering other than the majority rendering.

Where more than one rendering occurs in a chapter the simple
majority rendering is taken. Where there is an equal number o
differing renderings in a chapter, the minority rendering (fo
the section) is cited.

Sections of the Text: Chapters 1-39

Table 5.1

Ch.	5.1	2	3	4	5	6	9	10	11	12	13	14	15	16	17	18	21	23	25
1																			
2					x														
3					x						x	x	x						
4					x														
5	x	x	x	x				x											
6	x	o	x	x	o	x		.		x									
7	x	x	o	x	o						.			x	x	x			
8					x														
9					x														
10					x														
11	x	o	x	x	x				x									x	
12	o	x	x	x	x			x	x	x									
13	o	x	x		x	x					x		x						
14	x	o	x	x	x					.			x	.					
15	x	o	x							x									
16	x	o	x		o		x										x		
17	x	x	x	x	x		x							.					x
18											x								
19																			x
20	x	x	x		x			x	x										
21				x	x	x					x			x					
22	x	x	x		o			x	x										
23	o	x	x	x	x		x			x					x				
24	x	x	x	x	x												x		
25	x	x	x	x	o	x								x	(x)			x	
26	o	o	x	o	o		o								.	o			
27					o		o												
28	o	o	o	o	o	o													
29	o	o	o	x		o		o	o	.				o	.	o			
30	o	o	o	o		o		o	o					o			o		
31				o	x														o
32	o	o	o	o	o		o				.						o		
33	o	o	o	x	o						o	o	o	o			o	o	
34	o	o	o		o	o									o	o			
35	o	o	o	o	o	o				o				o					
36	o	o	x		o	o	o	o	.						o		o		
37	o	o	o		x	o													
38	o	o	o	o	o	o	o								.	o			
39	o	o	o	o	o	o									.	o			

131

The Greek Text of Ezekiel

<u>S1 and S2</u>

Although it is not the primary concern of this chapter, the relationship of S1 to S2 will be considered here also. The question is whether we have the work of two different translators or whether one of the two sections represents a revision. E. Tov has given a definition of the nature of a Septuagint revision:

> A given textual tradition can be considered a revision of the LXX if the following two conditions are met:
>
> (a) The LXX and the revision share a common textual basis, established by the recognition of distinctive agreements.
>
> (b) The reviser retouched the LXX in a certain direction, generally towards a more precise reflection of his Hebrew source. Other revisions aim at greater clarity as well as at improvement of the Greek language. (1976: 43)

(Cf. also Barthélemy 1963: 91). A few observations may be made here. Theoretically, a reviser could do his work so well and so thoroughly that it would be impossible to tell that a revision had taken place even if the unrevised text were available. We would be unable to distinguish between revision and new translation. In practice, however, it seems that LXX revisions were usually less thorough. When both a text and it revision are available, it is possible to see the "common textual basis" which Tov mentions. Yet "distinctive agreements" do not automatically indicate common textual basis, although Tov discounts other possibilities in the case of Jeremiah (1976: 20-22). However, it is difficult to prove much either way if there is a lack of these agreements.

The second condition mentioned by Tov seems to be less problematic. If a revision goes "in a certain direction", the

it should be possible to detect this direction on examination
of the deviation of a presumed revised text from what would be
the expected rendering. The reasons for a revision may be
linguistic and/or theological. We might thus categorise its
possible aims as:

1/ more literal Greek,

2/ more idiomatic Greek,

3/ more stereotyped Greek vocabulary,

4/ less stereotyped Greek vocabulary,

5/ alteration towards the MT,

6/ alteration away from the MT,

7/ updating the language of the text.

Several of these may be combined. It could be the case that
they may be to some extent contradictory too, e.g. alteration
towards the MT and more idiomatic Greek. Yet this does not
mean that the end result would be extremely confused. There
would be cases where only one factor could operate and in
these we could see what aims were guiding such a revision.

Nevertheless, the relationship between S1 and S2 cannot
be said to be characterised by any of these. There is no
marked change in the degree of "literalness" of the sections.
In both parts the Hebrew word order is followed closely, and
the majority of changes which take place between the sections
consist of replacing one word with a synonym. The addition or
omission of <<eimi>> in <5.3> does not alter the meaning of
the phrase, and the text makes sense either way.

One section does not seem to be distinctly more
stereotyped than the other. The examples cited above can be
put into four groups:

The Greek Text of Ezekiel

1. Stereotyped renderings in both sections.

S1	S2
εγω (κυριος)	εγω ειμι (κυριος)
ρομφαια	μαχαιρα
και ερεις	και ειπον
οχλος	συναγωγη
διασκορπιζειν	διασπειρειν
διαστελλειν	φυλασσειν
ρυεσθαι	εξαιρεισθαι
κληρονομια	κατασχεσις
κλημα	κλαδος

2. Stereotyped renderings in S1, variation in S2.

λεγειν προς	λεγειν τω/ προς
αδικια	ανομια/ αμαρτια
λαος	λαος/ εθνος
αφανισμος	ερημος/ απωλεια
ανομος	ασεβης/ αμαρτωλος
διαρπαγη	προνομη/ σκυλα

3. Stereotyped renderings in S2, variation in S1.

(επι)γινωσκειν	γινωσκειν
(δι)οτι	οτι
διασκορπιζειν/ διασπειρειν	λικμαν
εξαιρειν/ εξολεθρευσειν	απολλυειν
υπερηφανια/ φρυαγμα	υβρις

4. Variation in both sections.

κρατ-	ισχυ-
παραπτωμα/ ασεβεια	πλανη/ ανομημα

134

Sections of the Text: Chapters 1-39

Both sections have a substantial number of examples where the rendering is stereotyped (Group 1). Yet while there are cases where S2 has renderings which are more varied than those in S1 (Group 2), there are also cases where the reverse is true (Group 3). In a few instances, both sections have inconsistent renderings (Group 4). It is difficult to say if there exists any significant difference between the two sections in the amount of stereotyped renderings.

It would seem odd that a reviser who, for example, was sufficiently motivated to change <<romphaia>> to <<makhaira>>, should only sporadically change <<adikia>> and <<laos>>. The same problem exists if it is assumed that S1 was the revised text. There is an inconsistency between the extensive change from <<makhaira>> to <<romphaia>> and the sporadic alteration from <<ginesthai>> and <<hoti>> to <<epiginesthai>> and <<dioti>>.

Although certain cases of translation change might be linked to the change of meanings or usages in Greek (e.g. <<legein>> + <<pros>>/ + infinitive; <<hoti>>/ <<dioti>>; <<epiginesthai>>/ <<ginesthai>>), many of the other cases cannot. A substantial number of the renderings used appear in both sections, although with different hyponyms, e.g. the "sin" vocabulary.

The total effect of the difference between S1 and S2 can be seen in two short passages which are very similar. These are 3.18-19 and 33.8-9. If we compare the Greek of these, we can see how greatly their translations differ:

3.18-19	33.8-9
εν τω λεγειν με τω ανομω	εν τω ειπειν με τω αμαρτωλω
θανατω θανατωθηση	θανατω θανατωθηση
[και ου διεστειλω αυτω]	
ουδε ελαλησας	και μη λαλησης
του διαστειλασθαι τω ανομω	του φυλαξασθαι τον ασεβη
απο των οδων αυτου	απο της οδου αυτου
[του ζησαι αυτον]	
ο ανομος εκεινος τη αδικια	αυτος ο ανομος τη ανομια
αυτου αποθανειται	αυτου αποθανειται
και το αιμα αυτου εκ	το δε αιμα αυτου εκ
χειρος σου εκζητησω. και συ	της χειρος σου εκζητησω. συ δε
εαν διαστειλη τω ανομω	εαν προαπαγγειλης τω ασεβει
	[την οδον αυτου αποστρεψαι
	απ αυτης]
και μη αποστρεψη απο	και μη αποστρεψη απο
[της ανομιας αυτου και]	
της οδος αυτου, [ο ανομος]	της οδου αυτου,
εκεινος εν τη αδικια αυτου	ουτος τη ασεβεια αυτου
αποθανειται και συ την	αποθανειται και συ την
ψυχην σου ρυση.	ψυχην σαυτου εξηρησαι.

(Words in square brackets are translations of phrases which
are not common to both sections in the MT).

Some features do occur in both sections: the sporadic u
of <<de>>, the use of the subjunctive in negative future or
indefinite clauses, and the use of <<ekeinos>>. On the use o
the articular infinitive, however, see Chapter VI.

Overall, it seems that the best explanation for these
types of differences is that S1 and S2 had different
translators.

CHAPTER VI

SECTIONS OF THE TEXT — II

The Problem of Chapters 40-48

We now turn to the examination of the third section of
the book — chapters 40-48. One striking feature of the
examples listed so far is the dearth of evidence from S3. This
is because 40-48 deals with entirely different subject-matter
from the rest of Ezekiel. The description of the new temple
and its regulations requires a vastly different vocabulary
from that of oracles against nations or prophecies to Israel.
This change of subject-matter has made comparison difficult,
as the context can alter the meaning of words which are used
in other sections. In addition, much of the description is of
a highly repetitive nature, reducing even further the range of
vocabulary use for a given length of text. The lack of
evidence means that arguments about the nature of S3 are
weaker than those connected with S1 and S2.

The problem of S3 is further complicated by the fact that
there is not just the matter of deciding whether it is
distinct from S2 but also the question of its relationship to
S1. Indeed, this second part of the problem has engendered
more debate than the first. As we have seen in chapter II,
arguments in this area have not been free from methodological
weaknesses either.

Three points will be proposed here:
1) There is still a case for saying that S3 is distinct from
S2.
2) The text of S3 has had a different transmission history
from that of S1.

3) It is compatible with the available evidence to say that S
and S3 were the work of the same translator.

These points will now be dealt with in turn.

1. S3 and S2

It is of note that all who have argued for a division
of the Greek Ezekiel text are agreed in making a division
between ch.39 and ch.40 /1/. Although they might have been
misled by the witness of the divine names, they were probably
correct in seeing a difference between ch.40-48 and the
chapters preceding them. There still appears to be sufficient
evidence for splitting 26-48 into 26-39 and 40-48.

Of the examples already cited, only the following had
references in S3:

שחת	<2.13>	דלת	<2.29>
כתף	<2.14>	תועבה	<2.27>
חמאת	<2.19>	צוו	<5.7>
אכל	<2.21>	אמר	<5.5>
עם	<5.8>		

The evidence of the examples in the left column was seen to
invalid for various reasons. The evidence of the examples in
the right column seemed to point to a difference between S2
and S3. None of these cases is strong. Stronger evidence can
be found in the following examples:

‹6.1› סביב

4	סביב	κυκλω //	—
18	סביב	κυκλοθεν	—
27	סביב	‹ ›	κυκλω (1-6)
27	סביב	κυκλω	—
28	סביב	κυκλοθεν	—
2	סביב	κυκλω	—
2	סביבותיה	κυκλω αυτης	—
5	וסביבותיה	και ... κυκλω αυτης	κ. κ. της (5)
6	סביבותיה	κυκλω αυτης	—
7	סביבותיכם	κυκλω υμων	—
7	סביבותיכם	κυκλω υμων	—
12	סביבותיך	κυκλω σου	—
14	סביבותיך	κυκλω σου	κυκλωσουσιν (2)
15	סביבותיך	κυκλω σου	‹ › (2)/ ‹σου› (4)
5	סבובת	κυκλω	—
13	סבובת	κυκλω	—
10	סביב סביב	κυκλω	κ. κυκλω (3,6)/ κ. δι ολου (4)/ κ. του τοιχου δι ολου (4)
.12	סביב	κυκλοθεν	κυκλω (2,4)/ ‹ › (2)
.12	סביבותיכם	‹ ›	περικυκλω υμων (2,3, 4,6)
2.14	וסביבתי	κυκλω αυτου	‹ › (4)
5.33	מסביב	κυκλοθεν	—
5.37	מסביב	κυκλοθεν	—
5.57	וכל-סביבותיה	και παντων των κυκλω αυτης	‹ › (4)/ κ. π. τ. κ. σου (4,6)
5.57	מסביב	κυκλω	κυκλοθεν (3)
7.8	סביב	κυκλοθεν //	//
3.22	מסביב	κυκλοθεν	—
3.24	סביב	κυκλω	‹ › (3)
7.11	סביב	‹ ›	κυκλω (2-6)
7.11	סביב	κυκλω	—
8.23	מסביב	περικυκλω σου	κυκλω (1,5)

28.24	מכל סביבתם	απο των περι-κυκλω αυτων	α. τ. κυκλω α. (2,5
28.26	מסביבותם	εν τοις κυκλω αυτων	—
31.4	סביבות	κυκλω	—
32.22	סביבותיו	<>	—
32.23	סביבותיה	περικυκλω	—
32.24	סביבותיה	περικυκλω	—
32.25	סביבותיו	<> //	περικυκλω (αυτου) (4)
32.26	סביבותיו	περικυκλω	—
34.26	וסביבות	περικυκλω	—
36.3	מסביב	υπο των κυκλω υμων	απο τ. κ. υ. (1-6)/ υ. παντων τ. κ. υ (υ. των εχθρων των κ υ. (5)/ υ. των εθνω κ. υ. (6)/ υ. παντω εθνων τ. κ. υ. (3)/ υ. των εθνων των κ. (2,4,6)
36.4	מסביב	περικυκλω	τοις κυκλω (3)/ τοις π. αυτων (1,2, τοις π. (2)
36.7	מסביב	περικυκλω υμων	—
36.36	סביבותיכם	κυκλω υμων	—
37.2	סביב סביב	κυκλοθεν κυκλω	<κυκλοθεν> (1-3)/ <κυκλω> (1-3,6)
37.21	מסביב	απο παντων των περικυκλω αυτων	α. π. τ. π. αυτου (
39.17	מסביב	απο παντων των περικυκλω	α. π. τ. π. υμων (2 3,6)
40.5	סביב סביב	κυκλω	κυκλω κυκλω (3)
40.14	סביב סביב	κυκλω	κυκλω κυκλω (3)/ κ. τα περι την αυλη (4)
40.16	סביב סביב	κυκλοθεν	—
40.16	סביב סביב	κυκλω	κυκλοθεν (5)/ κυκλω κυκλω (3)
40.17	סביב סביב	κυκλω	<> (1)/ κυκλω κυκλω (3)
40.25	סביב סביב	κυκλοθεν	—
40.29	סביב סביב	κυκλω	κυκλω κυκλω (3)
40.30	סביב סביב	<>	κυκλω (1-6)/ κυκλω κυκλω (3)
40.33	סביב סביב	κυκλω	κυκλω κυκλω (3)

140

Sections of the Text: Chapters 40-48

40.36	סביב סביב	κυκλω	κυκλω κυκλω (3)
40.43	סביב סביב	κυκλω	κυκλοθεν (3)/ κυκλω κυκλω (3)
41.5	סביב סביב	κυκλοθεν	—
41.5	סביב	<>	κυκλω (3,4)
41.6	סביב סביב	κυκλω	κυκλοθεν (2)/ κυκλω κυκλω (3)
41.7	סביב סביב	κυκλω //	κυκλω κυκλω (3)
41.8	סביב סביב	κυκλω	κυκλω κυκλω (3)/ περικυκλω // (4)
41.10	סביב	το περιφερες //	—
41.10	סביב סביב	κυκλω	κυκλοθεν (3)/ κυκλω κυκλω (3)
41.11	סביב סביב	κυκλοθεν	κυκλω (5)/ εν (5)/ κυκλοθεν κυκλω (3)
41.12	סביב סביב	κυκλοθεν	κυκλοθεν κυκλω (3)/ <> (5)
41.16	סביב	κυκλω	—
41.16	סביב סביב	κυκλω	κυκλω κυκλω (3,4)/ παντα κυκλω (5)
41.17	סביב סביב	κυκλω	κυκλοθεν (2)/ κυκλω κυκλω (3)
41.19	סביב סביב	κυκλοθεν	κυκλοθεν κυκλω (3)
42.15	סביב סביב	κυκλοθεν διαταξει	//
42.16	סביב	//	//
42.17	סביב	//	//
42.20	סביב סביב	κυκλω	—
43.12	סביב סביב	κυκλοθεν	κυκλω κυκλω (3)
43.13	סביב	κυκλοθεν	—
43.17	אות סביב	κυκλοθεν κυκλουμενον αυτω	κυκλουμ. αυτω κυκλοθεν (1)
43.17	סביב	κυκλοθεν	—
43.20	סביב	κυκλω	//
45.1	סביב	κυκλοθεν	—
45.2	סביב	κυκλοθεν	—
45.2	סביב	κυκλοθεν	—
46.23	סביב	κυκλω	κυκλοθεν (4)
46.23	סביב	κυκλω	<> (1,3,4)
46.23	סביב	κυκλω	—

The Greek Text of Ezekiel

48.35   ם‎ל‎כ‎ב‎   κυκλωμα   κυκλω (2)

Cf. Thackeray (1903b: 401) and Herrmann (1923: 6). The absenc
of <<perikuklos>> from 39.17 onwards and the re-emergence of
the frequent use of <<kuklothen>> from 40.16 on give an
indication that a break around the end of 39 might have
occurred. In this instance it can be seen that S1 and S3
agree.

<6.2> εν τω ...

(+ Infinitive)

1.9	εν τω βαδιζειν αυτα	—
1.17	εν τω πορευεσθαι αυτα	—
1.19	εν τω πορευεσθαι	—
1.19	εν τω εξαιρειν	—
1.21	εν τω πορευεσθαι αυτα	—
1.21	εν τω εσταναι αυτα	—
1.21	εν τω εξαιρειν αυτα	—
1.24	εν τω πορευεσθαι αυτα	πτερυσ(σ)θαι α. (2-5)/ <> (2,3)
1.24	εν τω εσταναι αυτα	—
3.18	εν τω λεγειν με	—
3.20	εν τω αποστρεφειν	—
3.27	εν τω λαλειν με	—
5.13	εν τω συντελεσαι με	—
5.15	εν τω ποιησαι με	—
5.16	εν τω εξαποστειλαι με	—
6.8	εν τω γενεσθαι	του γεν. (4)/ ειναι (3)
9.8	εν τω κοπτειν αυτους	—
9.8	εν τω εκχεαι σε	εκχεεσθαι (2)/ εκκαλεσαι (2
10.3	εν τω εισπορευεσθαι	<εισ> (2,3)
10.6	εν τω εντελλεσθαι αυτον	—
10.11	εν τω πορευεσθαι αυτα	—
10.11	εν τω πορευεσθαι αυτα	—

10.11 εν τω πορευεσθαι αυτα   −

10.16 εν τω πορευεσθαι   −

10.16 εν τω εξαιρειν   εις το εξ. (5)

10.17 εν τω εσταναι αυτα   −

10.17 εν τω μετεωριζεσθαι αυτα   −

10.19 εν τω εξελθειν αυτα   εξαιρειν (2-6)

11.13 εν τω προφητευειν με   εν τω με προ. (3)

12.15 εν τω διασκορπισαι με   −

13.19 εν τω αποφθεγγεσθαι υμας   ενεκεν του απο. υ. (3)

15.7 εν τω στηρισαι με

16.21 εν τω αποτροπιαζεσθαι σε   του αποτ. (1) //

16.30 εν τω ποιησαι με

16.34 εν τω προσδιδοναι σε   εν τω γαρ π. (4)/ προσδιξ.
                                     (2-5)/ ⟨προσ⟩ (1,2,5)

16.52 εν τω δικαιωσαι σε   −

16.54 εν τω σε παροργισαι   παρ. σε (1)

16.61 εν τω αναλαβειν σε   αναλαμβανειν σε (4)

16.63 εν τω εξιλασκεσθαι με   εν τω με εξ. (4)/ εξιλασασ-
                                     θαι (2)

18.24 εν δε τω αποστρεψαι   και εν τω α. (3,4)/ ⟨δε⟩
                                     (1-3,6)

18.26 εν τω αποστρεψαι   εφ ω απ. (2)/ ⟨τω⟩ (6)/
                                     αποστρεφειν (3)

18.27 εν τω αποστρεψαι   επιστρεψαι (3)

20.26 εν τω διαπορευεσθαι με   −

20.41 εν τω εξαγαγειν με   εξαγειν (2)

20.42 εν τω εισαγαγειν με   −

20.44 εν τω ποιησαι με   εν τω με π. (3)/ ⟨με⟩ (3)

21.29 εν τω αποκαλυφθηναι   −

21.34 εν τω μαντευεσθαι σε   μαντευσασθαι (2)

23.30 εν τω εκπορνευσαι σε   −

23.39 εν τω σφαζειν αυτους   ⟨αυτους⟩ (5)

25.12 εν τω εκδικησαι αυτους   του εκδ. α. (2,3)/
                                     ⟨αυτους⟩ (2)

25.17 εν τω δουναι   επι του δ. (6)/
                                     εν τω δ. με (1,2,4)

26.15 εν τω στεναξαι   −

26.15 εν τω σπασαι   −

26.19 εν τω αναγαγειν με   απαγαγειν (5)/ αγαγειν (2-4)

28.22 εν τω ποιησαι με   -

29.16 εν τω αυτους ακολουθησαι   ακολουθησαι (4)/ <αυτους>
                                  (4)/ εν τω ακ. αυτ. (2-6)

30.18 εν τω συντριψαι με   εκτριψαι (3)/ <με> (3,5)

30.25 εν τω δουναι   διδοναι (3)/ δ. με (1-5)

31.10 εν τω υψωθηναι αυτον   -

32.7 εν τω σβεσθηναι σε   -

32.10 εν τω πετασθηναι   πετασθαι (1,3,6)/ πετεσθαι
                                  (2,3)/ πετασαι (2)/
                                  εκπετασαι με (4)/ εκσπασαι
                                  με (2,4)

33.8 εν τω ειπειν με   ειπαι (1,6)/ λεγειν (6)

33.13 εν τω ειπειν με   ειπαι (1,6)/ ειρηκεναι (6)

33.14 εν τω ειπειν με   ειπαι (1,6)

33.18 εν τω αποστρεψαι   -

33.19 εν τω αποστρεψαι   επιστρεψαι (5)

34.27 εν τω συντριψαι με   <με> (4,5)

36.20 εν τω λεγεσθαι αυτους   λ. αυτοις (4)

36.23 εν τω αγιασθηναι με   -

37.7 εν τω εμε προφητευσαι   -

37.13 εν τω ανοιξαι με   -

37.28 εν τω ειναι   -

38.14 εν τω κατοικισθηναι   -

38.16 εν τω αγιασθηναι με   -

39.26 εν τω κατοικισθηναι   κατοικηθηναι (3)/ <αυτους>
      αυτους   (1)

39.27 εν τω αποστρεψαι με   επι στρεψαι (4)
      αυτους

39.28 εν τω επιφανηναι με   -φαναι (2)/ -φανειμαι (3)

43.8 εν τω τιθεναι αυτους   θειναι (3)

44.7 εν τω προσφερειν υμας   -

44.10 εν τω πλανασθαι   πλανη(σει) (4)

44.15 εν τω πλανασθαι   οποτε επλανηθησαν (2,4)

44.17 εν τω εισπορευεσθαι αυτους -

44.17 εν τω λειτουργειν αυτους   -

44.19 εν τω εκπορευεσθαι αυτους   εισπορ. (4)/ εν τω εκει
                                  πορευσθαι (5)

44.21 εν τω εισπορευεσθαι αυτους

Sections of the Text: Chapters 40-48

45.1 εν τω καταμετρεισθαι υμας   ⟨κατα⟩ (4)

46.8 εν τω εισπορευεσθαι   —

46.10 εν τω εισπορευεσθαι αυτους   —

46.10 εν τω εκπορευεσθαι αυτους   —

In all but two instances this construction is a rendering of
the preposition ⟨⟨b⟩⟩ plus the infinitve construct. The two
exceptions are 3.27 and 11.13, where the MT has ⟨⟨k⟩⟩ instead.
The LXX Vorlage may have differed from the MT in these cases.

Although this construction may be in some measure
context-dependent, context cannot explain entirely the marked
difference between the sections. There is no significant
correspondence between the Greek tenses and the Hebrew forms
of the verb either. The clearest evidence is the almost
exclusive use of the aorist infinitive in S2, regardless of
context. S3 contrasts sharply as it uses only the present
infinitive, whereas S1 exhibits a mixture of both types. In
each section of the MT there is a variety of relationships
between the action of the main verbs and the action of their
infinitives /2/.

⟨6.3⟩ נשׂיא

7.27	נשׂיא	αρχων	και αρχων (1-6)
12.10	הנשׂיא	ο αρχων	τω αρχοντι (2-6)
12.12	והנשׂיא	και ο αρχων	αρχ. αυτων (1-6)
19.1	אל-נשׂיאי ישׂראל	επι τον αρχοντα του ισραηλ	—
21.17	בכל-נשׂיאי ישׂראל	εν πασι τοις αφηγουμενοις του ισραηλ	ηγουμενοις (6)
21.30	נשׂיא ישׂראל	αφηγουμενε του ισραηλ	βασιλευ (2)

145

22.6	נשיאי ישראל	οι αφηγουμενοι οικου ισραηλ	–
26.16	כל נשיאי הים	παντες οι αρχον- τες εκ των εθνων της θαλασσης	... <εκ των εθνων> (1,3,6)
27.21	וכל-(נ)שיאי קדר	και παντες οι αρχοντες κηδαρ	–
30.13	ונשיא	και αρχοντας	αρχοντες (1)
32.29	וכל-(נ)שיאיה	οι αρχοντες //	–
34.24	נשיא	αρχων	–
37.25	נשיא	αρχων	–
38.2	נשיא ראש	αρχοντα ρως	αρχοντας (2)/ αρχοντος (6)
38.3	נשיא ראש	αρχοντα ρως	–
39.1	נשיא ראש	αρχοντα ρως	–
39.18	נשיאי הארץ	αρχοντων της γης	–
44.3	את-הנשיא נשיא	διοτι ο ηγουμενος	ο ηγουμ. αρχων (3)/ τω ηγουμενω διοτι ο ηγουμενος (4,6)
45.7	ולנשיא	και τω ηγουμενω	–
45.8	(נ)שיאי	οι αφηγουμενοι του ισραηλ	<> (2)
45.9	נשיאי ישראל	οι αφηγουμενοι του ισραηλ	<> (2)/ ο αφηγουμενος (3,5)
45.16	לנשיא בישראל	τω αφηγουμενω του ισραηλ	των αφηγουμενων (4)
45.17	ועל-הנשיא	και δια του αφηγουμενου	–
45.22	הנשיא	ο αφηγουμενος	–
46.2	הנשיא	ο αφηγουμενος	–
46.4	הנשיא	ο αφηγουμενος	–
46.8	הנשיא	τον αφηγουμενον	τον ηγουμενον (1)
46.10	והנשיא	ο αφηγουμενος	–
46.12	הנשיא	ο αφηγουμενος	ο ηγουμενος (1)
46.16	הנשיא	ο αφηγουμενος	–
46.17	לנשיא	τω αφηγουμενω	τω ηγουμενω (1)
46.18	הנשיא	ο αφηγουμενος	ο ηγουμενος (1)

3.21	‮דניסא‬	τω αφηγουμενω	του αφηγουμενου (2)/ των αφηγουμενων (5)/ τω ηγουμενω (1)
3.21	‮דניסא‬	του αφηγουμενου	—
3.22	‮דניסא‬	των αφηγουμενων	τω αφηγουμενω (4,5)/ του αφηγουμενου (1,3)
3.22	‮דניסא‬	των αφηγουμενων	τω αφηγουμενω (3-5)/ τω ηγουμενω (1)

f. Herrmann (1923: 10) and Turner (1956: 15). The contexts of
he words do vary, but there is no consistent correlation
etween change of context and change of rendering. In all of
1 and S3, and in 34.24 and 37.25 in S2, the "prince" is a
rince over Israel. S2 consistently uses <<arkhòn>>, even in
4.24 and 37.25. <<arkhòn>> does not occur in S3, nor does
<aphègoumenos>> occur in S2.

The attestation at 44.3 and 45.7 to <<hègoumenos>> would
eem to point to a difference between S3 and S1. However, the
act that 967 differs from the B MSS in having <<hègoumenos>>
nstead of <<aphègoumenos>> in 46.8,12,17,18 and 48.21,22
hows that there was alteration from one form to another at
ome stage of transmission of the text. It is difficult to say
hich form is original, but such alteration means that little
eight should be laid on this case as an example of
ranslation difference between S1 and S3. This alteration is
ne of several instances of where the weight of apparent
ifferences between S1 and S3 is reduced by the conflict in
ttestation between 967 and the B MSS (see below).

‹6.4› שׂים (ק.)

4.2	ושׂים	και ταξεις	κ. δωσεις (4)
4.4	ושׂמת	και θησεις	κ. επιθ. (2)/ κ. στησει· (4)/ κ. ληψη (5)
5.5	שׂמתיה	τεθεικα αυτην	—
6.2	שׂים	στηρισον	—
7.20	שׂמהו	εθεντο αυτα	εθετο α. (4)/ ‹αυτα› // (2,6)
11.7	שׂמתכם	εταξατε	εφονευσατε (1,2)/ επαταξατε (1-6)
13.17	שׂים	στηρισον	-ξον (5)
14.4	ישׂים	ταξη	—
14.7	ישׂים	ταξη	—
15.7	בשׂומי	εν τω στηρισαι με	και ... (2)/ ‹με› (2,4,5
16.14	שׂמתי	εταξα	—
17.4	שׂמו	εθετο αυτα	ε. αυτο (3,4)/ ε. -τον (4)/ ε. -τω (3)
17.5	שׂמו	εταξεν αυτο	επαταξεν α. (4)/ ετ. αυτ (3)
19.5	שׂמתהו	εταξεν αυτον	-ξαν α. (2)/ επαταξεν α. (6)/ εξεταζεν (2)
20.28	וישׂימו	και εταξαν	—
21.2	שׂים	στηρισον	τηρησον (4,5)
21.7	שׂים	στηρισον	και σ. (1-4)
21.24	שׂים	διαταξον	-ξε (2)/ διδαξον (5)
21.25	תשׂים	διαταξεις	//
21.27	לשׂום	του βαλειν	τ. λαβειν (2)/ τ. περιβ. (4)
21.27	לשׂום	του βαλειν	—
21.32	אשׂימנה	θησομαι αυτην	διαθ. α. (3)
23.24	ישׂימו	και βαλει //	κ. βαλουσιν // (6)
23.41	שׂמת	ευφραινοντο	εξευφ. (2)/ -νονται (5)/ και ευφ. // (1,3,4)
24.7	שׂמתהי	τεταχα αυτο	τ. αυτον (4,5)
24.17	תשׂים	‹›	—
25.2	שׂים	στηρισον	—
26.12	ישׂימו	εμβαλει	—
28.21	שׂים	στηρισον	—

Sections of the Text: Chapters 40-48

29.2	שׂים	στηρισον	–
30.21	לשׁום	του δοθηναι	τ. δουναι (1)/ τ. δεθηναι (6)/ τ. επιτεθηναι (4)/ τ. επιθειναι (4)
35.2	שׂים	επιστρεψον	–
35.4	אשׂים	ποιησω	<> (1,4)
38.2	שׂים	στηρισον	–
39.21	שׂמתי	επηγαγον	–
40.4	ושׂים	και ταξον	–
44.5	שׂים	ταξον	–
44.5	ושׂמת	και ταξεις	–
44.8	ושׂמתון	και διεταξατε	κ. -ξασθε (2)/ κ. -ξα (2)/ κ. -ξαντο (3)/ κ. -ξατο (3)/ κ. δ. αυτοις (4)/ κ. δ. εαυτοις (4)/ κ. διετασσετε (1)

The Hebrew term is used in a wide variety of contexts. S1 and S2 agree in using <<stèrizein>> wherever the expression "to set one's face (against)" occurs. This phrase is absent from S3. Nevertheless S3 still appears to differ from S2 in preferring <<tassein>> and <<diatassein>>, a feature which it shares with S1. Neither of the Greek terms occurs in S2.

The next examples have more of a corroborative value. Independently they are weak.

<6.5> מלא (.ס)

3.3	תמלא	πλησθησεται	πληρωθησεται (3)
7.19	ימלאו	πληρωθωσι	–
9.7	ומלאו	και πλησατε	και πληρωσατε (2,3)
10.2	מלא	και πλησον	–
11.6	ומלאתם	ενεπλησατε	<εν> (3-5)
24.4	מלא	//	πληρη (3)
32.5	ומלאתי	και εμπλησω	–
35.8	ומלאתי	και εμπλησω	εμπληρω (3)

The Greek Text of Ezekiel

43.26   ומלאו   και πλησουσι   πληρωσουσι (1,3,4)/
                                    τελειωσουσι (3,4)/
                                    πλυνουσι (2)

Here the difference between S2 and S3 is just that of the
difference between <<empimplanai>> and <<pimplanai>> If the
variant <<plèròsousi>> attested by 967 and some other MSS at
43.26 is correct, this difference is strengthened, as
<<plèroun>> does not occur in S2. Cf. the rendering at 7.19.

<6.6>   לבש (.ק)

7.27   ילבש   ενδυσεται   —
26.16   ילבשו   εκστησονται //   —
34.3   תלבשו   περιβαλλεσθε   περιεβαλ(λ)εσθε (1,4)
42.14   ולבשו   και ενδυσονται   —
44.17   ילבשו   ενδυσονται   —
44.19   ולבשו   και ενδυσονται   —

Both <<enduein>> and <<periballein>> occur elsewhere in the
LXX as renderings for this term, although <<enduein>> is more
common. The contexts do vary, but this does not seem to affect
the general action — that of putting on clothes.

<6.7>   חטה

4.9   חטין   πυρους   —
27.17   בחטי   εν σιτου   —
45.13   החטים   του πυρου   των πυρων (1,3)

<<sitos>> is the more general term for "grain", whereas
<<puros>> denotes "wheat" in particular. However, the mention
of barley as well in 4.9 and 45.13 may have caused the
translator to be more specific. The attestation of the plural

in 45.13 by 967 and a few other MSS would, if correct, bring
S3 closer to S1.

Some further examples indicating the difference between
S2 and S3 will be found in the following sections of this
chapter as well. Yet it is clear from those cases already
cited that S2 and S3 do differ in their rendering of terms.

2. The Textual History of S3

One of the results of the investigation into the
witness of divine names was that S3 appeared to have had a
different textual history from the rest of the translation.
There are other examples which corroborate this finding. These
examples had formerly been used to show that S1 and S3 were
the work of different translators. As will be seen, the
witness of 967 shows that some degree of textual alteration
must have taken place. We have already noted the oscillation
between <<hègoumenos>> and <<aphègoumenos>> in ex. <6.3>. Cf.
also <6.5> and <6.7>.

The alterations occur too frequently to represent merely
scribal errors and so must be seen as the result of a (minor)
revision of the text. None of the changes noted in the text
brings about a substantial change in its meaning. This would
seem to indicate that the motivating factors were linguistic
or stylistic rather than purely theological.

The Greek Text of Ezekiel

<6.8> אחרי/אחר

3.12	אחרי קול	κατοπισθεν μου φωνην	<μου> (6)
5.2	אחריהם	οπισω αυτων	οπισθεν (4)/ εν μεσω (6)
5.12	אחריהם	οπισω αυτων	-
6.9	אחרי גלוליהם	οπισω των επιτηδευματων αυτων	-
9.5	ואחרי	οπισω αυτον	-
10.11	הראש ואחרי	η αρξη η μια	η α. η μ. οπισω αυτου (3-5)
12.14	אחריהם	οπισω αυτων	-
13.3	אחר רוחם	//	οπισω του πνευμα- τος αυτων (2-4,6)
14.7	מאחרי	απ εμου	-
14.11	מאחרי	απ εμου	-
16.23	אחרי כל-רעתך	μετα πασας τας κακιας σου	-
16.34	ואחריך	και μετα σε	και μετα σου (1,2,4,5)
20.16	אחרי גלוליהם	και οπισω των ενθυμηματων	-
20.24	ואחרי גלולי	και οπισω των ενθυμηματων	-
20.30	ואחרי שקוציהם	και οπισω των βδελυγματων αυτων	-
20.39	ואחר	και μετα ταυτα //	-
23.30	אחרי גוים	οπισω εθνων	ο. των ε. (4)
23.35	אחרי גוך	οπισω του σωματος σου	ο. τ. στοματος σ. (6)
29.16	אחריהם	οπισω αυτων	-
33.31	אחרי בצעם	και οπισω των μιασματων	-
41.15	על-אחריה	κατοπισθεν //	-
44.10	אחרי גלוליהם	κατοπισθεν των ενθυμηματων αυτων	οπισω των ειδωλων αυτων (4)/ οπισω (1)
44.26	ואחרי טהרתו	και μετα το καθαρισθηναι αυτον	<αυτον> (1)
46.12	אחרי צאתו	μετα το εξελθειν αυτον	-

The use of <<katopisthen>> in S3 was seen as evidence for distinguishing it from S2 (and even S1), cf. Herrmann (1923:

5) and Turner (1956: 14). Yet in 44.10 Papyrus 967 reads only <<opisð>>, raising doubts about the originality of <<katopisthen>>.

<6.9> לפני

2.10	לפני	ενωπιον εμου	ε. μου (2-5)
3.20	לפניו	εις προσωπον αυτου	-
4.1	לפניך	προ προσωπου σου	-
6.4	לפני	ενωπιον	-
6.5	לפני	<>	κατα προσωπον (2-6)
8.1	לפני	ενωπιον μου	ε. εμου (2,3)/ ε. <μου> (3)
8.11	לפניהם	προ προσωπου αυτων	εις προσωπον (3)/ εις πρ. αυτου (4)
9.6	לפני	εσωθεν	εως εν (3)/ εσωθεν <εν> (2)/ εσωθεν εν (5)/ <εσ.> εν (2,4)
14.1	לפני	προ προσωπου μου	-
16.18	לפניהם	προ προσωπου αυτων	-
16.19	לפניהם	προ προσωπου αυτων	-
16.50	לפני	ενωπιον μου	ε. εμου (2-6)
20.1	לפני	προ προσωπου μου	-
22.30	לפני	προ προσωπου μου	κατα προσωπου μου (3,5)
23.24	לפניהם	προ προσωπου αυτων	-
23.41	לפניה	προ προσωπου αυτης	εμπροσθεν αυτης (4)/ π. πρ. σου (1,3,4)/ π. πρ. αυτων (1-3)
28.9	לפני	ενωπιον	εν μεσω (2)
28.17	לפני	εναντιον	-
30.9	מלפני	<>	προ προσωπου μου (3,4)/ προ προσωπου σου (4)/ εκ πρ. μου (3,4)/ απο πρ. μου (4)
30.24	לפניו	//	// ενωπιον αυτου (3)
33.22	לפני בוא	πριν ελθειν	-
33.31	לפניך	εναντιον σου	ενωπιον σου (1,4)/ ενα. μου (5)

36.17	לפני	προ προσωπου μου	—
40.12	לפני	// επι προσωπον	επι κατα (3)/ και κατα (5)/ κατα πρ. (1-6)
40.15	על-לפני	//	επι προσωπον (3)
40.19	מלפני	//	//
40.19	לפני	//	//
40.22	לפניהם	//	//
40.26	לפניהם	εσωθεν //	ε. αυτων (4)
40.47	לפני	απεναντι	—
41.22	לפני	προ προσωπου	κατα πρ. (2)
42.4	ולפני	και κατεναντι	—
42.11	לפניהם	κατα προσωπον αυτων	κ. προσωπα α. (1)/ κ. πρ. αυτου (5)
43.24	לפני	εναντιον	—
44.3	לפני	εναντιον	εναντι (4,6)/ ενωπιον (1,2,6)
44.11	לפניהם	εναντιον	ενωπιον (1,2,6)
44.12	לפני	προ προσωπου	ενωπιον (4)
44.15	לפני	προ προσωπου με	—
46.3	לפני	εναντιον	ενωπιον (1)
46.9	לפני	εναντιον	ενωπιον (1,2,6)

Here we find the reading <<enantion>> in S3 strongly
challenged by 967 and sometimes by other witnesses as well. It
is difficult to say which form, <<enantion>> or <<enòpion>>,
was original. It is possible that both were used in S3
initially. The variation in the prepositions does not appear
to be affected by whether they are applied to Yahweh or to
mortals. Cf. Sollamo (1982: 70-80) and also ex. <6.10>.

Sections of the Text: Chapters 40-48

<6.10> עַיִן

1.4	כְּעֵין	ως ορασις	ως ομοιωμα (2,3,5)
1.7	כְּעֵין	ως	—
1.16	כְּעֵין	ως ειδος	—
1.18	עֵינִים	οφθαλμων	—
1.22	כְּעֵין	ως ορασις	—
1.27	כְּעֵין	ως οψιν	ως ορασιν (4-6)
4.12	לְעֵינֵיהֶם	κατ οφθαλμους αυτων	—
5.8	לְעֵינֵי	ενωπιον	—
5.11	עֵינִי	μου ο οφθαλμος	—
5.14	לְעֵינֵי	ενωπιον	—
6.9	עֵינֵיהֶם	τοις οφθαλμοις αυτων	τους οφθαλμους αυτων (3)
7.4	עֵינִי	ο οφθαλμος μου	—
7.9	עֵינִי	ο οφθαλμος μου	—
8.2	כְּעֵין	ως ορασις //	ως ορασις ως ειδος (1-6)
8.5	עֵינֶיךָ	τοις οφθαλμοις σου	—
8.5	עֵינִי	τοις οφθαλμοις μου	τους οφθαλμους (5)
8.18	עֵינִי	ο οφθαλμος μου	—
9.5	עֵינְכֶם	τοις οφθαλμοις υμων	—
9.10	עֵינִי	ο οφθαλμος μου	—
10.2	לְעֵינֵי	ενωπιον	—
10.9	כְּעֵין	ως οψις	—
10.12	עֵינִים	οφθαλμων	—
10.19	לְעֵינִי	ενωπιον εμου	—
12.2	עֵינִים	οφθαλμους	—
12.3	לְעֵינֵיהֶם	ενωπιον αυτων	—
12.3	לְעֵינֵיהֶם	ενωπιον αυτων	—
12.4	לְעֵינֵיהֶם	κατ οφθαλμους αυτων	ενωπιον αυτων (1,6)
12.4	לְעֵינֵיהֶם	<>	ενωπιον αυτων (1-6)
12.5	לְעֵינֵיהֶם	ενωπιον αυτων	εις οφθαλμους αυτων (2,3)/ <> (1-6)
12.6	לְעֵינֵיהֶם	ενωπιον αυτων	—
12.7	לְעֵינֵיהֶם	ενωπιον αυτων	—
12.12	לְעֵין	οφθαλμω	—

16.5	עיני	ο οφθαλμος μου	—
16.41	לעיני	ενωπιον	—
18.6	ועיניו	και τους οφθαλμους αυτου	—
18.12	עיניו	τους οφθαλμους αυτου	—
18.15	ועיניו	και τους οφθαλμους αυτου	—
20.7	עיניו	των οφθαλμων αυτου	<> (1)
20.8	עיניהם	των οφθαλμων αυτων	—
20.9	לעיני	ενωπιον	εν μεσω (5)
20.9	לעיניהם	ενωπιον αυτων	—
20.14	לעיני	ενωπιον	—
20.14	לעיניהם	κατ οφθαλμους αυτων	—μων (2)
20.17	עיני	ο οφθαλμος μου	—
20.22	לעיניהם	ενωπιον	—
20.24	עיניהם	οι οφθαλμοι αυτων	—
20.41	לעיני	κατ οφθαλμους	—
21.11	לעיניהם	κατ οφθαλμους αυτων	—
21.28	בעיניהם	ενωπιον αυτων	—
22.16	לעיני	κατ οφθαλμους	ενωπιον (2,6)
22.26	עיניהם	τους οφθαλμους αυτων	—
23.16	עיניה	οφθαλμων αυτης	—μους (3)
23.27	עיניך	τους οφθαλμους σου	—
23.40	עיניך	τους οφθαλμους σου	—
24.16	עיניך	οφθαλμων σου	—
24.21	עיניכם	οφθαλμων υμων	—
24.25	עיניהם	οφθαλμων αυτων	—
28.18	לעיני	εναντιον	—
28.25	לעיני	ενωπιον	—
33.25	ועיניכם	<>	οφθαλμους (2-6)/ οφθαλμος (2,3)
36.23	לעיניהם	κατ οφθαλμους αυτων	—
36.34	לעיני	κατ οφθαλμους	—
37.20	לעיניהם	ενωπιον αυτων	—
38.16	לעיניהם	ενωπιον αυτων	—
38.23	לעיני	εναντιον	εναντι (4)/ ενωπιον (2,5)
39.27	לעיני	ενωπιον	—

40.4   בָּעֵינֶיךָ   εν τοις οφθαλμοις σου   ⟨εν⟩ (1,3-5)
43.11   לְעֵינֵיהֶם   εναντιον αυτων   ενωπιον (1,6)
44.5   בְּעֵינֶיךָ   τοις οφθαλμοις σου   ⟨⟩ (1)

For the sake of completeness every usage of ⟨⟨'yn⟩⟩ has been
included, although the main form of interest is ⟨⟨l'yny⟩⟩.

This example and the previous one contain all the
occurrences of ⟨⟨enantion⟩⟩ in S3. Yet here too the witness of
967 raises doubts about the strength of the reading. Sollamo
notes that the rendering ⟨⟨enòpion⟩⟩ is "particularly popular
in Ez" (1982: 150; cf. p. 148).

The importance of these differences between 967 and the
other witnesses, especially the B MSS, is not only that they
show that some revision had occurred at an early stage in the
history of the text, but also that they weaken the argument
for seeing S1 and S3 as the work of different translators. In
each of the above examples - ⟨6.8-10⟩ - the witness of 967
brings the translation technique of S3 closer to that of S1,
cf. also ⟨6.3,5,7⟩. This fact should be of use to us in
comparing S1 and S3, to which task we now turn.

3. The Relationship between S1 and S3

This relationship is one area where there has been
strong disagreement. Thackeray had argued that a' (1-27) and
g' (40-48) were the work of the same person, but Herrmann,
Danielsmeyer and Turner all maintained that ch.40-48 were
rendered by a third, different translator. It may have been
the case that Thackeray was guided to his two-translator view
for Ezekiel by analogy with his two-translator hypothesis for
Jeremiah rather than solely by the linguistic evidence.

Nevertheless, he may not have been far wrong. It is true that there are differences between S1 and S3. Yet these are not as significant as has been affirmed. The evidence for distinguishing S3 from S1 certainly is not "weighty", as Turner contended (1956: 14).

Indeed, it will be maintained here that the evidence available is at least compatible with the suggestion that S1 and S3 are the work of the same person. There cannot be complete certainty with this, for even if the sections exhibited almost no differences, our knowledge of the range of translation styles is so limited that we cannot say how similar the work of two contemporary translators could be.

We have already seen that some of the differences between the sections have been due to early sporadic revision and scribal alteration. The witness of the divine names and certain other terms (as in examples <2.18> and <6.3,8-10> above) cannot be used as evidence of differing translation technique. However, the effect of textual variation is not the only distorting factor here.

To a great extent, the problem of assessing the relationship between S1 and S3 resolves into one of determining how much a change of context can change a translation. The contexts in S3 often differ strongly from those in S1. We might thus expect at least some change of rendering. It is the extent of this change which is difficult to predict.

Changes of context can be divided into two different types. Firstly, there is that change of context which so alters the meaning or connotation of a word that a change of rendering would be necessary if a sensible translation is to be made (unless the semantic range of the initial Greek

equivalent extends to the new meaning). For example, the word
<<p'r>> - "hair" - had three different renderings:

<6.11> פאר

24.17	פארך	το τριχωμα σου	—
24.23	ופארכם	και αι κομαι υμων	<και> (1,6)
44.18	פארי	και κιδαρεις	<και> (3,4)

Although the Greek terms in S1 generally mean "hair", while
the term in S3 denotes a head-dress of some sort, this change
in meaning in S3 is forced on the translator by the fact that
the text in 44.18 states that "<<p'ry>> of linen shall be on
their heads". The rendering "hair" would be quite
inappropriate, thus necessitating a different translation.

Secondly, there is the change of context which so alters
the meaning or connotation of a word that a change of
rendering would be justifiable, though not necessary. In this
case the original rendering could be retained without
destroying the sense of the text, though a translator might
also wish to use what he felt was a more accurate equivalent.

Most of the differences between S1 and S3 fall under this
second type of context change. If we leave aside prepositions
and particles, and omit ch.16 and 36.23c-38 for the time
being, we find that there are only 158 Hebrew lexical forms
which occur in all three sections. There are a further 78
forms which occur only in S1 and S3. This gives us a total of
236 terms shared by S1 and S3 at least. (These are listed in
Appendix D). Yet out of those 236 terms, 147 are rendered by
the same form in both sections and 16 more have such a variety
and distribution of rendering as to be of ambiguous value,
e.g. <<'mr>>. A further 26 exhibit textual problems, either of
possible differing Vorlage or of an inner-Greek nature or of a

combination of factors. In the case of another 20 the context
would require a translation change in order to preserve the
sense of the passage. This leaves us with just 27 terms where
S3 differs from S1. Only 6 of those seem to be relatively free
from the effects of context change. They either occur in the
same context in both sections or else are reasonably
independent of context. These 6 cases are cited below:

<6.12> פתח

8.3	אל-פתח	επι τα προθυρα	—
8.7	אל-פתח	επι τα προθυρα	—
8.8	פתח	θυρα	—
8.14	אל-פתח	επι τα προθυρα	—
8.16	פתח	επι των προθυρων	ε. τ. θυρων (4,5)/ ε. τ. προθυρον (1,2)
10.19	פתח	επι τα προθυρα	—
11.1	בפתח	επι των προθυρων	—
33.30	ובפתחי	και εν τοις πυλωσι	—
40.11	פתח	της θυρας	<> (5)
40.13	פתח	// πυλη	πυλην (1)
40.13	פתח	// πυλην	πυλης (4)
40.38	ופתחה	και τα θυρωματα αυτης	κ αστου παστοφοριου η(ν) θυρα (4)
40.40	לפתח	//	//
41.2	הפתח	του πυλωνος	—
41.2	הפתח	του πυλωνος	—
41.3	הפתח	του θυρωματος	—
41.3	והפתח	και το θυρωμα	κ. την θυραν (3,4)
41.3	הפתח	//	//
41.11	ופתח	και αι θυραι	κ. αι θυριδες (2)
41.11	פתח	της θυρας	—
41.11	ופתח	και η θυρα	—
41.17	הפתח	<>	—
41.20	הפתח	//	//

Sections of the Text: Chapters 40-48

42.2	פתח	//		//
42.4	ופתחיהם	και τα θυρωματα αυτων		κ. το θυρωμα α. (6)
42.11	ופתחיהם	και κατα τα φωτα αυτων		-
42.12	ופתחי	και κατα τα θυρωμα αυτων		κ. κ. τα οχυρωματα α. (5)
42.12	פתח	// και κατα τα θυρωμα		-
46.3	פתח	κατα τα προθυρα		κ. προθυρων (3)
47.1	אל-פתח	επι τα προθυρα		-

Cf. Herrmann (1923: 17). This is the strongest example in the argument against the identity of translators. The use of <<thuròma>> is limited to S3 in Ezekiel, where it also occurs as a rendering of <<dlt>>, cf. ex. <2.20>. All the references in both S1 and S3 are to temples too.

It might be suggested, however, that the abundance of technical description in S3 could have caused the translator to vary his renderings in such a way.

<6.13> גור (.ק)

14.7	אשר-יגור	των προσηλυτευοντων		τ. προσκειμενων (2,5) / τ. επικειμενων (5)
47.22	הגרים	τοις παροικουσιν		τ. κατοικ. (2,4)/ τ. προσοικ. (2)/ τ. προκειμενοις (2)
47.23	אשר-גר הגר	προσηλυτων εν τοις προσηλυτοις //		των π. ε. τ. π. (2)

Cf. Herrmann (1923: 16). The meaning of the term <<gwr>> seems unaffected by context. The word <<prosèluteuein>> is found only in 14.7 in all of the LXX.

161

The Greek Text of Ezekiel

<6.14> עֶלְיוֹן

9.2	הָעֶלְיוֹן	της υψηλης	<> (2,6)
41.7	עַל-הָעֶלְיוֹנָה	επι τα υπερωα	−
42.5	הָעֶלְיוֹנֹת	οι υπερωοι	//

Cf. Turner (1956: 15). <<huperòos>> occurs only in S3, although <<hupsèlos>> is found in both sections. All three references are in the context of temple descriptions.

<6.15> קַדְמוֹנִי

10.19	הַקַּדְמוֹנִי	της απεναντι	<> (2)
11.1	הַקַּדְמוֹנִי	την κατεναντι	την απεναντι (2)
38.17	קַדְמֹנִים	των εμπροσθεν	−
47.18	הַקַּדְמוֹנִי	την προς ανατολας	−

In S1 and S3 this Hebrew term is used in an adjectival and geographical sense. In 10.19 and 11.1 it is applied to a gate and in 47.18 to a sea. The rendering in 47.18 might imply a different understanding of the term ("the eastern one") from that in S1 ("the opposite one"). This could have been influenced though by the occurrence of similar words — <<qdym>> and <<qdymh>> — in the same verse.

<6.16> חָמָס

7.11	הֶחָמָס	//	//
7.23	חָמָס	ανομιας	ανομιων (1,3,4)
8.17	חָמָס	ανομιας	−
12.19	מֵחֲמַס	εν ασεβεια	δι(α τας) ασεβειας (2,6)
28.16	חָמָס	ανομιας	ανομια (6)/ <> (4,6)
45.9	חָמָס	αδικιαν	−

Cf. Herrmann (1923: 16) and Turner (1956: 15). The Hebrew term
seems fairly independent of context. The rendering in 12.19
might indicate that the translator had not fixed on a
stereotyped rendering of the term.

<6.17> רחק (.ק)

8.6	לרחקה	του απεχεσθαι	τ. ανεχ. (3)/ τ. α αυτους (4)
11.15	רחקו	μακραν απεχετε	μ. απεχειν (2)
44.10	רחקו	αφηλαντο	αφειλ. (2)/ αφειλοντο (2,3,6)/ μακρυνθεντες (4)

This expression occurs in similar contexts in S1 and S3.
Although <<aphairein>> is found in both sections, it is only
in 44.10 that it is used in the sense (apparently) of "to go
away from".

These six cases of translation change cannot be easily
explained on the grounds of context or Vorlage. Yet it is not
unreasonable to expect that a translator might simply have
changed his mind in these instances. Indeed, we note that
there was variation of rendering in these examples within S1
itself. It must be remembered too that a considerable amount
of text lies between the renderings. This material could
easily have choked out any conscious memory the translator had
of his previous renderings.

The 21 examples where the change of context between S1
and S3 might justify the translation change will be considered
next. As mentioned before, the problem is that we cannot
easily predict how much translation change we should expect to
find with such a context change as we have in S3 (assuming
that the same translator were to have worked on both parts of

the text). This difficulty can work in two ways. It means that
the case for seeing the two sections as the work of one
translator cannot be completely certain. But it also means
that the argument for seeing the two sections as the work of
two translators is weakened as well, because the possibility
that most of the difference is due to context cannot be ruled
out. It will be maintained here that the context change is
strong and that the translation change is at least
justifiable. If this proposal is correct, then the case for
different translators is substantially weakened.

<6.18> מלך

1.2	המלך יויכין	του βασιλεως ιωακιμ	<βασιλεως> (2,5)
7.27	המלך	<>	(ο) βασιλε (2-6)
17.12	מלך-בבל	βασιλευς βαβυλωνος	–
17.12	את-מלכה	τον βασιλεα αυτης	<> (2)
17.16	המלך	ο βασιλευς	του -λεως (1,3,4,6 / <> (3)
19.9	אל-מלך בבל	προς βασιλεα βαβυλωνος	–
21.24	מלך בבל	βασιλεως βαβυλωνος	–
21.26	מלך-בבל	βασιλευς βαβυλωνος	ο β. β. (3-5)
24.2	מלך-בבל	βασιλευς βαβυλωνος	ο β. β. (2,4)
26.7	מלך בבל	βασιλεα βαβυλωνος	βασ. βασιλεα βαβ. (2)
26.7	מלך מלכים	βασιλεως βασιλεων	βασιλεως βασ. (3)/ β. βαβυλωνος (6)
27.33	מלכי-ארץ	βασιλεις της γης	–
27.35	ומלכיהם	και οι βασιλεις αυτων	–
28.12	על-מלך צור	επι τον αρχοντα τυρου	// (1)/ ε. τ. α. σωρ // (6)
28.17	מלכים	βασιλεων	–
29.2	מלך מצרים	βασιλεα αιγυπτου	-λει α. (5)/ -λεως α. (6)/ β. -τω (5)
29.3	מלך-מצרים	<>	βασιλευς αιγυπτου (2)/ βασιλευ αιγυπτου (2-6)/ βασιλεα αιγυπτου (2,6)

Sections of the Text: Chapters 40-48

29.18	מלך־בבל	βασιλευς βαβυλωνος	ο β. β. (4,6)
9.19	מלך־בבל	βασιλει βαβυλωνος	−λεα βαβ. (2,5)
50.10	מלך־בבל	βασιλεως βαβυλωνος	β. βαβυλωνιων (3)
50.21	מלך־מצרים	βασιλεως αιγυπτου	−
50.22	מלך־מצרים	βασιλεα αιγυπτου	−
50.24	מלך בבל	βασιλεως βαβυλωνος	<> (6)
50.25	מלך בבל	βασιλεως βαβυλωνος	−
50.25	מלך־בבל	βασιλεως βαβυλωνος	−
51.2	מלך־מצרים	βασιλεα αιγυπτου	−
52.2	מלך־מצרים	βασιλεα αιγυπτου	τον β. α. (4)
52.10	ומלכיה	και οι βασιλεις αυτων	−
52.11	מלך־בבל	βασιλεως βαβυλωνος	−
52.29	מלכיה	οι αρχοντες //	−
57.22	ומלך	και αρχων	−
57.22	למלך	<>	εις βασιλεα (2−4)/ εις βασιλειαν (4)
57.24	מלך	αρχων	−
43.7	ומלכיה	και οι ηγουμενοι αυτων	−
43.7	מלכיה	των ηγουμενων	τ. ηγαπημενων (5)/ <> (5)/ τ. η. αυτων (1,4,5)
43.9	מלכיה	των ηγουμενων αυτων	−

Cf. Turner (1956: 15). The rendering <<hègoumenos>> in S3 is
unusual, and does not occur elsewhere in the LXX. All the
references to kings in S1 are to actual rulers of countries
around the time of the Exile. However, the references to kings
in 43.7,9, being in the context of the future temple, are less
distinct. The LXX translator may have understood or intended
them to include the subsequent rulers of Israel, in which case
the term <<basileus>> would have been inappropriate both
historically, as the monarchy was not continued, and
eschatologically, as the temple vision made provision for a
"prince", not a "king", cf. ex. <6.3>. Accordingly, the
references to the "corpses" in 43.7,9 and the "high places" in
. 7 are given the more general translation of "killings" (cf.

165

43.8) and "in their midst" respectively.

<6.19> נוח (.ה)

5.13	והנחותי	<> //	—
16.39	<והניחו>	και αφησουσι σε	—
16.42	והנחתי	και επαφησω	—
21.22	והנחתי	και εναφησω	επαφησω (3-5)/ εαν αφησω (2)
22.20	<והנחתי>	και συναξω	συνταξω (3)/ κ. σ. κ επαφησω (4)/ εισαξω επαφησω (4)
24.13	עד-הניחי	εως ου εμπλησω	—
37.1	ויניחני	και εθηκε με	—
37.14	<והנחתי>	και θησομαι	—
40.2	ויניחני	και εθηκε με	κ. ηγαγε(ν) (3,4)
40.42	<וינייו>	επιθησουσι	θησουσι (1)
42.13	<יניחו>	θησουσι	αποθησονται (4)
42.14	<יניחו>	//	—
44.19	<והניחו>	και θησουσιν	—
44.30	להניח	του θειναι	ειναι (6)

One set of the two Hiphil forms of the Hebrew verb is
differentiated from the other by means of angular brackets.
Both classifications of the verb have been included as the
translator may not have recognised such a differentiation.
S1 the verb is used mostly to express the "turning away" of
the wrath of God (in [16.42], 21.22; 24.13). The exact mean
in the MT in 22.20 is unclear, and BHS suggests an emendati
In S3, on the other hand, most of the uses consist of
physically "setting" things in a certain place (in 40.2,42;
42.13; 44.19). In 44.30 a slighly more abstract idea is
expressed: that of "setting" a blessing on a house.

Sections of the Text: Chapters 40-48

<6.20> בגד

16.16	מבגדיך	εκ των ιματιων σου	—
16.18	אֶת-בגדי	τον ιματισμον	—
16.39	בגדיך	τον ιματισμον	τα ιματια (1,3,4)
18.7	יכסה-בגד	περιβαλει	π. εν ιματιω (3)/ π. ιματιον (2-6)
18.16	כסה-בגד	περιβαλει	περιβαλει (5)/ π. ιματιον (2-6)
23.26	אֶת-בגדיך	τον ιματισμον σου	—
26.16	וְאֶת-בגדי	και τον ιματισμον	—
27.20	בבגדי	μετα κτηνων //	—
42.14	בגדיהם	του στολισμου αυτων	τους λογισμους α. (5)
42.14	בגדים	ιματια	—
44.17	בגדי	στολας	—
44.19	אֶת-בגדיהם	τας στολας αυτων	—
44.19	בגדים	στολας	—
44.19	בבגדיהם	εν ταις στολαις αυτων	—

Cf. Herrmann (1923: 15). The only rendering in S1 suitable for comparison is 23.26. Ch.16 is to be excluded (see chapter VII), while the Greek at 18.7,16 represents the translation of a phrase. In S3 the garments referred to are those of the priests, whereas in 23.26 (and ch.16) the garments are those worn by adulterous women. Significantly, the rendering <<himatia>> occurs in 42.14 too, where the priests are to put off their holy attire and don other "garments" when they go near the people.

<6.21> עבד (.ק)

20.39	עבדו	//	—
20.40	יעבדני	δουλευσουσι μοι	δουλευσι μ. (4)
29.18	עבד	εδουλευσαν	-σεν (1-4,6)/ -λωσεν (2)/ -λωσαν (5)

167

29.20	עָבַד	εδουλευσαν	-σαν (3,6)/
			-λωσεν (5)
34.27	הָעֹבְדִים	των καταδουλωσαμενων αυτους	—
48.18	לְעֹבְדֵי	τοις εργαζομενοις	—
48.19	הָעֹבֵד	οι δε εργαζομενοι	—
48.19	יַעַבְדוּהוּ	εργωνται αυτης	—

In 20.40 the verb is used of the service of the house of
Israel to Yahweh. In 48.18,19 the "service" is that of workin◄
the land.

<6.22> קרב (.ק)

9.1	קָרְבוּ	ηγγικεν	—
12.23	קָרְבוּ	ηγγικασιν	—
18.6	יִקְרָב	προσεγγιει	εγγιει (6)
37.7	וָאַקְרִבוּ	και προσηγαγε	—
42.14	וְקָרְבוּ	// απτωνται	—
44.15	יִקְרְבוּ	προσαξουσι	εγγιουσι(ν) (4)
44.16	יִקְרְבוּ	προσελευσονται	εισελευσ. (2)/ π. μοι (6)◄

Again, there is a marked context change between S1 and S3. I◄
9.1 the LXX records that the vengeance (MT: guard) of the ci◄
"has come". In 12.23 we are told that the days of fulfilment
"have come", while in 18.6 <<qrb>> is used of approaching a
woman for sexual intercourse. On the other hand, the context
in 44.15,16 is that of the priests "approaching" to minister
to Yahweh. The reading 42.14 may represent theological rathe◄
than linguistic considerations on the part of the translator

<6.23> קרב (.ה)

22.4	ותקריבי	και ηγγισας	προσηγγ. (4)
43.22	תקריב	λημψονται	λημψη (1) //
43.23	תקריב	προσοισουσι	και π. (3) / -οισεις (1)
43.24	והקרבתם	και προσοισετε	κ. π. αυτους (2,4)
44.7	בהקריבכם	εν τω προσφερειν υμας	-
44.15	להקריב	του προσφερειν	-
44.27	יקריב	προσοισουσιν	-οισει (1,3,4)/ και π. (2)
46.4	אשר-יקרב	προσοισει	-οισουσιν (3)

The context change here is similar to that in the preceding
example. In 22.4 the reference is to having "brought near" the
days, whereas in S3 the term is always used in the sense of
"offering" something in the temple. <<prospherein>> is
frequently used in this cultic sense in the LXX.

<6.24> טמא (.ו)

5.11	טמאת	εμιανας	εμιαναν (2)
9.7	טמאו	μιανατε	-
18.6	טמאה	μιανη	εμιανεν (6)
18.11	טמא	εμιανε	-
18.15	טמא	εμιανε	μειανει (5)
20.26	ואטמא	και μιανω	-
22.11	טמא	εμιαινεν	-νον (2,3,4)/ -νεν (2-5)
23.17	ויטמאו	και εμιαινον	κ. εμιαναν (1,4)/ εμιανον (5)
23.38	טמאו	εμιανον	εμια(ι)ναν (1,2,4,6)
33.26	טמאתם	<>	εμιανατε (2-6)
36.17	ויטמאו	και εμιαναν	-
36.18	טמאוה	<>	εμιαναν αυτην (2-6)

43.7   יחללו   βεβηλωσουσιν   –

43.8   ויחללו   και βεβηλωσαν   –

Only here (i.e. S3) in the LXX is this particular verb
rendered by <<bebèloun>>. In most instances in the LXX it is
translated by <<miainein>>. Both <<miainein>> and <<bebèloun>
are found in S1 and S3. In all the contexts the concept is
that of defilement or profanation. Yet while in S1 (and S2)
there are references to defiling the temple (9.7), sanctuary
(5.11; 23.28) and people (18.6, 11, 15), it is only in S3 that
there is mention made of defiling the name of God (43.7,8).
The term <<bebèloun>> is also used in S1, with different
hyponyms, to describe profanation of the divine name, cf.
20.9,14,22,39,(44), whereas <<miaiein>> is reserved for the
subjects mentioned above.

<6.25>   שרת   (.פ)

20.32	לשרת	του λατρευειν	τ. δουλευειν (1)
40.46	לשרתו	λειτουργειν αυτω	του λ. α. (1)
42.14	ישרתו	λειτουργουσιν //	λειτουργησουσιν (.
43.19	לשרתי	του λειτουργειν μοι	του λευι λειτ. (2 <μοι> (4)
44.11	משרתים	λειτουργουντες	–
44.11	ומשרתי	λειτουργουντες	–
44.11	לשרתם	του λειτουργειν αυτοις	λειτουργουντες α. (4)/ μου λ. α. (1 <του> (2-4)
44.12	ישרתו	ελειτουργουν	-χησαν (4)/ ελιτουργειν (2)
44.15	לשרתי	του λειτουργειν μοι	<του> (2,4,5)
44.16	לשרתי	του λειτουργειν μοι	–
44.17	בשרתם	εν τω λειτουργειν αυτους	–
44.19	משרתם	λειτουργουσιν	–
44.27	לשרת	του λειτουργειν	–

Sections of the Text: Chapters 40-48

45.4	משרתי	τοις λειτουργουσιν	-
45.4	לשרת	λειτουργειν	-
45.5	משרתי	τοις λειτουργουσι	-
46.24	משרתי	οι λειτουργουντες	-

The difference between the two sections is two-fold. Firstly, the "service" performed in S1 is to wood and stones and not to Yahweh in the cult, as in S3 (except for 44.12). Secondly, the "service" in S1 is done by foreign peoples, while in S3 it is rendered by the priests alone. In the LXX <<leitourgein>> is used almost invariably in depicting cultic service to Yahweh, cf. TDNT IV pp. 221-2. Almost half of the occurrences of <<latreuein>> refer by contrast to the serving of false or "other" gods.

<6.26> נגד (.ה)

23.36	והגד	και αναγγελεις	απαγγελλεις (3,4)/ επαγγελεις (4)/ απαγγελεις (2-6)
24.19	הלא-תגיד	ουκ αναγγελεις	ο. αναγγελλεις (1-3)/ ο. απαγγελλεις (2-4)/ ο. απαγγειλης (1,2)/ ο. απαγγελεις (2-6)
37.18	הלא-תגיד	ουκ αναγγελεις	ουκ αναγγελλεις (1,3)/ ουκ απαγγελλεις (2,4)/ ου καταγγελλεις (2)/ ουκ απαγγελεις (1-6)
40.4	הגד	και δειξεις	-
43.10	הגד	δειξον	υποδειξον (4)

Cf. Turner (1956: 15). In 23.36 and 24.19 <<ngd>> is used in the normal sense of conveying a message, while in S3 it is used of conveying information about the plan of the temple. The LXX translator may have visualised a more pictorial method of presentation, such as drawing a plan. Cf. ex. <6.27>.

171

The Greek Text of Ezekiel

<6.27> כתב (.ק)

2.10	כתובה	γεγραμμενα	—
2.10	וכתוב	και εγεγραπτο	—
24.2	כתב	γραψον	—
37.16	וכתב	και γραψον	—
37.16	וכתוב	και γραψεις	συγγρ. (2)
37.20	תכתב	εγραψας	συνεγρ. (2)/ συ επεγρ. (4)
43.11	וכתב	και διαγραψεις	διαγραφεις (2)

Cf. ex. <6.26>. In S1 the word clearly is used in the sense o
"to write". In 43.11, however, the translator may have
understood that the plan of the temple was to be drawn. The
term <<diagraphein>> occurs twice in 43.11, and the noun
<<diagraphè>> appears in the following verse. <<diagraphein>>
is also used twice in the sense "to draw" in S1 – 4.1 and
8.10. (In 4.1 Ezekiel is asked to "draw" the city of Jerusale
on a clay tablet as part of his way of conveying a message.)

<6.28> יתר (.נ)

14.22	נותרה	υπολελειμμενοι	—
34.18	הנותרים	και το λοιπον	κ. το καταλοιπ (1,4,6)/ κ. το επιλοιπον (5,6
39.14	את-הנותרים	// τους καταλελειμμενους	—
48.15	הנותר	τας περισσας	—
48.18	והנותר	και το περισσον	—
48.21	והנותר	το δε περισσον	—

Cf. Herrmann (1923: 9). In 14.22 the "remainder" is the peop
who survive the judgments sent against Jerusalem. In S3, by
contrast, the "remainder" refers to areas of land which have
not yet been allocated. <<perissos>> would be more suitable
S3 as it conveys the sense of positive "excess".

Sections of the Text: Chapters 40-48

<6.29> גב

(1.18)	וגביהן	ουξ οι νωτοι αυτων	—
(1.18)	וגבתם	και οι νωτοι αυτων	—
10.12	וגביהם	και οι νωτοι αυτων	αι νωτοι (5)
16.24	גב	οικημα πορνειον	—
16.31	גבך	το πορνειον σου	—
16.39	גבך	το πορνειον σου	—
43.13	גב	το υψος	—

Cf. Turner (1956: 14). Here the issue of the difference of the
context is compounded by the problem of the similarity of
different words. Certain forms of the word <<gb>>, which can
mean "back", are similar to the word <<gbh>>, which means
"height". In 10.12 (and in 1.18) the context is that of a
description of creatures in a vision. (For ch.16 see later).
The translator understood <<gb>> to refer to the back of these
creatures. In 43.13 the altar is being described and thus a
reference to its height fits the context well. A number of
English translations follow the LXX rendering here, and BHS
suggests correcting the text to read <<gbh>>. It may be that
the LXX Vorlage had <<gbh>>, but it is also possible that the
context dictated the rendering. Cf. ex. <6.30>.

<6.30> קומה

13.18	כל-קומה	πασης ηλικιας	—
17.6	קומה	τω μεγεθει	<> (1,2)
19.11	קומתו	τω μεγεθει αυτης	εν τω ... (1,2,4)
31.3	קומה	τω μεγεθει	τω γενει (3)/ εν τω ... (1,2)
31.5	קמתו	το μεγεθος αυτου	—
31.10	בקומה	τω μεγεθει	—
31.14	בקומתם	εν τω μεγεθει αυτων	—
40.5	וקומה	και το υψος αυτου	—

173

In S1 the "size" of the head (13.18) and of a vine (17.6;
19.11) is meant. In S3, however, the context demands a linear
measurement of a wall — something for which a measuring-rod
was used. A rendering which just conveyed the idea of "size"
would be inexact.

<6.31> תורה

7.26	ותורה	και νομος	—
22.26	תורתי	νομον μου	τον ν. μ. (2,4)
43.11	וכל-תורתו	<> //	—
43.12	זאת תורת	και την διαγραφην	κατα τ. δ. (3)/ αυτη η δ. (4)
43.12	תורת	<>	ο νομος (1-6)
44.5	ולכל-תורתו	και κατα παντα τα νομιμα αυτου	... κριματα α. (1)/ ... νομηματα α. (3)
44.24	ואת-תורתי	και τα νομιμα μου	<μου> (2)

Here the difference between S1 and S3 is that between "the
law" and "laws". (The rendering in 43.12a may have been cause
by a misreading of the text, cf. ex. <6.27>). The translator
of S3 may have felt that <<ta nomima>> was a better rendering
of the specific regulations than the more general <<nomos>>.

<6.32> דרום

21.2	אל-דרום	επι δαρωμ	δαρωρ (2,3)/ δαχυχ (6)/ δαρουμ (4,6)/ δαρουμι (4)/ δαχωμ (5)/ δαχων (1-6)/ δαρων (1)
40.24	דרך הדרום	κατα νοτον	την οδον την προς ν. (4)
40.24	דרך הדרום	προς νοτον	προς τον ν. (3)/ κατα ν. (
40.27	דרך הדרום	προς νοτον	—
40.27	דרך הדרום	προς νοτον	//

0.28	הדרום	προς νοτον	—
0.28	הדרום	<>	προς νοτον (2-4)
0.44	דרך הדרום	προς νοτον	κατα ν. (1)/ προς τον ν. (5)
0.45	דרך הדרום	προς νοτον	προς τον ν. (1)
1.11	לדרום	προς νοτον	—
2.12	דרך הדרום	προς νοτον	—
2.13	הדרום	προς νοτον	—
2.18	הדרום	//	//

cf. Herrmann (1923: 16) and Turner (1956: 14). We had noted in chapter II that the use of the translation/ transliteration distinction was of doubtful value. In this example and in the one following we see that context might influence the choice of transliteration or translation too. In 21.2-3 (LXX: 20.46-7) the prophet is told to preach towards the south. The LXX has taken this as referring to a location, rather than to just a direction. Hence it has transliterated the terms for "south", and we have <<thaiman>>, <<darom>> and <<nageb>> all in the same verse. The references to "south" in S3 are by contrast directional. This distinction was admitted by Herrmann even though he felt S3 was the work of a third translator (1923: 16).

<6.33> נגב

21.2	השדה נגב	ηγουμενον ναγεβ //	<ηγ.> (2)/ -μενου ν. (4)/ -μενων ν. (5)/ η. αγεβ (2)/ η. ναγεθ (2)/ η. ναγεμ (3,4,6)
21.3	הנגב	ναγεβ	<> (2)/ ναγεμ (3,4)/ ναγεω (3,5)/ ναβεγ (1)/ ναγες (5)/ μαρεβ (1)/ δαβελ (3)//
21.3	מנגב	απο απηλιωτου	—
21.9	מנגב	απο απηλιωτου	και α. α. (1)

40.2	נכבד	απεναντι	—
46.9	נגב	της προς νοτον	την π. ν. (3-5)
46.9	נגב	της προς νοτον	⟨της⟩ (3)
47.19	ופאת נגב	και τα προς νοτον	⟨και τα⟩ (1)
47.19	נגבה	και λιψ	κ. λιβος (3,4)/ κ. λημψη (5)
48.10	ונגבה	και προς νοτον	—
48.16	ופאת-נגב	και απο των προς νοτον	—
48.17	ונגבה	και προς νοτον	—
48.28	אל-פאת נגב	εως των προς λιβα	ε. το π. λ. (2)/ ε. την π. λ. (6) ⟨των⟩ (1,3,5)/ ε. τ π. θαλασσαν (4)
48.33	ופאת-נגבה	και τα προς νοτον	—

This example presents the same issues as the one preceding i
We can note in this case that even within S3 there is a
substantial variety of rendering.

<6.34> זרק (ק.)

10.2	וזרק	και διασκορπισον	—
36.25	וזרקתי	και ρανω	—
43.18	ולזרק	και προσχεειν	-χεεις (1)

In 10.2 we find that hot coals are the object of ⟨⟨zrq⟩⟩,
while in 43.18 it is blood which is to be "scattered".

<6.35> שכן (ק.)

17.23	ושכנו	και αναπαυσεται	—
17.23	תשכנה	// αποκατασταθησεται	-σονται (4)
31.13	ישכנו	απεπαυσαντο	-σατο (4,5)/ επανεπ- (2,5)

Sections of the Text: Chapters 40-48

| 43.7 | אשכן | // κατασκηνωσει | – |
| 43.9 | ושכנתי | και κατασκηνωσω | -σκηνω (6) |

The usual LXX rendering of this example is <<kataskènoun>>.
Again the contexts in S1 and S3 differ strongly. In 17.23
birds "rest" in the branches of a cedar, while in 43.7,9 there
is the promise that Yahweh will "rest" among the Israelites
forever. So in this instance the choice in S3 of
<<kataskènoun>>, which can mean "to settle", would be more
appropriate than <<anapauesthai>>.

<6.36> מאכל

4.10	ומאכלך	και το βρωμα σου	–
47.12	כל-עץ-מאכל	παν ξυλον βρωσιμον	π. ξ. βρωμα (6)
47.12	למאכל	εις βρωσιν	–

Cf. Herrmann (1923: 16). The differences between usages here
could be said to be similar to the differences between three
English expressions: (the colloquial noun) "eats", "eatable",
and "for eating". In 4.10 Ezekiel is to weigh out his daily
ration of "food". In 47.12a the construction implies that the
trees bear "edible" fruit (or else are themselves "edible"),
while in 47.12b the fruit the trees bear is to serve for food,
i.e. "for eating". The differences are expressed in the LXX.

<6.37> חלק (.פ)

| 5.1 | וחלקתם | και διαστησεις αυτους | κ. διαθησεις α. (3)/ ... αυτοις (6)/ ... αυτας (4,6)/ ... αυτα (6)/ ... αυτην (2,6) |
| 47.21 | וחלקתם | και διαμεριειτε | κ. διαμερισετε (1)/ κ. διεμετρησεν (2) |

Cf. Herrmann (1923: 15). In 5.1 the verb is used of "dividing"
Ezekiel's hair. In 47.21 it is the land which is to be divided
among Israel.

<6.38> אציל

| 13.18 | כל-אצילי | παντα αγκωνα | παντων α. (4) |
| 41.8 | אצילה | διαστημα | -ματα (1,3)/ <> (1) |

Here 13.18 refers to a joint in the arm, whereas in 41.8 an
architectural term appears to be implied. Commentators and
translations are unsure of the exact nature of this meaning,
as was the LXX translator. The term <<diastèma>> is probably
"filler" word, which the translator used when he was uncertai
about his text (see below).

Ex. <6.12-38> show at least that we are not comparing
like with like. Their evidence is ambiguous. Although the
translator of S1 may be called "literalistic" in that the
Hebrew word order is closely followed and that a number of
terms have stereotyped renderings, we have seen enough
examples to know that even in S1 there was not total
consistency. Within S1 too there was variation according to
context, cf. ex. <2.15; 7.45-52>.

The 6 cases which exhibited translation change
independent of context do not seem to present a strong
argument. Only one, ex. <6.12>, had enough frequency of item
to make it at least noteworthy. The rest had only
corroborative value. To have just 6 instances of moderate
translation change out of 236 cases does not seem a strong
argument in favour of seeing different translators for S1 an
S3 /3/.

Sections of the Text: Chapters 40-48

It might be asked whether there is positive evidence
which would bring S1 and S3 even closer. Thackeray gave some
examples of usages common to a' and g' but absent from b'.
These were intended to "prove the identity of translators a'
and g'" (1903b: 404; cf. 1921: 120). The weaknesses of many of
these examples have already been noted, cf. ex. <2.1-9;
2.24-36>, and they do not prove identity of translators. They
only show a similarity of rendering, which has already been
demonstrated.

There are, however, two cases which do make it more
likely, if not conclusive, that S1 and S3 were the work of the
same translator. The first of these is the rendering of
<<brk>>:

<6.39> ברך

7.17	וכל־ברכים	και παντες μηροι	—
21.12	וכל־ברכים	και παντες μηροι	—
47.4	ברכים	εως των μηρων	εως των γονατων (4,6)/ ευλογιας (1)

The word <<brk>> is generally taken to mean "knee", which in
Greek is <<gonu>>, not "thigh", which is <<mèros>>. It occurs
25 times in the OT and is translated in 21 instances by
<<gonu>>. Only in Genesis 50.23 (mistakenly for <<yrk>> ?) and
here in Ezekiel is it translated by <<mèros>>. The usual
hyponym of <<mèros>> is <<yrk>> or <<yrkh>>. This agreement in
a slightly unusual rendering does point to the closeness of S1
and S3.

A second noteworthy case is where the renderings in S1
and S3 disagree. This is found with <<gdr>>:

<6.40> (גדרת) / גדר

13.5	ותגדרו גדר	και συνηγαγον ποιμνια	κ. ου σ. π. (4)/ κ. σ. ποιμνιον (1,3-5)
22.30	גדר-גדר	αναστρεφομενον ορθως	<ορθως> (4) //
42.7	וגדר	και φως	κ. το φ. (5)/ κ. φ. εστιν (3)
42.10	ברחב גדר החצר דרך	κατα το φως του εν αρχη περιπατου	και τ. φ. ... (6)/ καθως τ. φ. ... (1) κ. φως τουτο εν ... (1)/ ... εν α. του περ. (1-3,5)
42.12	דרך בפני הגדרת הגינה	ως επι φως διαστηματος καλαμου //	-

13.5 and 22.30 also contain the only two occurrences of the
verb <<gdr>> in Ezekiel. The sole occurrence of the closely
related noun <<gdrt>> is listed here too.

There is general agreement that <<gdr>> and <<gdrt>>
denote a wall of some sort. This meaning is corroborated by
the LXX as well, for in 7 out of the ten occurrences of
<<gdr>> outside Ezekiel (in Numbers, Psalms, Proverbs,
Ecclesiastes and Isaiah) the rendering is <<phragmos>>.
However, it seems that the translator of neither section knew
what <<gdr>> meant at all. In S1 none of the translations
gives any sense of a "wall". Indeed, two completely differen
renderings are given, both of which make sense in Greek and
fit into the general context:
13.5   "and they brought together flocks"
22.30   "living uprightly"
In S3 quite a different set of renderings appears. Yet the u
of the terms <<phòs>> and <<diastèma>> is significant. Both
these words appear to be "fillers", which the translator use
when he was uncertain as to what his text meant. <<diastèma:
occurs 11 times in Ezekiel (41.6,8,8,8; 42.5,5,12,13; 45.2;
48.15,17) and has at least 8 different hyponyms in those 11
occurrences /4/. <<phòs>> is found 5 times in S3 (41.11;
42.7,10,11,12) and apart from 42.7 it is difficult to say w
certainty what its hyponyms are. Indeed, the intended meani

f these two Greek words themselves in S3 are unclear. It does
ppear, therefore, that the translator of S3 was simply
ttempting to avoid leaving a gap in his translation.

Hence we see that the translations of both sections show
 lack of understanding of the meaning of this word. This is
ot a general LXX feature, since, as noted above, several
ther LXX books do give what seems a correct rendering. This
ase still does not make it absolutely certain that S1 and S3
ere by the same translator. Yet it does at least point in
hat direction.

Deciding the exact relationship of S3 to the rest of the
ook has proved more difficult than was the case with S1 and
2. The data on which to work is not as extensive, nor is it
s easy to evaluate, as the material from the earlier
ections. The distortion caused by context and the subsequent
extual alterations have also complicated the picture.
evertheless, the evidence does seem compatible with the view
hat S1 and S3 were the work of the same translator.

CHAPTER VII

SECTIONS OF THE TEXT - III

Two Unusual Subsections

In this chapter we shall refer briefly to two smaller
sections of the Greek text of Ezekiel. These are chapter 16
and 36.23c-38. Both of these subsections have noteworthy
features which make them stand out from the main sections in
which they are found. Consequently their evidence has usually
been excluded from consideration in earlier chapters.

Chapter 16

The unusual nature of this chapter was first noted by
Thackeray, though not in his earlier articles. He commented in
his Schweich lectures that ch.16 was:

> just such another passage, like the Uriah episode,
> as the original translators would readily omit,
> containing a scathing indictment of Jerusalem
> under the figure of a harlot making advances to
> every passer-by (1921: 26)

Thackeray considered the Greek in our present text to be a
later supplement (1921: 38). However, he does not seem to have
made any attempt to support his suggestion in detail,
mentioning only the use of <<parodos>>. N. Turner also saw 16
as exhibiting unusual qualities. In his view, though, the
chapter was to be seen, along with many others, as
incorporating older strata of material (1956: 21). He viewed
the section as a composite. In general, though, the suggestion
that 16 differs from the rest of the Greek translation of S1
has been ignored.

The Greek Text of Ezekiel

The investigations into the Greek text in chapters V a
VI have, by and large, yielded little indication of composi
sections. This might make us suspect that possibly Thackera
and Turner were misled here. Yet there does seem to be stro
evidence to show that 16 exhibits at least some peculiariti

In this instance we are more fortunate than in the cas
of 40-48, because we are in a better position to assess the
effect of context on translation technique. This is due to
fact that chapter 23 deals with subject-matter similar to t
of 16. Ch.16 allegorises Jerusalem as a lascivious prostitu
and 23 depicts both Jerusalem and Samaria as equally
libidinous sisters. In both chapters there is strong sexual
imagery. The Hebrew vocabulary of these chapters is quite
similar too. This should enable us to make a more controlle
comparison of the renderings in 16.

If we examine ch. 23 first we find that there is littl
evidence for suggesting, as does Turner (1956: 21), that it
too contains parts of different translations. The Greek tex
does indeed present us with some vocabulary which is found
nowhere else in S1:

<7.1> διαπαρθενευειν 23.3   <7.11> βαθυς 23.32
<7.2> καταλυμα 23.21   <7.12> πλατυς 23.32
<7.3> ηγουμενος 23.6,12   <7.13> πλεοναζειν 23.32
<7.4> επιθεσις 23.11   <7.14> μεθη 23.33
<7.5> υακινθος 23.6   <7.15> εκλυσις 23.33
<7.6> στρατηγος 23.6   <7.16> εορτη 23.34
<7.7> ιππευς 23.6,12   <7.17> νεομηνια 23.34
<7.8> ιππαζεσθαι 23.6,12   <7.18> μακροθεν 23.40
<7.9> ευπαρυφος 23.12   <7.19> στιβιζεσθαι 23.40
<7.10> γραφις 23.14   <7.20> κλινη 23.41

Sections of the Text: Two Subsections

⟨7.21⟩ ποικιλμα 23.15	⟨7.37⟩ στρωννυναι 23.41
⟨7.22⟩ τιαρα 23.15	⟨7.38⟩ τραπεζα 23.41
⟨7.23⟩ βαπτος 23.15	⟨7.39⟩ ανακρουειν 23.42
⟨7.24⟩ τρισσος 23.15,23	⟨7.40⟩ ταραχη 23.46
⟨7.25⟩ κοιτη 23.17	⟨7.41⟩ παιδευειν 23.48
⟨7.26⟩ ονος 23.20	⟨7.42⟩ νεοτης 23.3
⟨7.27⟩ αιδοιον 23.20,20	⟨7.43⟩ μοιχευειν 23.43
⟨7.28⟩ ιππευειν 23.23	⟨7.44⟩ πατρις 23.15
⟨7.29⟩ αρμα 23.24	⟨7.45⟩ λαλημα 23.10
⟨7.30⟩ θυρεος 23.24	⟨7.46⟩ προστιθεναι 23.14
⟨7.31⟩ πελτη 23.24	⟨7.47⟩ ζωγραφειν 23.14,14
⟨7.32⟩ καταλοιπος 23.25,25	⟨7.48⟩ εμπυρος 23.37
⟨7.33⟩ μισος 23.29	⟨7.49⟩ ευφραινειν 23.41
⟨7.34⟩ πονος 23.29	⟨7.50⟩ αρμονια 23.42
⟨7.35⟩ μοχθος 23.29	⟨7.51⟩ αναγειν 23.46
⟨7.36⟩ ποτηριον 23.31,32,33,33	⟨7.52⟩ κατακεντειν 23.47

Yet 41 of these 52 examples — ⟨7.1-41⟩ — have hyponyms which
are not found elsewhere in S1. (In 7 cases — ⟨7.2, 21, 22, 26,
33, 34, 40⟩ — it is difficult to say exactly what the Vorlage
implied by the LXX was.) In 3 instances — ⟨7.42-44⟩ — the
hyponyms are only found in 16 and 23, and hence these indicate
a difference of translation technique between 16 and 23 with
these items of vocabulary. Only 7 cases exist — ⟨7.45-52⟩ —
where the hyponyms are translated differently elsewhere, and
most of the differences can be explained on the grounds of
context.

Chapter 23 also has some vocabulary which is common to 16
and 23 but is not found in the rest of S1:

⟨7.53⟩ λουειν 16.4,9; 23.40
⟨7.54⟩ μαστος 16.4,7; 23.3,21
⟨7.55⟩ ασχημονευειν 16.7,22,39; 23.29
⟨7.56⟩ κοσμειν 16.11,13; 23.40,41

<7.57> μισειν 16.23,37; 23.28

<7.58> εκδυνειν 16.39; 23.26

<7.59> εραστης 16.33,36,37; 23.5,9,22

<7.60> πορνεια 16.15,22,25,33,34,36,41; 23.7,8,8,11,
11,14,17,18,19,27,29,30,35

<7.61> ψελιον 16.11; 23.42

<7.62> μοιχασθαι/ μοιχευειν 16.32; 23.37,37,43

<7.63> μοιχαλις 16.38; 23.45,45

<7.64> ελαιον

<7.65> πορνη 16.30,31,35; 23.43,44

<7.66> λιθοβολειν 16.40; 23.27

<7.67> τικτειν 16.4,5; 23.4

<7.68> ιματισμος 16.18,39; 23.26

<7.69> μυκτηρ 16.12; 23.25

<7.70> ξιφος 16.40; 23.47

<7.71> εμπιπραναι 16.41; 23.47

Out of these 19 cases 14 — <7.53-66> — have hyponyms which
appear only in 16 and 23. This leaves us with really only 5
cases where 16 and 23 agree against the rest of S1. Yet these
5 cases — <7.67-71> — are not very strong as evidence either.
<<tiktein>> is a rendering of the Hiphil of <<yld>> in 16 and
of the Qal in 23. See <6.13> for the background of <7.68>, and
<5.4> for the background of <7.70>. The rendering of <7.69>
has already been explained on the basis of context, see
<2.15>. The hyponym of <<empipranai>> only appears once
outside 16 and 23 — in 5.4.

Hence we see that chapter 23 (a) does not deviate from
what we might expect for a chapter in S1 and (b) does not al
itself with 16 more than what could be explained by similari
of context.

However, when we come to examine ch.16 we find a
different situation. Thackeray had mentioned the rendering o

Sections of the Text: Two Subsections

<<'br>> by <<parodos>>. This is unique in Ezekiel, although
there is a degree of inconsistency:

<7.72> עבר (.ק)

5.14	כל-עובר	παντος διοδευοντος	δια παντος διοδευονται (3)
5.17	יעבר-בך	διελευσονται επι σε	διελευσεται (3-5)
9.4	עבר	διελθε	-
9.5	עברו	πορευσθε	-
14.15	עובר	ο διοδευων	-
14.17	תעבר	διελθατω	διελετω (1-6)
16.6	ואעבר	διηλθον	-
16.8	ואעבר	διηλθον	ηλθον (2-3)
16.15	על-כל-עובר	επι παντα παροδον	-
16.25	לכל-עובר	παντι παροδω	-
29.11	תעבר-בה	διελθη εν αυτη	-
29.11	תעבר-בה	διελθη αυτην	-
33.28	מאין עובר	δια το μη ειναι διαπορευομενον	παραπορευομενον (4) πορευομενον (3)
35.7	עבר ושב	ανθρωπους και κτηνη	ανθρωπον και κτηνος (1,3)/ ανθρωπον και κτηνη (4,6)/ ανθ. κ. κτ. παραπορευομενον και αναστρεφοντα (4)
36.34	כל-עובר	παντος παροδευοντος	διοδευοντος (2,4)
39.11	העברים	των επελθοντων	απελθοντων (3)
39.11	את-העברים	//	-
39.14	עברים	επιπορευομενους	περιερχομενους (3)
39.14	את-העברים	<>	και τους παραπορευομενους (1,3)/ μετα των περιερχομενων (3,4)
39.15	ועברו העברים	και πας ο διαπορευομενος	παντες οι διαπορευομενοι (1,3)/ κ. π. ο δ. .. και διερχομενος (4)
47.5	לעבר	διελθειν	-

It should also be noted that in 16.6,8 the renderings are

187

consistent with what is found elsewhere in S1. It is possib]
that the somewhat rare <<parodos>> had overtones which suite
the context of 16.15,25.

However, it is not only with this unusual form that 16
deviates from the usual rendering in S1. For example:

<7.73> קבץ

11.17	וקבצתי	και εισδεξομαι	συναξω (4)
16.37	מקבץ	συναγω	και συναγαγω (5)/ αναγω (5)
16.37	וקבצתי	και συναξω	—
20.34	וקבצתי	και εισδεξομαι	—
20.41	בקבצי	και εισδεχεσθαι	εισδεξασθαι (1)/ εισδεξομαι (1-5)
22.19	קבץ	εισδεχομαι	εισδεξομαι (1,3,4)
22.20	[קבצת]	εισδεχεται	εισδεξεται (3)
22.20	אקבץ	εισδεξομαι	εισδεχομαι (3)
28.25	בקבצי	και συναξω	—
29.5	תקבץ	περισταλης	συσταλης (2)/ περισταλησῃ (1)
29.13	אקבץ	συναξω	αναξω (2,5)
34.13	וקבצתים	και συναξω αυτους	—
36.24	וקבצתי	και αθροιζω	—
37.21	וקבצתי	και συναξω	—
38.8	מקבצת	συνηγμενην	-μενων (1-6)/ ηθροισμενην (4)
39.17	הקבצו	συναχθητε	—
39.27	בקבצי	και συναγαγειν με	εξαγαγειν (4)/ <με> (1)

Here the usual rendering in S1 is <<eisdekhesthai>>, but ch.
agrees with S2 in using <<sunagein>>.

Other instances of the way 16 differs from S1 can be se
in some of the examples already given:

Sections of the Text: Two Subsections

Example	Hebrew	16 Rendering	Usual S1 Rendering
<2.13>	שחת	υπερκεισθαι	εξαλειφειν
<5.4>	חרב	ξιφος	ρομφαια
<5.19>	חזק	αντιλαμβανεσθαι	κρατειν
<5.5>	אמר ל	λεγειν τη	λεγειν προς την
<6.8>	אחרי	μετα	οπισω

Like ch.23, ch.16 has a number of items of Greek vocabulary
which occur nowhere else in S1. These number 65 in all. Yet 24
of these (as opposed to 7 in ch.23) represent translations of
Hebrew terms which occur elsewhere in S1 as well. A number of
these are quite rare in the LXX:

Example	Reference	Occurrence in LXX (outside 16)	Where listed
<7.74>	μεγαλαυχειν	16.50	4	
<7.75>	ανομημα	16.49,49,50	14	<2.27> /<5.19>
<7.76>	αποτροπιαζεσθαι	16.21	0	<6.25>
<7.77>	προσδιδοναι	16.33,34	2	
<7.78>	πορνειον	16.25,31,39	0	
<7.79>	κομιζειν	16.52,54,58	24	
<7.80>	διαπεταζειν	16.8	22	
<7.81>	παροδος	16.15,25	5	<7.72>
<7.82>	επαφιεναι	16.42	3	<6.21>
<7.83>	νηπιοτης	16.22,43,60	1	
<7.84>	ομορειν	16.26	2	
<7.85>	αποπλυνειν	16.9	3	
<7.86>	υπαρχειν	16.49	>50	
<7.87>	αγρος	16.7	>50	
<7.88>	ασχημοσυνη	16.8	>20	

189

<7.89>	μισθωμα	16.31,32,33,	6	
		33,34,34,41		
<7.90>	οικημα	16.24	2	
<7.91>	πορνικος	16.24	1	
<7.92>	πολλαχως	16.26	1	
<7.93>	περιτιθεναι	16.11	>30	
<7.94>	αφιεναι	16.39	>50	
<7.95>	ιματιον	16.16	>80	<6.13>
<7.96>	ακοη	16.56	>20	
<7.97>	αιωνιος	16.60	>60	

Although a few of these examples can be explained on the grounds of context, many of them cannot. The comparative rarity of about half of them is striking too. Although Thackeray's explanation of why the chapter was omitted may be questioned, it appears that his feeling about the Greek was right. Chapter 16 does seem to be different from the rest of S1.

Chapter 36.23c-38

About this subsection less needs to be said. It has been generally accepted that it represents a different type of text from the rest of S2. There does not seem to be any indication that this view is incorrect. Although Thackeray's attention was drawn to the text by the use of the divine name in the B manuscript, his inferences have not been invalidated. Several examples of the difference in translation technique may be noted in conclusion:

Sections of the Text: Two Subsections

Verse	Form in 36.23c-38	Form in S2	Where listed
36.23	κατ οφθαλμους	ενωπιον	⟨6.10⟩
36.24	αθροιζειν	συναγειν	⟨7.73⟩
36.24	γεων	χωρων	—
36.33,37	αδωναι κυριος	....	—
36.34	ανθ ων οτι	ανθ ων	—
36.34	παροδευειν	διαπορευεσθαι	⟨7.72⟩
36.35	κηπος τρυφης	παραδεισος	—
36.35	ηφανισμενος	ερημος	⟨5.12⟩
36.36,38	εγω κυριος	εγω ειμι κυριος	⟨5.3⟩

CHAPTER VIII

CONCLUSIONS

The aim of this study has been to answer the question of
whether the Greek text of Ezekiel as we now have it is
homogeneous. In order to do this, three distinct problems have
had to be resolved. The first of these was the general issue
of deciding what valid principles and methods could be
employed in splitting up a translated text. The second was the
more specific task of explaining the apparently inconsistent
evidence of the divine names in the Greek and Hebrew texts of
Ezekiel. The clarification of both of these matters enabled us
then to proceed to the third and main problem — the
examination of the text itself to see if differing sections
could be isolated.

Each of these three components of the argument —
methodology, divine names, and sections of the text — have
contributed to our understanding of the nature of the
Septuagint. We shall consider the contribution of each in
turn. In some respects, the findings of the first two
components have as much significance as those of the third.

Methodology

The development of a methodology of translation
criticism called attention to several features about the
nature of a translation. The first feature was the range of
factors which had to be borne in mind when the change in
translation of a particular term was being examined. It was
noted in Chapter II that elements which could distort our
assessment of the homogeneity of a translation included: the

193

effect of the Vorlage in dictating the contents of the
translation; the influence of context on the meaning of words;
the textual variation which could occur, particularly within
the Greek witnesses; the frequency and distribution of given
terms; the conventions and resources of the translator's
receptor language; and the types of variation which could
occur simply as phenomena associated with the progression of a
translation. These factors give an indication of the
complexity of the processes underlying our Greek text. Any
attempt at translation criticism, or even at a general
evaluation of a translation, needs to cater for such
processes, if valid results are to be obtained.

A second feature noted was the fact that there is a wide
range of variation to be found within even a homogeneous text.
This more empirical observation became clearer as lists of
renderings were assembled, not only in chapter II, but also in
chapters V to VII.

For example, in S1 (excluding ch.16) instances could be
found of renderings which: 1) are rigorously stereotyped, 2)
are usually stereotyped but susceptible to strong context
change, 3) oscillate seemingly randomly between two or three
forms, 4) oscillate between several forms but show a strong
preference for one of them ("weighted" oscillation), 5) change
gradually from one predominant form to another, 6) change
abruptly from one stereotyped form to another, 7) vary
considerably according to context /1/. The fact that all these
were found in one homogeneous section should make us wary of
inferring too much from the general characterisation of a
translation /2/. This affects directly how a text is assessed
for the purposes of textual criticism. It also means that a
multiple translator hypothesis cannot be dismissed just by
citing several examples showing inconsistencies in the
renderings of certain terms and then inferring, as did Ziegle

(1953), that any other cases of translation change in the text
must be the result of inconsistency in the "translator".

These two features are clearly related to one another.
The second gives us a better insight than before into the
nature of the variation that can occur within a translation.
The first enables us to deal with the influences behind some
of that variation, particularly when questions of homogeneity
are involved.

Consideration of these features in the case of Ezekiel
brought to light a third matter. This is the fact that many
previously cited examples of translation change were either
invalid or else much weaker than had been thought. The number
of these examples in the case of Ezekiel makes it likely that
such arguments for other books have similar weaknesses. Only
in the books of Kingdoms and Jeremiah has it been generally
accepted that the "Septuagint" text is not homogeneous. The
book of Ezekiel was, as we have seen, a disputed case.
However, multiple translator theories have been proposed for
Genesis, Leviticus, Joshua, Psalms, Isaiah, Daniel, Baruch,
Amos, and also the Pentateuch and the Minor prophets as units
/3/. These merit re-assessment.

Divine Names

The second component of the argument, the case of the
divine names, brings us to an entirely different area. The
conclusions regarding them were somewhat negative for the
purposes of the present study, though it was essential that
such a significant case should be resolved. The outcome was
that the forms of the Greek equivalents for <<'dny yhwh>>
probably were not what was written in the Old Greek, and hence

this case could not be used in the translation criticism of
Ezekiel.

Yet this is not the only conclusion to be drawn from the
divine names issue. If the present forms of the nomina sacra
are the results of scribal activity, then the diversity of
renderings in the Greek MSS gives us an indication of the
extent of that scribal activity. The breadth and variety of
the Greek substitute names demonstrate that even our earliest
witnesses have had a long textual history.

The distribution of the types of readings is another
factor of note. This is probably another indication of the
practice of circulating a large book in two or three rolls.
Such an inference would corroborate other evidence to the same
effect and would indicate that it may not be unlikely to find
at least a change of text-type in the middle of other large
LXX books. In this respect our findings in the case of Ezekiel
should not be surprising.

The case for holding that <<yhwh>> was not translated
throughout the LXX is further strengthened by the nomina sacra
evidence in Ezekiel. Moreover, the originality of the form
<<'dny>> in the Hebrew text of Ezekiel seems quite likely too.
Almost half of the occurrences of <<'dny>> in the Old
Testament are found in the phrase <<'dny yhwh>> in Ezekiel
/4/. Earlier writers, especially Baudissin (1929), had taken
the witness of the Greek MSS as evidence that <<'dny>> was a
later expansion in the Hebrew manuscripts. If it is the case
that the Hebrew form <<yhwh>> was retained in the LXX text,
then the present Greek equivalents for <<'dny yhwh>> are late
developments, and cannot be used as evidence in discussions of
the origins and early development of the term <<'dny>> in the
Hebrew text. Investigations which relied on the testimony of
the LXX here will have to be re-examined.

<u>Sections of the Text</u>

The main conclusion of this study has been that the
Greek translation of Ezekiel is not homogeneous. It was seen
that the text could be split up into three distinct large
sections: 1-25 (S1), 26-39 (S2), and 40-48 (S3). There were in
addition at least two sub-sections - ch.16 and 36.23c-38 -
which showed marked translation differences from their
surrounding text.

This conclusion does differ from views which had been
propounded previously, although many of its components have
been suggested before. The same boundaries for the main
sections had been deduced by N. Turner (1956), but his
three-translator theory was found to be less convincing. On
the other hand, it seemed that Thackeray was probably closest
to the truth in suggesting that two translators were
responsible for the three sections.

The relationship of S1 to S2 was seen to be that of two
different translations, rather than that of translation and
revision. This goes against the recent tendency to ascribe
differences within a translated text or between certain MSS as
due to the effects of partial revision. The most notable
examples of such revision hypotheses are the conclusions of
Barthélemy (that parts of Kingdoms in many MSS represent the
Kaige recension) and Tov (that part of the LXX of Jeremiah is
a revised text). The result here does not invalidate such
conclusions, but it does mean that multiple-translator
theories as opposed to translator-reviser theories cannot be
rejected entirely.

As noted above, the division between S1 and S2 was seen
to lie between ch.25 and 26, and not ch.27 and 28, as most
have held. A number of grammatical and lexical studies have

197

relied on this latter division and thus need to be corrected
/5/.

The exact nature of S3 proved difficult to elucidate. It
seemed to be distinct from S2, but its relationship with S1
was less certain. The marked change in subject-matter and the
restricted vocabulary made it difficult to come to a definite
conclusion. However, the evidence available did seem to concur
with the view expressed that S1 and S3 were the work of the
same translator. Nevertheless, there were signs that S3 had
had a different textual history from either S1 or S2. The
distribution of the various forms of the nomina sacra pointed
to the possibility of this difference. Further evidence, in
the form of conflicting readings between the witness of the
leading MSS, 967 and B, showed that minor revision had
occurred too.

The immediate practical implication of these divisions in
the Greek text of Ezekiel is that a number of text-critical
judgments will have to be re-evaluated. Ziegler's LXX edition
has been carefully done, and in most cases his assessment of
the text may well be sound. Nevertheless, some readings will
need to be re-examined, as Ziegler considered the book to be
homogeneous (apart from 36.23c-38). Those readings which lie
close to boundaries between sections or which rely on evidence
outside their own section would be most in need of
re-evaluation.

The lack of homogeneity of our text raises two questions
The first is that of how the LXX of Ezekiel came to have such
a variety of translation types. The section S1 consists of
almost exactly half of the whole Greek text and it would thus
be understandable if we had found only two sections, 1-25 and
26-48. This might be taken as a division of labour. However,
the uneven division of 26-48 into 29-39 and 40-48 raises

complications. It is possible that two contemporaneous translators were assigned uneven lengths of text, perhaps according to their abilities, but other possibilities come to mind too. If, as is suggested by the nomina sacra, the text of Ezekiel circulated in three rolls, then different translations of the book might have got mixed in some way. It would be useful to have a detailed study of whether the linguistic differences between the sections pointed to a chronological difference.

The picture is further complicated by the occurrence of the small sections. The near total MS agreement on their occurrence could be taken as an indication of the narrowness of the textual tradition. It might also prompt the suggestion that one particular LXX manuscript may have been selected to become the "authentic" text — an archetype, in fact. Unfortunately, we can only speculate at this stage.

The second question raised by the lack of homogeneity in Ezekiel is whether this is typical of a LXX book. As mentioned earlier, attempts have been made to analyse the translations of other parts of the LXX, though little consensus has been reached. Much therefore needs to be examined. If we wish not only to refine our text-critical, lexical and grammatical data about the LXX, but also to gain information which could further understanding of its origins and early history, then the question of homogeneity of translation must be investigated. The correct application of translation criticism could yield valuable results in this investigation.

NOTES TO CHAPTERS

Chapter I

/1/ Epiphanius, "On Weights and Measures", PG 43 col
241-244.

/2/ The issue of the divine names in Ezekiel has had quite a
complicated history, even apart from the translator problem. A
fuller account of the whole discussion of the matter will be
given in chapter III.

/3/ The papyrus will be referred to from here on as (P.) 967.
Others have classified it differently. Aland (1976) registers
it as AT 146 [010], while van Haelst (1976) gives it the
catalogue number 315. See also note /4/.

/4/ Estimates of the date ranged from the late second century
A.D. to the late third century A.D. (Cf. Johnson, Gehman, Kase
1938: 5). Convenient summaries of the contents and other
features, including dating, are given by Aland (1976: 30-33,
206-7) and van Haelst (1976: 115-7).

/5/ The Chester Beatty leaves contained:
11.25-12.6; 12.12-18; 12.23-13.6; 13.11-17; 13.20-14.3;
14.6-10; 14.15-20; 14.23-15.7; 16.5-11; 16.16-22; 16.28-34;
16.39-45; 16.48-53; 16.57-17.1; 17.6-10; 17.15-21.

/6/ The Scheide collection contained:
19.12-20.15; 20.40-44; 21.4-25.4; 26.10-28.18; 29.12-32.30;
34.6-36.23; 37.1-4; 38.1-39.29.

/7/ The translation of this quotation is a slightly adapted
form of that given in the English edition of Würthwein's "The

Text of the Old Testament" (1980: 182), which cites Ziegler.
Cf. also Ziegler's introduction in his Göttingen edition of
Ezekiel (1952: 28).

/8/ There are quite a few references and allusions in Qumran
material to the subject-matter of the book of Ezekiel.
Unfortunately, very little direct manuscript evidence of its
text has appeared. Fitzmyer lists the following portions of
text: 4.9,10; 4.16-5.1; 5.11-17; 7.9-12; 9.4; 16.31-33; 37.23
(?); 44.15. To this must be added a fragment containing
10.17-11.10, which is reproduced on the endpapers of both
volumes of the Hermeneia edition of Zimmerli's commentary on
Ezekiel (1979; 1983). The text of this fragment is given in
Appendix C.

There was also a scroll that could not be unrolled
(Brownlee 1963: 11-28). Y. Yadin also reported finding some
fragments of an Ezekiel scroll at Masada (Yadin 1978:
187-189). The text of this does not seem to have been
published.

/9/ I would like to thank Mrs. Turner for giving me permission
to refer to her work.

/10/ The fragments in the Galiano edition (1971b: 7-76)
contained:
28.19-29.12; 32.30-34.6; 37.4-28; 40.1-43.9.
Cf. also Galiano's descriptions (1968: 72; 1970: 133-8) and
his observations on the closeness of 967 and the Antinoopolis
fragments (1971a: 51-61).

/11/ Jahn's fragments included:
12.3-4; 12.6-7; 12.15-16; 12.18-19; 13.7-9; 13.18; 14.3-4;
14.10-13; 14.21-22; 15.7-16.3; 16.11-14; 16.23-26; 16.35-37;
16.45-46; 16.53-55; 17.1-5; 17.11-14; 17.21-24; 17.24-19.12;
20.5-8; 20.13-41; 20.44-21.3; 25.5-26.10; 43.9-48.35.

Notes

His edition of the text ("Der griechische Text des Buches Ezechiel") included extensive text-critical notes.

/12/ Muraoka gave his views in a paper entitled "A Re-examination of the Two-translator Theory of a Septuagint Book", which was read at an IOSCS conference in 1971. Although a summary of it appeared in print (Muraoka 1972b [=BIOSCS 5]: 9), the full paper was never published, as far as I can ascertain. Cf. Muraoka 1972a: 91; 1973: 22.

Chapter II

/1/ A bibliography of the subject can be found in "A Classified Bibliography of the Septuagint" (Brock, Fritsch, Jellicoe 1973: 34-7), to which must be added the works mentioned by Orlinsky (1975: 89-90) and Tov (1981: 48-63).

/2/ As E. Tov has noted, "the nature and scope of translation technique needs to be better defined in scholarship." (1975: 805). The term "translation technique" is at present used to denote at least four different concepts:
1) How certain terms are rendered by a particular translation.
2) The nature of the rendering, i.e. its classification according to "literalness", faithfulness, consistency, linguistic features and so on.
3) The principles guiding the choice of renderings.
4) The renderings which are characteristic of a certain "translator".
The term is used here to denote the first concept.

/3/ The term "hyponym" has been constructed because there does not seem to be an exact single word in English (or at least the English of biblical scholarship) to denote this concept, which occurs frequently here.

The hyponym ("underlying word") of a given expression could be defined as that unit of language of which the expression is a translation. If <<oikos>> is a translation of <<byt>>, then <<byt>> is a hyponym of <<oikos>>. The two main hyponyms of <<ethnos>> in Ezekiel are <<'m>> and <<gwy>>.

/4/ The evidence of the translation of a given term is normally presented in a fixed format. An explanation of the conventions and abbreviations used is given in the preface.

/5/ The literature on this is already extensive. An indication of the approaches used can be had from such journals as "Computers and the Humanities" and "Association for Literary and Linguistic Computing Journal". A useful, though slightly dated introduction to the use of the computer in literary study is given by S. Hockey in her book "A Guide to Computer Applications in the Humanities" (1980).

/6/ In other statistical approaches, e.g. those of Y. T. Radday, the decision about where to split up a text is usually based on literary-critical arguments.

/7/ Turner seems to be using Thackeray's division of the text (a'=1-27, b'=28-39) rather than his own (a'=1-25, b'=26-39).

/8/ The occurrence of such small sections, approximately a chapter or so in size, is not as rare as might be expected. Apart from the instances where the Greek text has a plus section over against the MT, other suggested small sections are: Exodus 38, suggested by Gooding in "The Account of the Tabernacle" (1959: 40-63, 99); Numbers 22-24, suggested by A. Wifstrand, cf. Aejmelaeus in "Parataxis in the Septuagint" (1982a: 173); Isaiah 66, suggested by Ziegler (1934: 42-46); Jeremiah 52, suggested by Thackeray (1903a: 260), but cf. Tov

(1976: 79); and Ezekiel 36.23c-38 (see chapter VII). In general, however, the issue of small sections in the LXX has received little attention.

/9/ Similar criticisms have been made of the method of Soisalon-Soininen by Gooding in his review of Soisalon-Soininen's work, "Die Infinitive in der Septuaginta". Cf. JTS 18 (1967): 451-455.

/10/ Aejmelaeus, for example, is aware of these latter issues, and devotes some discussion to them (1982a: 168-184). Yet none of the proponents of the "numerical" approach seems to have given a detailed treatment of the statistical factors involved.

/11/ Some of the results of statistical analysis on literary material can be quite striking in the way they differ from what one might expect. For example, Y. T. Radday relates that the probability according to one particular test of Kant having written Kant is 8 %, and of Goethe having written Goethe 22 % (Radday et alii 1982: 469).

Chapter III

/1/ There are slight differences among scholars about the number of single and double divine names in Ezekiel:

	<<yhwh>>	<<'dny yhwh>>
Dalman	-	227
Cornill	218	228
Herrmann	218	217
Baudissin	-	217

The figures arrived at here were 217 for <<yhwh>> and 217 for <<'dny yhwh>>. The discrepancies seem to be due a) to a

different text, b) to a misprint (?). This latter reason seems
to be the case with the figure 227/8. Unlike Herrmann and
Baudissin, Dalman and Cornill did not list the occurrences of
the forms, and so it is impossible to be sure of the real
reason for the discrepancy. Anyhow, it is extremely easy to
miscount these words.

/2/ Again, there are different figures given by different
writers. Below is a table of the figures given by several
scholars on the occurrence of <<kurios kurios>> in ch.1-39 of
B:

Cornill	58
Herrmann	56
Baudissin	54
Harford	54

55 occurrences were counted here.

/3/ In all Dalman suggested the deletion of <<'dny>> in seven
passages: Job 28.28; I Kg 3.10,15; II Kg 7.6; Ez 13.9; 23.49;
24.24; 28.24 (Dalman 1889: 27-33). He excluded the book of
Daniel from consideration here.

/4/ According to Herrmann, Daechsel's communication on this
was delivered verbally (Herrmann 1913: 81). I have not found
any indication that it was ever printed.

/5/ At that stage (1938) only 6 occurrences of <<kurios (o)
theos>> were to be found in the Scheide fragments: 24.3,9;
34.17; 37.3; 39.5,29. It should be noted that the Chester
Beatty papyri attested 7 more instances.

/6/ See chapter I: The Effect of Papyrus 967.

/7/ At the time of writing only the first volume of the
English translation of Zimmerli's commentary was available.

Notes

References containing the date 1979 refer to this translation, while references containing the date 1969 refer to the German edition.

/8/ See also chapter IV.

Chapter IV

/1/ Cf. Ziegler 1959: 57-58.

/2/ This occurs at the beginning of section XV (= CD 15). Cf. Vermes 1968: 108.

/3/ Amos may contain some parallels, but these are not as numerous. See Janzen's tables on the distribution of the divine name in the OT (1973: 155-161).

/4/ Chapter 35.15 has only <<yhwh>> in the MT, but the Greek manuscripts are unanimous in having <<kurios (o) theos>>, which is a strong indication that the Greek Vorlage was <<yhwh 'lhym>>. Cf. the uniformity of the manuscripts at other <<yhwh 'lhym>> references.

/5/ For the discussion on the form of the divine name in the early Greek texts see (in addition to the editions of the texts published):
Swete: Introduction, (1914: 34-40); Waddell: "The Tetragrammaton in the LXX" (1944); Kahle: Cairo Genizah (1959: 218-222); Dunand: "Papyrus grecs bibliques" (1966 and 1971); Siegal: "The Employment of Palaeo-Hebrew Characters for the Divine Names at Qumran in the Light of Tannaitic Sources" (1971); Roberts: Manuscript, Society and Belief in Early Christian Egypt (1979: 26-48); Skehan: "The Divine Name at

Qumran, in the Masada Scroll, and in the Septuagint" (1980);
Metzger: Manuscripts of the Greek Bible (1981: 33-35); and
Pietersma: "Kyrios or Tetragram: A Renewed Quest for the
Original Septuagint" (1984: 85-101). I would like to thank
Professor Pietersma for giving me the opportunity to read and
make use of the manuscript of the above article prior to its
publication.

/6/ This possibility has already been suggested by H.
Stegemann, according to Zimmerli (1969: 1256). As far as I am
aware, Stegemann has not yet published any detailed treatment
of this issue in Ezekiel.

/7/ Origen seems to imply that <<yhwh>> was pronounced as
<<kurios>> by some. His main remarks are found in his
commentary on Ps 2, (PG 12, col 1104):

> Mention must be made of the word pronounced 'Kurios'
> by the Greeks and 'Adonai' by the Hebrews. God is
> given ten names by the Hebrews. One of these is
> 'Adonai' and is translated as 'Lord' [Kurios]. In some
> places it is pronounced 'Adonai' by the Hebrews and
> 'Kurios' by the Greeks, the form of what has been
> written in Scripture dictating this. When Iae is
> found, it is pronounced 'Kurios' by the Greeks, but
> not by the Hebrews, as in 'Praise the Lord, for praise
> is good' [LXX: Ps 146.1]. 'Lord' [Kurion] is said
> there instead of Iae. The beginning of the Psalm is
> 'Allelouia' according to the Hebrews. There is a
> four-character, ineffable word among them, which is
> also written on the gold plate of the high priest and
> is pronounced 'Adonai'. (This is not what is spelled
> by the tetragram.) Among the Greeks, however, it is
> pronounced 'Kurios', and in the most accurate of the
> texts the name is found in Hebrew characters, not the
> present day Hebrew characters, but the very ancient

208

ones. They say that in the Exile Ezra gave them other
characters besides the former ones. We mentioned this
since the tetragram is found as 'Kurios' in 'but in
the law of the Lord', and in 'for the Lord knows the
way of the just', and now 'against the Lord and
against his Christ'.

Chapter VI

/1/ Cf. chapter I. Thackeray, Schäfers, Herrmann,
Danielsmeyer and Turner all distinguished 40-48 from the
preceding chapters on the grounds of translation differences.
Baudissin and Harford (cf. chapter III) separated 40-48 from
the rest of the Greek text because they believed that the
initial translation of the book had been made before the
temple section had been appended to the Hebrew text. Ch.40-48
were thus translated later, when they were accepted as being
part of the Ezekiel text.

/2/ Soisalon-Soininen notes that in general the aorist
infinitive occurs much more often than the present in the LXX
(1965: 148). Although he goes on to observe that 40-48 clearly
differs from this overall pattern, he dismisses the deviation
on the grounds that the context requires the frequent use of
the present infinitive. This might well be so for many
occurrences in S3, but there still are cases where the aorist
infinitive would make sense, for example 43.8; 44.10,12.

/3/ It is true that 147 out of the 236 terms had approximately
the same translation in both sections. Yet this high figure
can be slightly misleading. Apart from ch.16 and 36.23c-38,
there were 80 out of 158 terms which had the same translation
for all three sections. This fact means that even S1 and S2,

which we have seen to be the work of different translators,
had at least 80 terms with the same renderings. Most of these
terms, however, were items of vocabulary which had a
stereotyped rendering throughout the LXX. As in textual
criticism, the important factor is not the number of the
witnesses but their individual "weight". The 6 cases of
translation difference between S2 and S3 lack this weight.

/4/ In 41.6 the LXX differs strongly from the MT. Here the
translator may have departed from his text out of
considerations of piety. Cf. Gooding, "Temple Specifications:
A Dispute in Logical Arrangement between the MT and the LXX"
(1967b) p. 153.

Chapter VIII

/1/ Examples of these types of renderings are:
  1) <5.6>, <5.8>, <<5.9>
  2) <2.15>, <5.4>
  3) <5.1>, <5.2>
  4) <2.21>, <5.5>, <6.1>
  5) <2.28>, <5.16>
  6) <2.27>, <5.10>, <5.22>
  7) <5.19>, <5.20>, <6.4>.

/2/ A similar point, from a different perspective, has been
made by Barr in his study "The Typology of Literalism in
Ancient Biblical Translations" (1979), especially pp. 305-314
= [31]-[40].

/3/ See note /1/ to chapter II.

/4/ <<'dny>> occurs 222 times in Ezekiel (TDOT vol 1 p. 63

inaccurate here). In 217 of those occurrences it appears in the phrase <<'dny yhwh>>. The divine name form <<'dny>> occurs 449 times in the Old Testament in all.

/5/ For example, Thackeray's Grammar (1909),
Soisalon-Soininen's study "Die Infinitive in der Septuaginta" (1965), and Sollamo's "Renderings of Hebrew Semiprepositions in the Septuagint" (1979).

Appendix A

The Distribution of the Forms of <<yhwh>> in the Massoretic
Text of Ezekiel.

The figures presented here are based on the text of BHS. Other
Massoretic manuscripts may give slightly different results.
The key to the categories is as follows:

CC   the divine name comes at the end of a construct chain:
      "the ... of <<>>"

YD   the divine name comes in the phrase:
      <<yd' ky 'ny ...>> - "... know that I am ..."

KM   the divine name comes in the phrase:
      <<kh 'mr ...>> - "thus says <<>>""

NE   the divine name comes in the formula:
      <<n'm ...>> - "says ..."

AM   the divine name is the subject of <<'mr>>:
      "... said"

DB   the divine name is the subject of <<dbr>>:
      "I ... have spoken"

MS   miscellaneous forms not included above

AD   the divine name is used in direct address
      to God, i.e. as a vocative.

The classification is dictated by the nature of the most
frequently occurring forms rather than by preconceived
grammatical or lexical considerations. The divine names in,
for example, the book of Jeremiah would require a quite
different set of categories.

Table A.1 : Occurrence of the Single <<yhwh>> Form in Ezekiel

CC	YD	KM	NE	AM	DB	MS	AD
1.3a	5.13	11.5b	13.6a	4.13	5.15	8.12a	O
1.3b	6.7	21.8	13.7	9.4	5.17	8.12b	
1.28	6.10	30.6a	16.58	23.36	12.25a	9.9a	
3.12	6.13		37.14b	44.2a	17.24b	9.9b	
3.14	6.14			44.5a	21.22	11.15	
3.16	7.4				21.37	13.6b	
3.22	7.9				22.14	14.4b	
3.23	7.27				24.14a	14.7	
6.1	11.10				26.14a	14.9	
7.1	11.12				30.12	20.1	
7.19	12.15				34.24b	21.4	
8.14	12.16				36.36b	22.28b	
8.16a	12.20					30.3	
8.16b	13.14					33.30	
8.16c	13.21					34.24a	
10.4a	13.23					35.10	
10.4b	14.8					40.46	
10.18	15.7					41.22	
10.19	16.62					42.13	
11.1	17.21					43.24a	
11.5a	17.24a					43.24b	
11.14	20.12					44.3	
11.23	20.26					45.1	
11.25	20.38					45.4	
12.1	20.42					45.23	
12.8	20.44a					46.3	
12.17	21.10					46.4	
12.21	22.16					46.9	
12.26	22.22					46.12	
13.1	24.27					46.13	
13.2	25.5					46.14	
13.5	25.7					48.9	
14.2	25.11					48.14	
14.12	25.17					48.35	
15.1	26.6						
16.1	28.22b						
16.35	28.23						
17.1	28.26						
17.11	29.6						
18.1	29.9						
20.2	29.21						
21.1	30.8						
21.3a	30.19						
21.6	30.25						
21.13	30.26						
21.23	32.15						
22.1	33.29						
22.17	34.27						
22.23	34.30						
23.1	35.4						
24.1	35.9						
24.15	35.12						
24.20	35.15						
25.1	36.11						
26.1	36.23a						
27.1	36.36a						
28.1	36.38						
28.11	37.6						
28.20	37.13						
29.1	37.14a						
29.17	37.28						
30.1	38.23						
30.20	39.6						

Appendix A

CC	YD	KM	NE	AM	DB	MS	AD
31.1	39.7						
32.1	39.22						
32.17	39.38						
33.1							
33.22							
33.23							
34.1							
34.7							
34.9							
35.1							
36.1							
36.16							
36.20							
37.1a							
37.1b							
37.4							
37.15							
38.1							
40.1							
43.4							
43.5							
44.4a							
44.4b							
44.5b							
48.10							

The groups CC and MS can be further subdivided according to the words linked with <<yhwh>>:

Table A.2 : <<yhwh>> in Group CC

Phrase	Occurrences	References			
דבר-יהוה (the word of Yahweh)	: 57	1.3 11.14 12.21 14.2 16.35 20.2 21.13 22.23 24.20 28.1 29.17 32.1 34.1 36.1 38.1	3.16 12.1 12.26 14.12 17.1 21.1 21.23 23.1 25.1 28.11 30.1 32.17 34.7 36.16	6.1 12.8 13.1 15.1 17.11 21.3 22.1 24.1 26.1 28.20 30.20 33.1 34.9 37.4	7.1 12.17 13.2 16.1 18.1 21.6 22.17 24.15 27.1 29.1 31.1 33.23 35.1 37.15
כבוד-יהוה (the glory of Yahweh)	: 10	1.28 10.4 43.5	3.12 10.18 44.4	3.23 11.23	10.4 43.4
יד-יהוה (the hand of Yahweh)	: 6	1.3 37.1	3.14 40.1	3.22	33.22
בית-יהוה (the house of Yahweh)	: 6	8.14 44.4	8.16 44.5	10.19	11.1
היכל-יהוה (the temple of Yahweh)	: 2	8.16	8.16		
רוח-יהוה (spirit of Yahweh)	: 2	11.5	37.1		
דברי-יהוה (the words of Yahweh)	: 1	11.25			
עם-יהוה (the people of Yahweh)	: 1	36.20			
מקדש-יהוה (the sanctuary of Yahweh)	: 1	48.10			
ביום-יהוה (in the day of Yahweh)	: 1	13.5			
ביום-עברת-יהוה (in the day of the wrath of Yahweh)	: 1	7.19			
Total	: 88				

Appendix A

Table A.3 : <<yhwh>> in Group MS

Phrase	Occurrences		References			
ליהוה (to Yahweh)	: 11		30.3 45.23 46.14	42.13 46.4 48.9	43.24 46.12 48.14	45.1 46.13
לפני יהוה (before Yahweh)	: 5		41.22 46.9	43.24	44.3	46.3
אין יהוה ראה (Yahweh does not see)	: 2		8.12	9.9		
<<'ny yhwh>> + verb (I Yahweh will/have ...)	: 4		14.4	14.7	14.9	34.24
וראה ... כי אני יהוה (and ... shall see that I am Yahweh)	: 1		21.4			
Inf + <<'t-yhwh>> (to ... Yahweh [Object])	: 2		20.1	45.4		
יהוה שם/שמה (Yahweh is there)	: 2		35.10	48.35		
<<yhwh>> [Subj.] + verb (Yahweh will/has ...)	: 4		8.12	9.9	13.6	22.28
מעל יהוה (from Yahweh)	: 1		11.15			
מאת יהוה (from Yahweh)	: 1		33.30			
אל-יהוה (to Yahweh)	: 1		40.46			

Total	: 34					

217

Table A.4 : Occurrences of <<yhwh 'lhym>> in the Book of
Ezekiel.

Phrase	Occurrences		References			
אני יהוה אלהיכם (I am Yahweh your God)	:	4	20.5	20.7	20.19	20.20
אני יהוה אלהיהם (I am Yahweh their God)	:	4	28.26	34.30	39.22	39.28
יהוה אלהי-ישראל בא (Yahweh God of Israel came in)	:	1	44.2			
Total	:	9				

CC	YD	KM	NE	AM	DB	MS	AD
0	20.20 28.26 34.30 39.22 39.28	0	0	0	0	20.5 20.7 20.19 44.2	0

Table A.5 : Occurrences of <<'dny yhwh>> in Ezekiel.

CC	YD	KM	NE	AM	DB	MS	AD
6.3a	13.9	2.4	5.11	0	0	0	4.14
8.1	23.49	3.11	11.8				9.8
25.3a	24.24	3.27	11.21				11.13
36.4a	28.24	5.5	12.25b				21.5
	29.16	5.7	12.28b				37.3
		5.8	13.8b				
		6.3b	13.16				
		6.11	14.11				
		7.2	14.14				
		7.5	14.16				
		11.7	14.18				
		11.16	14.20				
		11.17	14.23				
		12.10	15.8				
		12.19	16.8				
		12.23	16.14				
		12.28a	16.19				
		13.3	16.23				
		13.8a	16.30				
		13.13	16.43				
		13.18	16.48				
		13.20	16.63				
		14.4a	17.16				
		14.6	18.3				
		14.21	18.9				
		15.6	18.23				
		16.3	18.30				
		16.36	18.32				
		16.59	20.3b				
		17.3	20.31				
		17.9	20.33				
		17.19	20.36				
		17.22	20.40				
		20.3a	20.44b				
		20.5a	21.12				
		20.27	21.18				
		20.30	22.12				
		20.39	22.31				
		21.3b	23.34				
		21.29	24.14b				
		21.31	25.14				
		21.33	26.5				
		22.3	26.14b				
		22.19	26.21				
		22.28a	28.10				
		23.22	29.20				
		23.28	30.6b				
		23.32	31.18				
		23.35	32.8				
		23.46	32.14				
		24.3	32.16				
		24.6	32.31				
		24.9	32.32				
		24.21	33.11				
		25.3b	34.8				
		25.6	34.15				
		25.8	34.30b				
		25.12	34.31				
		25.13	35.6				
		25.15	35.11				
		25.16	36.14				
		26.3	36.15				

CC	YD	KM	NE	AM	DB	MS	AD
		26.7	36.23b				
		26.15	36.32				
		26.19	38.18				
		27.3	38.21				
		28.2	39.5				
		28.6	39.8				
		28.12	39.10				
		28.22a	39.13				
		28.25	39.20				
		29.3	39.29				
		29.8	43.19				
		29.13	43.27				
		29.19	44.12				
		30.2	44.15				
		30.10	44.27				
		30.13	45.9b				
		30.22	45.15				
		31.10	47.23				
		31.15	48.29				
		32.3					
		32.11					
		33.25					
		33.27					
		34.2					
		34.10					
		34.11					
		34.17					
		34.20					
		35.3					
		35.14					
		36.2					
		36.3					
		36.4b					
		36.5					
		36.6					
		36.7					
		36.13					
		36.22					
		36.33					
		36.37					
		37.5					
		37.9					
		37.12					
		37.19					
		37.21					
		38.3					
		38.10					
		38.14					
		38.17					
		39.1					
		39.17					
		39.25					
		43.18					
		44.6					
		44.9					
		45.9a					
		45.18					
		46.1					
		46.16					
		47.13					

Appendix A

Table A.6 : Comparison of Distribution of <<yhwh>> and <<'dny yhwh>> Forms.

		CC	YD	KM	NE	AM	DB	MS	AD	Total
יהוה	:	88	62	3	4	5	12	34	0	208
יהוה אלהים	:	0	5	0	0	0	0	4	0	9
אדני יהוה	:	4	5	122	81	0	0	0	5	217
Total	:	92	72	125	85	5	12	38	5	434

The word <<'dny>> also occurs 5 times by itself: 18.25,29; 21.14; 33.17,20.

Appendix B

The Distribution of the Forms of the
Divine Name in the Greek Textual Witnesses of
the Book of Ezekiel.

This appendix shows what forms in the Greek witnesses and
their daughter translations correspond to the words <<yhwh>>
and <<'dny yhwh>> in the Massoretic text. The edition of the
MT used is that of BHS, i.e. that based on the Leningrad
manuscript B19a. Information concerning the Greek manuscripts
is taken mostly from the Ziegler edition of the Septuagint of
Ezekiel. The readings of 967 (i.e. Papyrus 967) have been
taken from the various editions of its text. The manuscripts
are grouped according to Ziegler's classification. This
grouping corresponds mostly with that used in the citation of
variants in the translation examples. However, for the sake of
clarity some omissions and alterations have been made. Several
fragmentary witnesses have been left out, as have marginal
readings found in the texts mentioned below. Citations from
early commentaries have mostly been omitted also. The Old
Latin readings have been given separately.

The witnesses cited are:

1) "The B-Text":

          B   Vaticanus, 4th century
          967   Papyrus 967, 3rd century
          Bo   Bohairic translation

Ziegler classes the Old Latin citations along with these three
witnesses, but in the appendix these are placed lower down.

2) "The Alexandrian Text":

A	Alexandrinus, 5th century
26	10th century
106	14th century
410	13th century
544	11th century
Arab	Arabic translation
Aeth	Ethiopic translation

3) "The Hexaplaric Recension":

Q	Marchalianus, 6th century
88	Chisianus, 10th century
Syh	Syrohexaplaric translation
62	11th century
147	12th century
407	9th century

62 exhibits Aquila-type readings. Ziegler splits the
manuscripts into two sub-groups: Q-88-Syh and 62-147-407.

4) "The Lucianic Recension":

22	11-12th century
36	11th century
48	10-11th century
51	11th century
96	11th century
231	10-11th century
763	11th century
311	12th century
538	12th century
V	Venetus, 8th century
46	13-14th century
449	10-11th century

These manuscripts are divided into three subgroups:
22-36-48-51-96-231-763, 311-538 and V-46-449.

5) "The Catena Group":

87	10th century
91	11th century
490	11th century
49	11th century
90	11th century
764	13-14th century
130	12-13th century
233	10th century
534	11th century

The three subgroups are: 87-91-490, 49-90-764 and 130-233-534

6) "Codices mixti":

```
239   written 1046
306   11th century
403   written 1542
613   13th century
```

At times these witnesses follow the Alexandrian group.

7) The Old Latin (La):

Readings of the Old Latin have been taken from the respective editions of the texts mentioned here.

```
W     Codex Wirceburgensis, 6th century
Tyc   Citations from Liber Regularum Tyconii,
      edited by F.C. Burkitt
S     Fragmenta Sangallensia, 9th century
C     Codex Constantiensis, 5th century
```

The top lines contain the chapter and verse references, while the bottom line contains the form of the context of the words (see Appendix A).

The following are the symbols for the main part of the appendix:

```
.     <<kurios>>, in MT <<yhwh>>, in VL <<Dominus>>
ak    <<adònai kurios>>, in MT <<'dny yhwh>>,
      in VL <<Adonai Dominus>>
kt    <<kurios (o) theos>>, in MT <<yhwh 'lhym>>,
      in VL <<Dominus Deus>>
kk    <<kurios kurios>>, in VL <<Dominus Dominus>>
ka    <<kurios adònai>>
kak   <<kurios adònai kurios>>
akt   <<adònai kurios (o) theos>>
at    <<adònai theos>>
ki    <<kurios (tou) israèl>>
kti   <<kurios (o) theos (tou) israèl>>
kkt   <<kurios kurios (o) theos>>
kka   <<kurios kurios adònai>>
t     <<(o) theos>>
akk   <<adònai kurios kurios>>
o     lacuna in text
—     omission in text (this is also indicated by no entry)
*     something other than mentioned here.
```

The chapter and verse system follows that of the Massoretic Text.

In cases of homoioteleuton the same reading has been entered twice. This occurs at 12.28a/28b (in 410) and 33.25/27 (in

B-967-Bo). There are also several instances where there is not
complete certainty about a reading. These are: 14.6 (in Aeth),
16.3,35; 28.26; 36.23a (in 967), and 24.14b (in S).

Table B.1 (opposite) shows the distribution of the readings:

Ch. Vs.	1. 3a	1. 3b	1. 28	2. 4	3. 11	3. 12	3. 14	3. 16	3. 22	3. 23	3. 27	4. 13	4. 14	5. 5
MT	.	.	.	ak	ak	.	.	.	.	.	ak	.	ak	ak
967	.	.	.	.	.	.	.	.	.	.	.	kti	kti	.
Bo	.	.	.	.	.	.	.	.	.	.	.	kti	kti	.
A	.	.	.	kk	kk	.	.	.	.	.	kk	kti	*	ak
26	.	.	.	kk	kk	.	.	.	.	.	kk	kti	*	ak
106	.	.	.	kk	kk	.	.	.	.	.	kk	kti	kti	ak
410	.	.	.	kk	kk	.	.	.	.	.	kk	kti	kti	kak
544	.	.	.	kk	kk	.	.	.	.	.	kk	kti	*	.
Aeth	.	.	.	kk	kk	.	.	.	.	.	kk	kti	kti	ak
Arab	.	.	.	kk	kk	.	.	.	.	.	kk	kti	kti	ak
Q	.	.	.	kk	kk	.	.	.	.	.	ak	kti	kti	ak
38	.	.	.	kk	kk	.	.	.	.	.	ak	kti	kti	ak
Syh	.	.	.	kk	kk	.	.	.	.	.	ak	kti	kti	ak
52	.	.	.	*	kt	.	.	.	.	.	ak	kti	kti	ak
147	.	.	.	.	.	.	.	.	.	.	ak	kti	kti	ak
407	.	.	.	.	kk	.	.	.	.	.	ak	kti	kti	kak
22	.	.	.	ka	ak	.	.	.	.	.	ak	kti	kti	ak
36	.	.	.	ka	ak	.	.	.	.	.	ak	kti	kti	ka
48	.	.	.	ka	ak	.	.	.	.	.	ak	kti	kti	ak
51	.	.	.	ka	ak	.	.	.	.	.	ak	kti	kti	ak
96	.	.	.	ka	ak	.	.	.	.	.	ak	kti	kti	ak
231	o	o	.	ka	ak	.	.	.	.	.	ak	kti	kti	ak
763	.	.	.	ka	ak	.	.	.	.	.	ak	kti	kti	ak
311	.	.	.	ka	ak	.	.	.	.	.	ak	kti	kti	ak
538	.	.	.	ak	ak	.	.	.	.	.	.	kti	kti	ak
V	.	.	.	ak	.	.	.	.	.	.	ak	kti	kti	ak
46	.	.	.	.	kk	.	.	.	.	.	ak	kti	ki	ka
449	.	.	.	ka	ak	.	.	.	.	.	ak	kti	kti	ak
87	.	.	.	kk	kk	.	.	.	.	.	kk	kti	kti	ak
91	.	.	.	kk	kk	.	.	.	.	.	kk	kti	kti	ak
490	.	.	.	kk	kk	.	.	.	.	.	kk	kti	kti	ak
49	.	.	.	kk	kk	.	.	.	.	.	kk	kti	kti	ak
90	.	.	.	kk	kk	.	.	.	.	.	kk	kti	kti	ak
764	.	.	.	kk	kk	.	.	.	.	.	kk	kti	kti	ak
130	.	.	.	kk	kk	.	.	.	.	.	kk	kti	kti	ka
233	.	.	.	kk	.	.	.	.	.	.	kk	kti	kti	ak
534	.	.	.	kk	kk	kk	.	.	.	.	kk	kti	kti	ka
239	.	.	.	kk	.	.	.	.	.	.	kk	kti	kti	ak
306	.	.	.	kk	.	.	.	.	.	.	kk	kti	kti	ak
403	.	.	.	kk	kk	.	.	.	.	.	kk	kti	*	ak
613	.	.	.	kk	kk	.	.	.	.	.	kk	kti	kti	ak

La:
W
Tyc
S
C

| Form | CC | CC | CC | KM | KM | CC | CC | CC | CC | CC | KM | AM | AD | KM |

Ch. Vs.	5.7	5.8	5.11	5.13	5.15	5.17	6.1	6.3a	6.3b	6.7	6.10	6.11	6.13	6.1
MT	ak	ak	ak	.	.	.	.	ak	ak	.	.	ak	.	.
B 967	.	.	.	.	.	.	.	.	.	.	.	.	.	.
Bo	.	.	ak	.	.	.	.	.	.	.	.	.	.	.
A	ak	ak	ak	.	.	.	.	ak	ak	.	.	ak	.	.
26	ak	ak	ak	.	—	.	.	ak	ak	.	.	.	.	.
106	kak	ak	ak	.	.	.	.	.	ak	.	.	.	.	.
410	ak	ak	ak	.	.	.	.	ak	.	.	.	.	.	.
544	ak	ak	ak	.	.	.	.	ak	ak	.	.	.	.	.
Aeth	ak	ak	ak	.	.	.	.	.	ak	.	.	.	.	.
Arab	ak	ak	ak	.	.	.	.	ak	ak	.	.	ak	.	.
Q	ak	ak	ak	.	.	.	.	ak	ak	.	.	ak	.	.
88	ak	ak	ak	.	.	.	.	ak	ak	.	.	ak	.	.
Syh	ak	ak	ak	.	.	.	.	ak	ak	.	.	ak	.	.
62	ak	ak	ak	.	.	.	.	ak	ak	.	.	ak	.	.
147	ak	ak	ak	.	.	.	.	ak	ak	.	.	ak	.	.
407	ak	ak	ak	.	.	.	.	ak	ak	.	.	ak	.	.
22	ak	ak	ak	.	.	.	.	ak	ak	.	.	ak	.	.
36	ak	ak	ak	.	.	.	.	kak	ak	.	.	ak	.	.
48	ak	ak	ak	.	.	.	.	ak	ak	.	.	ak	.	.
51	ak	ak	ak	.	.	.	.	ak	ak	.	.	ak	.	.
96	ak	ak	ak	.	.	.	.	ak	ak	.	.	ak	.	.
231	ak	ak	ak	.	.	.	.	ak	ak	.	.	ak	.	.
763	ak	ak	ak	.	.	.	.	ak	ka	.	.	ak	.	.
311	ak	ak	ak	.	.	.	.	ak	ak	.	.	.	.	.
538	ak	ak	ak	.	.	.	.	ak	ak	.	.	.	.	.
V	ak	ak	ak	.	.	.	.	ak	ak	.	.	ak	.	.
46	ak	ak	ak	.	.	.	.	.	ak	.	.	.	.	.
449	ak	ka	ak	.	.	.	.	ak	ak	.	.	ak	.	.
87	ak	ak	ak	.	.	.	.	ak	ak	.	.	ak	.	.
91	ak	ak	ak	.	.	.	.	ak	ak	.	.	ak	.	.
490	ak	ak	ak	.	.	.	.	ak	ak	.	.	ak	.	.
49	ak	ak	ak	.	.	.	.	ak	ak	.	.	.	.	.
90	ak	ak	ak	.	.	.	.	ak	ak	.	.	.	.	.
764	ak	ak	ak	.	.	.	.	ak	ak	.	.	.	.	.
130	ak	ak	ak	.	.	.	.	ak	ak	.	.	.	.	.
233	ak	ak	ak	.	.	.	.	ak	ak	.	.	.	.	.
534	ak	ak	ak	.	.	.	.	ak	ak	.	.	.	.	.
239	ak	ak	ak	.	.	.	.	.	ak	.	.	.	.	.
306	ak	ak	ak	.	.	.	.	.	ak	.	.	.	.	.
403	ak	ak	ak	.	.	.	.	ak	ak	.	.	.	.	.
613	ak	ak	ak	.	.	.	.	ak	ak	.	.	.	.	.
La: W Tyc S C														
Form	KM	KM	NE	YD	DB	DB	CC	CC	KM	YD	YD	KM	YD	YD

228

Table B.1

Ch. Vs.	7.1	7.2	7.4	7.5	7.9	7.19	7.27	8.1	8.12a	8.12b	8.14	8.16a	8.16b	8.16c
MT	.	ak	.	ak	.	.	.	ak	.	.	.	.	.	.
B 967	.	.	.	.	.	−	.	.	.	.	.	.	.	.
Bo	.	.	.	.	kt	−	.	.	.	.	.	.	.	.
A	.	ak	.	.	.	.	.	ak	.	.	.	.	.	.
26	.	ak	.	.	.	.	.	.	.	.	.	.	.	.
106	.	ak	.	kk	.	.	.	ak	.	.	.	.	.	.
410	.	.	.	ak	.	.	.	ak	.	.	.	.	.	.
544	.	ak	.	ak	.	.	.	.	.	.	.	.	.	.
Aeth	.	ak	.	ak	.	.	.	ka	.	.	.	.	.	.
Arab	.	ak	.	.	.	.	.	ak	.	.	.	.	.	.
Q	.	ak	.	ak	.	.	.	ak	.	.	.	.	.	.
88	.	ak	.	kk	.	.	.	ak	.	.	.	.	.	.
Syh	.	ak	.	kk	.	.	.	ak	.	.	.	.	.	.
62	.	ak	.	ak	.	.	.	ak	.	.	.	.	.	.
147	.	.	.	ak	.	.	.	ak	.	−	.	.	.	.
407	.	.	.	ak	.	.	.	ak	.	.	.	.	.	.
22	.	ak	.	ak	.	.	.	ak	.	.	.	.	.	.
36	.	ka	.	ak	.	.	.	kak	.	.	.	.	.	.
48	.	ak	.	ak	.	.	.	ak	.	.	.	.	.	.
51	.	ak	.	ak	.	.	.	ak	.	.	.	.	.	.
96	.	ak	.	ak	.	.	.	ak	.	.	.	.	.	.
231	.	ak	.	ak	.	.	.	ak	.	.	.	.	.	.
763	.	ak	.	ak	.	.	.	ak	.	.	.	.	.	.
311	.	ak	.	ak	.	.	.	ak	.	.	.	.	.	.
538	.	a	.	ak	.	.	.	ak	.	.	.	.	.	.
V	.	ak	.	ak	.	.	.	ak	.	.	.	.	.	.
46	.	ak	.	ak	.	.	.	ak	.	.	.	.	.	.
449	.	ak	.	ak	.	.	.	ak	.	.	−	.	.	.
87	.	ak	.	.	.	.	.	ak	.	.	.	.	.	.
91	.	ak	.	kk	.	.	.	ak	.	.	.	.	.	.
490	.	ak	.	kk	.	.	.	ak	.	.	.	.	.	.
49	.	ak	.	kk	.	.	.	ak	.	.	.	.	.	.
90	.	ak	.	kk	.	.	.	ak	.	.	.	.	.	.
764	.	ak	.	kk	.	.	.	ak	.	.	.	.	.	.
130	.	ak	.	kk	.	.	.	ak	.	.	.	.	.	.
233	.	ak	.	kk	.	.	.	ak	.	.	.	.	−	.
534	.	ak	.	.	.	.	.	ak	.	−	.	.	.	.
239	.	ak	.	ak	.	.	.	ak	.	.	.	.	.	.
306	.	ak	.	ak	.	.	.	ak	.	.	.	.	.	.
403	.	ak	.	kk	.	.	.	.	.	.	.	.	.	.
613	.	ak	.	kk	.	.	.	.	.	.	.	.	.	.
La: W Tyc														
S	o	o	o	o	o	−	.	.	.	.	.	.	.	.
C	o	o	o	o	o	o	o	−	.	.	.	.	.	.
Form	CC	KM	YD	KM	YD	CC	YD	CC	MS	MS	CC	CC	CC	CC

229

Ch. Vs	9.4	9.8	9.9a	9.9b	10.4a	10.4b	10.18	10.19	11.1	11.5a	11.5b	11.7	11.8	11.10
MT	.	ak	.	.	.	.	.	.	.	.	.	ak	ak	.
B 967	−	.	.	.	.	.	.	.	.	−	.	.	.	.
Bo	−	.	.	.	.	.	.	.	.	.	.	.	ak	.
A	.	ak	.	−	.	.	.	.	.	.	.	ak	ak	.
26	.	ak	.	.	.	.	.	.	.	.	.	ak	ak	.
106	.	ak	.	.	.	.	.	.	.	.	.	ak	ak	.
410	.	ak	.	.	.	.	.	.	.	.	.	ak	ak	.
544	.	ak	.	.	.	.	.	.	.	.	.	ak	ak	.
Aeth	.	ak	.	−	.	.	.	.	.	.	.	ak	ak	.
Arab	.	ak	.	−	.	.	.	.	.	.	.	ak	ak	.
Q	.	ak	.	.	.	.	.	.	.	.	.	ak	ak	.
88	.	ak	.	.	.	.	.	.	.	.	.	ak	kk	.
Syh	.	ak	.	.	.	.	.	.	.	.	.	ak	kk	.
62	.	ak	.	.	.	.	.	.	.	.	.	ak	ak	.
147	.	ak	.	.	.	.	.	.	.	.	.	ak	ak	.
407	.	ak	.	.	.	.	.	.	.	.	.	ak	ak	.
22	.	ak	.	.	.	.	.	.	.	.	ak	.	ak	.
36	.	ak	.	.	.	.	.	.	.	.	kak	.	ak	.
48	.	ak	.	.	.	.	.	.	.	.	ak	.	ak	.
51	.	ak	.	.	.	.	.	.	.	.	ak	.	ak	.
96	.	ak	.	.	.	.	.	.	.	.	ak	.	ak	.
231	.	ak	.	.	.	.	.	.	.	.	ak	.	ak	.
763	.	ak	.	.	.	.	.	.	.	.	ak	.	ak	.
311	.	ak	.	.	.	.	.	.	.	.	ak	.	ak	.
538	.	ak	.	.	.	.	.	.	.	.	.	ak	ak	.
V	.	ak	.	.	.	.	.	.	.	.	ak	ak	ak	.
46	−	ak	.	.	.	.	.	.	.	.	ak	ak	ak	.
449	.	ak	.	.	.	.	.	.	.	.	ak	ak	ak	.
87	.	ak	.	.	.	.	.	.	−	.	ak	ak	ak	.
91	.	ak	.	.	.	.	.	.	−	.	ak	ak	ak	.
490	.	ak	.	.	.	.	.	.	−	.	ak	ak	ak	.
49	.	ak	.	.	.	.	.	.	.	.	ak	ak	ak	.
90	.	ak	.	.	.	.	.	.	.	.	ak	ak	ak	.
764	.	ak	.	.	.	.	.	.	.	.	ak	ak	ak	.
130	.	ak	.	.	.	.	.	.	.	.	.	ak	ak	.
233	.	ak	t	.	.	.	.	.	.	.	.	ak	ak	.
534	.	ak	.	.	.	.	.	.	.	.	.	ka	ak	.
239	.	ak	.	.	.	.	.	.	.	.	.	ak	ak	.
306	.	ak	.	.	.	.	.	.	.	.	.	ak	ak	.
403	.	ak	.	.	.	.	.	.	.	.	.	ak	ak	.
613	.	ak	.	.	.	.	.	.	.	.	.	ak	ak	.
La: W Tyc S C	−	.	.	.	.	.	.	.	.	−	.	.	.	.
Form	AM	AD	MS	MS	CC	CC	CC	CC	CC	CC	KM	KM	NE	YD

Table B.1

Ch. Vs.	11. 12	11. 13	11. 14	11. 15	11. 16	11. 17	11. 21	11. 23	11. 25	12. 1	12. 8	12. 10	12. 15	12. 16
MT	.	ak	.	.	ak	ak	ak	.	.	.	.	ak	.	.
B	−	.	.	.	.	.	.	.	.	.	.	kk	.	.
967	o	o	o	o	o	o	o	o	.	o	o	o	o	.
Bo	−	.	.	.	.	.	.	.	.	.	.	.	.	.
A	.	ak	.	.	ak	ak	ak	.	.	.	.	kk	.	.
26	.	ak	.	.	ak	ak	ak	.	.	.	.	kk	.	.
106	.	ak	.	.	ak	ak	ak	.	.	.	.	kk	.	.
410	.	ak	.	.	ak	ak	ak	.	.	.	.	kk	.	.
544	.	ak	.	.	ak	ak	ak	.	.	.	.	.	.	.
Aeth	.	ak	.	.	ak	ak	ak	.	.	.	.	.	.	.
Arab	−	ak	.	.	ak	ak	ak	.	.	.	.	kk	.	.
Q	.	ak	.	.	ak	ak	ak	.	.	.	.	kk	.	.
88	.	ak	.	.	ak	ak	ak	.	.	.	.	kk	.	.
Syh	.	ak	.	.	ak	ak	ak	.	.	.	.	kk	.	.
62	.	ak	.	.	ak	ak	ak	.	.	.	.	ak	.	.
147	.	ak	.	.	ak	ak	ak	.	.	.	.	.	.	.
407	.	ak	.	.	ak	ak	ak	.	.	.	.	.	.	.
22	.	ak	.	.	ak	ak	ak	.	.	.	.	ak	.	.
36	.	ak	.	.	ak	ak	ak	.	.	.	.	ak	.	.
48	.	ak	.	.	ak	ak	ak	.	.	.	.	ak	.	.
51	.	ak	.	.	ak	ak	ak	.	.	.	.	ak	.	.
96	.	ak	.	.	ak	ak	ak	.	.	.	.	ak	.	.
231	.	ak	.	.	ak	ak	ak	.	.	.	.	ak	.	.
763	.	ak	.	.	ak	ak	ak	.	.	.	.	ak	.	.
311	.	ak	.	.	ak	ak	ak	.	.	.	.	ak	.	.
538	.	ak	.	.	ak	.	ak	.	.	.	.	kk	.	.
V	.	ak	.	.	ak	ak	.	.	.	.	.	ak	.	.
46	−	ak	.	.	ak	ak	ak	.	.	.	.	kk	.	.
449	.	ak	.	.	ak	ak	ak	.	.	.	.	ak	.	.
87	.	ak	.	.	ak	ak	ak	.	.	.	.	kk	.	.
91	.	ak	.	.	ak	ak	ak	.	.	.	.	kk	.	.
490	.	ak	.	.	ak	ak	ak	.	.	.	.	kk	.	.
49	.	ak	.	.	ak	ak	ak	.	.	.	.	kk	.	.
90	.	ak	.	.	ak	ak	ak	.	.	.	.	kk	.	.
764	.	ak	.	.	ak	ak	ak	.	.	.	.	kk	.	.
130	.	ak	.	.	ak	ak	ak	.	.	.	.	kk	.	.
233	.	ak	.	.	ak	.	ak	.	.	.	.	kk	.	.
534	−	ak	.	.	ak	ak	ak	.	.	.	.	.	.	.
239	.	ak	.	.	ak	ak	ak	.	.	.	.	kk	.	.
306	.	ak	.	.	ak	ak	ak	.	.	.	.	kk	.	.
403	.	ak	.	.	ak	ak	ak	.	.	.	.	kk	.	.
613	.	ak	.	.	ak	ak	ak	.	.	.	.	kk	.	.
La: W Tyc S	.	.	.	.	.	.	o	o	o	o	o	o	o	o
C	o	o	o	o	o	o	o	o	o	o	o	o	.	.
Form	YD	AD	CC	MS	KM	KM	NE	CC	CC	CC	CC	KM	YD	YD

Ch. Vs.	12. 17	12. 19	12. 20	12. 21	12. 23	12. 25a	12. 25b	12. 26	12. 28a	12. 28b	13. 1	13. 2	13. 3	13. 5
MT	.	ak	.	.	ak	.	ak	.	ak	ak	.	.	ak	.
B	.	.	.	.	.	.	.	.	.	.	.	.	.	.
967	.	.	o	o	o	.	.	—	—	—	.	.	.	.
Bo	.	.	.	.	.	.	.	.	.	.	.	.	.	.
A	.	ak	.	.	ak	.	ak	.	ak	ak	.	.	ak	.
26	.	ak	.	.	ak	.	ak	.	ak	ak	.	.	ak	.
106	.	ak	.	.	ak	.	ak	.	ak	ak	.	.	ak	.
410	.	ak	.	.	ak	.	ak	.	ak	ak	.	.	ak	.
544	.	ak	.	.	ak	.	ak	.	ak	ak	.	.	ak	.
Aeth	.	ak	.	.	ak	.	ak	.	ak	ak	.	.	ak	.
Arab	.	ak	.	.	ak	.	ak	.	ak	ak	.	.	ak	.
Q	.	ak	.	.	ak	.	ak	.	ak	ak	.	.	ak	.
88	.	ak	.	.	ak	.	ak	.	ak	ak	.	.	ak	.
Syh	.	ak	.	.	ak	.	ak	.	ak	ak	.	.	ak	.
62	.	ak	.	.	ak	.	ak	.	ak	ak	.	.	.	.
147	.	ak	.	.	ak	.	ak	.	ak	ak	.	.	.	.
407	.	ak	.	.	ak	.	ak	.	ak	ak	.	.	.	.
22	.	ak	.	.	ak	.	ak	.	ak	ak	.	.	ak	.
36	.	ak	.	.	ak	.	ak	.	ak	ak	.	.	ak	.
48	.	ak	.	.	ak	.	ak	.	ak	ak	.	.	ak	.
51	.	ak	.	.	ak	.	ak	.	ak	ak	.	.	ak	.
96	.	ak	.	.	ak	.	ak	.	ak	ak	.	.	ak	.
231	.	ak	.	.	ak	.	ak	.	ak	ak	.	.	ak	.
763	.	ak	.	.	ak	.	ak	.	ak	ak	.	.	ak	.
311	.	ak	.	.	ak	.	ak	.	ak	ak	.	.	ak	.
538	.	ak	.	.	ak	.	ak	.	ak	ak	.	.	ak	.
V	.	ak	.	.	ak	.	ak	.	ak	ak	.	.	ak	.
46	.	ak	.	.	ak	.	ak	.	ak	ak	.	.	ak	.
449	.	ak	.	.	ak	.	ak	.	ak	ak	.	.	ak	.
87	.	ak	.	.	ak	.	ak	.	ak	ak	.	.	ak	.
91	.	ak	.	.	ak	.	ak	.	ak	ak	.	.	ak	.
490	.	ak	.	.	ak	.	ak	.	ak	ak	.	.	ak	.
49	.	ak	.	.	ak	.	ak	.	ak	ak	.	.	ak	.
90	.	ak	.	.	ak	.	ak	.	ak	ak	.	.	ak	.
764	.	ak	.	.	ak	.	ak	.	ak	ak	.	.	ak	.
130	.	ak	.	.	ak	.	ak	.	ak	ak	.	.	ak	.
233	.	ak	.	.	ak	.	ak	.	ak	ak	.	.	ak	.
534	.	ak	.	.	.	.	ak	.	ak	ak	.	.	ak	.
239	.	ak	.	.	ak	.	ak	.	ak	ak	.	.	ak	.
306	.	ak	.	.	ak	.	ak	.	ak	ak	.	.	ak	.
403	.	ak	.	.	ak	.	ak	.	ak	ak	.	.	ak	.
613	.	ak	.	.	ak	.	ak	.	ak	ak	.	.	ak	.
La:														
W														
Tyc														
S														
C	.	o	o	o	o	o	o	o	o	o	o	o	o	o
Form	CC	KM	YD	CC	KM	DB	NE	CC	KM	NE	CC	CC	KM	CC

Table B.1

Ch. Vs.	13. 6a	13. 6b	13. 7	13. 8a	13. 8b	13. 9	13. 13	13. 14	13. 16	13. 18	13. 20	13. 21	13. 23	14. 2
MT	.	.	.	ak	ak	ak	ak	.	ak	ak	ak	.	.	.
B	.	.	−	.	.	.	.	.	.	.	kk	.	.	.
967	o	o	o	o	o	o	.	.	o	o	o	.	.	.
Bo	.	.	.	.	.	.	.	.	.	.	.	.	.	.
A	.	.	.	ak	ak	ak	ak	.	ak	ak	kk	.	.	.
26	.	.	.	ak	.	ak	ak	.	ak	ak	kk	.	.	.
106	.	.	.	ak	ak	ak	kak	.	ak	ak	.	.	.	.
410	.	.	.	ak	ak	ak	ak	.	ak	ak	kk	.	.	.
544	.	.	.	ak	ak	ak	ak	.	ak	ak	kk	.	.	.
Aeth	.	.	.	ak	ak	ak	ak	.	ak	ak	kk	.	.	.
Arab	.	.	.	ak	ak	ak	ak	.	ak	ak	kk	.	.	.
Q	.	.	.	ak	ak	ak	ak	.	ak	ak	kk	.	.	.
88	.	.	.	ka	ak	ak	ak	.	ak	ak	kk	.	.	.
Syh	.	.	.	ak	ak	ak	ak	.	ak	ak	kk	.	.	.
62	.	.	.	ak	ak	ak	ak	.	ak	ak	ak	.	.	.
147	.	.	.	ak	ak	ak	ak	.	ak	ak	kk	.	.	.
407	.	.	.	ak	ak	.	ak	.	ak	ak	kk	.	.	.
22	.	.	.	ak	ak	ak	ak	ak	ak	ak	ak	.	.	.
36	.	.	.	ak	ak	ak	ak	ak	ak	ak	ka	.	.	.
48	.	.	.	ak	ak	ak	ak	ak	ak	ak	ak	.	.	.
51	.	.	.	ak	ak	ak	ak	ak	ak	ak	ak	.	.	.
96	.	.	.	ak	ak	ak	ak	ak	ak	ak	ak	.	.	.
231	.	.	.	ak	ak	ak	ak	ak	ak	ak	ak	.	.	.
763	.	.	.	ak	ak	ak	ak	ak	ak	ak	ak	.	.	.
311	.	.	.	ak	ak	ak	ak	ak	ak	ak	ak	.	.	.
538	.	.	.	ak	ak	ak	ak	.	ak	ak	.	.	kk	.
V	.	.	.	ak	ak	ak	ak	ak	ak	ak	ak	.	.	.
46	.	−	.	ak	ak	ak	ak	.	ak	ak	ak	.	.	.
449	.	.	.	ak	ak	ak	ak	ak	ak	ak	ak	.	.	.
87	.	−	.	ak	ak	ak	ak	.	ak	ak	kk	.	.	.
91	.	−	.	ak	ak	ak	ak	.	ak	ak	kk	.	.	.
490	.	−	.	ak	ak	ak	ak	.	ak	ak	kk	.	.	.
49	.	−	.	ak	ak	ak	ak	.	ak	ak	kk	.	.	.
90	.	−	.	ak	ak	ak	ak	.	ak	ak	kk	.	.	.
764	.	−	.	ak	ak	ak	ak	.	ak	ak	kk	.	.	.
130	.	.	.	ak	ak	ak	ak	.	ak	ak	kk	.	.	.
233	.	.	.	ak	ak	ak	ak	.	ak	ak	kk	.	.	.
534	.	.	.	ak	ak	ak	ak	.	ak	ak	kk	.	.	.
239	.	.	.	ak	ak	ak	ak	.	ak	ak	kk	.	.	.
306	.	.	.	ak	ak	ak	ak	.	ak	ak	kk	.	.	.
403	.	.	.	ak	ak	ak	ak	.	ak	ak	kk	.	.	.
613	.	.	.	ak	ak	ak	ak	.	ak	ak	kk	.	.	.
La:														
W														
Tyc														
S	o	o	o	o	o	o	o	o	.	.	.	.	.	.
C														
Form	NE	MS	NE	KM	NE	YD	KM	YD	NE	KM	KM	YD	YD	CC

Ch. Vs.	14. 4a	14. 4b	14. 6	14. 7	14. 8	14. 9	14. 11	14. 12	14. 14	14. 16	14. 18	14. 20	14. 21	14. 23
MT	ak	.	ak	.	.	.	ak	.	ak	ak	ak	ak	ak	ak
B	.	.	kk	.	.	.	.	.	.	.	.	.	.	.
967	o	o	o	.	.	.	o	o	o	.	.	.	o	kt
Bo	.	.	.	.	.	.	.	.	.	.	.	.	.	.
A	ak	.	kkt	.	.	.	ak	.	ak	.	.	.	ak	.
26	.	.	kt	.	.	.	.	.	ak	.	.	.	ak	.
106	ak	.	kk	.	.	—	ak	.	ak	ak	ak	ak	ak	ak
410	ak	.	kt	.	.	.	ak	.	ak	ak	ak	ak	ak	ak
544	.	.	kt	.	.	.	ak	.	ak	.	.	.	ak	.
Aeth	ak	.	ak	.	.	—	ak	.	ak	ak	ak	ak	ak	ak
Arab	ak	.	kkt	.	.	.	ak	.	ak	ak	ak	ak	ak	ak
Q	ak	.	kk	.	.	.	ak	.	ak	ak	ak	ak	ak	ak
88	ak	.	kk	.	.	.	ak	.	ak	ak	ak	ak	ak	ak
Syh	ak	.	kk	.	.	.	ak	.	ak	ak	ak	ak	ak	ak
62	ak	.	ak	.	.	.	ak	.	ak	ak	ak	ak	ak	ak
147	ak	.	.	.	.	.	.	ak	ak	ak	ak	ak	ak	ak
407	ak	.	kk	.	.	.	ak	.	ak	ak	ak	ak	ak	ak
22	ak	.	ak	.	.	.	ak	.	ak	ak	ak	ak	ak	ak
36	ak	.	ak	.	.	.	ak	.	ak	ka	ak	ak	ak	ak
48	ak	.	ak	.	.	.	ak	.	ak	ak	ak	ak	ak	ak
51	ak	.	ak	.	.	.	ak	.	ak	ak	ak	ak	ak	ak
96	ak	.	ak	.	.	.	ak	.	ak	ak	ak	ak	ak	ak
231	ak	.	ak	.	.	.	ak	.	ak	ak	ak	ak	ak	ak
763	ak	.	ak	.	.	.	ak	.	ak	ak	ak	ak	ak	ak
311	ak	.	ak	.	.	—	ak	.	ak	ak	ak	ak	ak	ak
538	ak	.	kk	.	.	.	ak	.	ak	ak	ak	ak	ak	ak
V	ak	.	ak	.	.	.	ak	.	ak	ak	ak	ak	ak	ak
46	ak	.	ak	.	.	.	ak	.	ak	ak	ak	ak	ak	ak
449	ak	.	ak	.	.	.	ak	.	ak	ak	ak	ak	ak	ak
87	ak	.	kt	.	.	.	ak	.	ak	ak	ak	ak	ak	ak
91	ak	.	kt	.	.	.	ak	.	ak	ak	ak	ak	ak	ak
490	ak	.	kt	.	.	.	ak	.	ak	ak	ak	ak	ak	ak
49	ak	.	kt	.	.	.	ak	.	ak	ak	ak	ak	ak	ak
90	ak	.	kt	.	.	.	ak	.	ak	ak	ak	ak	ak	ak
764	ak	.	kt	.	.	.	ak	.	ak	ak	ak	ak	ak	ak
130	akk	.	kkt	.	.	.	ak	.	ak	ak	ak	ak	ak	ak
233	ak	.	kkt	.	.	.	ak	.	ak	ak	ak	ak	ak	ak
534	ak	.	kt	.	.	.	ak	.	ak	ak	ak	ak	ak	ak
239	ak	.	kkt	.	.	.	ak	.	ak	ak	ak	ak	ak	ak
306	ak	.	kkt	.	.	.	ak	.	ak	ak	ak	ak	ak	ak
403	.	.	kt	.	.	.	.	.	ak	ak	.	ak	ak	ak
613	.	.	kt	.	.	.	.	.	ak	ak	.	ak	ak	ak
La:														
W														
Tyc														
S	.	.	.	.	.	.	.	.	.	—	.	.	.	.
C														
Form	KM	MS	KM	MS	YD	MS	NE	CC	NE	NE	NE	NE	KM	NE

Table B.1

Ch. Vs.	15.1	15.6	15.7	15.8	16.1	16.3	16.8	16.14	16.19	16.23	16.30	16.35	16.36	16.43
MT	.	ak	.	ak	.	ak	ak	ak	ak	ak	ak	.	ak	ak
B	.	.	.	.	.	.	.	.	.	.	.	.	.	.
967	.	.	o	o	o	.	kt	o	kt	o	.	.	.	kt
Bo	.	.	.	.	.	.	.	.	.	.	.	.	.	.
A	.	ak	.	.	.	.	ak	.	.	.	.	.	ak	.
26	.	ak	.	.	.	.	.	.	.	.	.	.	ak	.
106	.	ak	.	ak	.	ak	ak	ak	ak	ak	ak	.	ak	ak
410	.	ak	.	ak	.	ak	ak	ak	ak	ak	ak	.	ak	ak
544	.	ak	.	.	.	.	.	.	.	.	.	.	ak	.
Aeth	.	ak	.	ak	.	ak	ak	ak	ak	ak	ak	.	ak	ak
Arab	.	ak	.	ak	.	ak	ak	ak	ak	ak	ak	.	ak	ak
Q	.	ak	.	ak	.	ak	ak	ak	ak	ak	ak	.	ak	ak
88	.	ak	.	ak	.	ak	ak	ak	ak	ak	ak	.	ak	ak
Syh	.	ak	.	ak	.	ak	ak	ak	ak	ak	ak	.	ak	ak
62	.	ak	.	ak	.	ak	kt	ak	ak	ak	ak	.	akt	ak
147	.	.	.	ak	.	ak	ak	ak	ak	ak	ak	.	ak	ak
407	.	.	.	ak	.	ak	ak	ak	ak	ak	ak	.	ak	ak
22	.	ak	.	ak	.	ak	ak	ak	ak	ak	ak	.	ak	ak
36	.	ak	.	ak	.	ak	ak	ak	ak	ak	ak	.	ak	ak
48	.	ak	.	ak	.	ak	ka	ak	ak	ak	ak	.	ak	ak
51	.	ak	.	ak	.	ak	ak	ak	ak	ak	ak	.	ak	ak
96	.	ak	.	ak	.	ak	ak	ak	ak	ak	ak	.	ak	ak
231	.	ak	.	ak	.	ak	ak	ak	ak	ak	ak	.	ak	ak
763	.	ak	.	ak	.	ak	ak	ak	ak	ak	ak	.	ak	ak
311	.	ak	.	ak	.	ak	ak	ak	ak	ak	ak	.	ak	ak
538	.	ak	.	ak	.	ak	ak	ak	ak	ak	ak	.	ak	ak
V	.	ak	.	ak	.	ak	ak	ak	ak	ak	ak	.	ak	ak
46	.	ak	.	ak	.	ak	ak	ak	ak	ak	ak	.	ak	ak
449	.	ak	.	ak	.	ak	ak	ak	ak	ak	ak	.	ak	ak
87	.	ak	.	ak	.	ak	ak	ak	ak	ak	ak	.	ak	ak
91	.	ak	.	ak	.	ak	ak	ak	ak	ak	ak	.	ak	ak
490	.	ak	.	ak	.	ak	ak	ak	ak	ak	ak	.	ak	ak
49	.	ak	.	ak	.	ak	ak	ak	ak	ak	ak	.	ak	ak
90	.	ak	.	ak	.	ak	ak	ak	ak	ak	ak	.	ak	ak
764	.	ak	.	ak	.	ak	ak	ak	ak	ak	ak	.	ak	ak
130	.	ak	.	ak	.	ak	ak	ak	ak	ak	ak	.	ak	ak
233	.	ak	.	ak	.	ak	ak	ak	ak	ak	ak	.	ak	ak
534	.	ak	.	ak	.	ak	ak	ak	ak	ak	ak	.	ak	ak
239	.	ak	.	ak	.	ak	ak	ak	ak	ak	ak	.	ak	ak
306	.	ak	.	ak	.	ak	ak	ak	ak	ak	ak	.	ak	ak
403	.	ak	.	.	.	.	.	.	.	.	.	.	ak	.
613	.	ak	.	.	.	.	.	.	.	.	.	.	ak	.
La:														
W														
Tyc														
S	.	.	.	.	.	.	.	.	.	.	.	.	.	.
C														
Form	CC	KM	YD	NE	CC	KM	NE	NE	NE	NE	NE	CC	KM	NE

Ch.	16.	16.	16.	16.	16.	17.	17.	17.	17.	17.	17.	17.	17.	17.
Vs.	48	58	59	62	63	1	3	9	11	16	19	21	22	24a
MT	ak	.	ak	.	ak	.	ak	ak	.	ak	ak	.	ak	.
B														
967	o	.	–	kt	.	.	.	kt	.	kt	kt	.	.	o
Bo	.	.	.	.	.	.	.	.	.	.	.	.	.	.
A	.	.	ak	.	.	.	.	.	.	.	.	.	.	.
26	.	.	ak	.	.	.	.	.	.	.	.	.	.	.
106	ak	.	ak	.	ak	.	ak	ak	.	ak	ak	.	ak	.
410	ak	.	ak	.	ak	.	ak	ak	.	ak	ak	.	akk	.
544	.	.	ak	.	.	.	.	.	.	.	.	.	.	.
Aeth	ak	.	ak	.	ak	.	ak	ak	.	ak	ak	.	ak	.
Arab	ak	.	ak	.	ak	.	ak	ak	.	ak	ak	.	ak	.
Q	ak	.	ak	.	ak	.	ak	ak	.	ak	ak	.	ak	.
88	ak	.	ak	.	ak	.	ak	ak	.	ak	ak	.	ak	.
Syh	ak	.	ak	.	ak	.	ak	ak	.	ak	ak	.	ak	.
62	ak	.	ak	.	ak	.	at	ak	.	ak	ak	.	ak	.
147	ak	.	ak	.	ak	.	ak	ak	.	ak	ak	.	ak	.
407	ak	.	ak	.	ak	.	ak	ak	.	ak	ak	.	ak	.
22	ak	.	ak	.	ak	.	ak	ak	.	ak	ak	.	ak	.
36	ak	.	ak	.	ak	.	ak	ak	.	ak	ak	.	ak	.
48	ak	.	ak	.	ak	.	ak	ak	.	ak	ak	.	ak	.
51	ak	.	ak	.	ak	.	ak	ak	.	ak	ak	.	ak	.
96	ak	.	ak	.	ak	.	ak	ak	.	ak	ak	.	ak	.
231	ak	.	ak	.	ak	.	ak	ak	.	ak	ak	.	ak	.
763	ak	.	ak	.	ak	.	ak	ak	.	ak	ak	.	ak	.
311	ak	.	ak	.	ak	.	ak	ak	.	ak	ak	.	ak	.
538	ak	.	ak	.	ak	"	ak	ak	.	ak	ak	.	ak	.
V	ak	.	ak	.	ak	.	ak	ak	.	ak	ak	.	ak	.
46	ak	.	ak	.	ak	.	ak	ak	.	ak	ak	.	ak	.
449	ak	.	ak	.	ak	.	ak	ak	.	ak	ak	.	ak	.
87	ak	.	ak	.	ak	.	ak	ak	.	ak	ak	.	ak	.
91	ak	.	ak	.	ak	.	ak	ak	.	ak	ak	.	ak	.
490	ak	.	ak	.	ak	.	ak	ak	.	ak	ak	.	ak	.
49	ak	.	ak	.	ak	.	ak	ak	.	ak	ak	.	ak	.
90	ak	.	ak	.	ak	.	ak	ak	.	ak	ak	.	ak	.
764	ak	.	ak	.	ak	.	ak	ak	.	ak	ak	.	ak	.
130	ak	.	ak	.	ak	.	ak	ak	.	ak	ak	.	ak	.
233	ak	.	ak	.	ak	.	ak	ak	.	ak	ak	.	ak	.
534	ak	.	ak	.	ak	.	ak	ak	.	ak	ak	.	ak	.
239	ak	.	ak	.	ak	.	ak	ak	.	ak	ak	.	ak	.
306	ak	.	ak	.	ak	.	ak	ak	.	ak	ak	.	ak	.
403	.	.	ak	.	.	.	.	kk	.	.	.	.	.	.
613	.	.	ak	.	.	.	.	kk	.	.	.	.	.	.
La:														
W														
Tyc														
S														
C	o	.	–	.	.	.	.	o	o	o	o	.	.	.
Form	NE	NE	KM	YD	NE	CC	KM	KM	CC	NE	KM	YD	KM	YD

Table B.1

Ch. Vs.	17. 24b	18. 1	18. 3	18. 9	18. 23	18. 30	18. 32	20. 1	20. 2	20. 3a	20. 3b	20. 5a	20. 5b	20. 7
MT	.	.	ak	ak	ak	ak	ak	.	.	ak	ak	ak	kt	kt
B	.	.	.	.	.	.	-	.	.	.	.	.	kt	kt
967	.	.	.	.	.	.	-	.	.	.	.	.	-	kt
Bo	.	.	.	.	-	.	.	.	.	.	.	-	kt	kt
A	.	.	ak	ak	kk	ak	ak	.	.	.	ak	kt	kt	kt
26	.	.	.	.	kk	ak	ak	.	.	.	.	kt	kt	kt
106	.	.	ak	ak	.	ak	ak	.	.	ak	ak	kt	-	kt
410	.	.	ak	ak	.	ak	ak	.	.	ak	ak	akt	kt	kt
544	.	.	.	.	kk	ak	ak	.	.	.	ak	kt	kt	kt
Aeth	.	.	ak	ak	.	ak	ak	.	.	ak	ak	ak	kt	kt
Arab	.	.	ak	ak	.	ak	ak	.	.	ak	ak	ak	kt	kt
Q	.	.	ak	ak	kk	ak	ak	.	.	ak	ak	kt	kt	kt
88	.	.	ak	ak	kk	ak	ak	.	.	ak	ak	ak	kt	kt
Syh	.	.	ak	ak	kk	ak	ak	.	.	ak	ak	kk	kt	kt
62	.	.	ak	ak	*	ak	ak	.	.	ak	ak	ak	kt	kt
147	.	.	ak	ak	.	ak	ak	.	.	ak	ak	kt	kt	kt
407	.	.	ak	ak	.	ak	ak	.	.	ak	ak	kt	kt	kt
22	.	.	ak	ak	ak	ak	ak	.	.	ak	ak	ak	kt	kt
36	.	.	ak	ak	ak	ak	ak	.	.	ak	ak	ak	kt	kt
48	.	.	ak	ak	ak	ak	ak	.	.	ak	ak	ak	kt	kt
51	.	.	ak	ak	ak	ak	ak	.	.	ak	ak	ak	kt	kt
96	.	.	ak	ak	ak	ak	ak	.	.	ak	ak	ak	kt	kt
231	.	.	ak	ak	ak	ak	ak	.	.	ak	ak	ak	kt	kt
763	.	.	ak	ak	ak	ak	ak	.	.	ak	ak	ak	kt	kt
311	.	.	ak	ak	ak	ak	ak	.	.	ak	ak	ak	kt	kt
538	.	.	ak	ak	ak	ak	ak	.	.	ak	ak	ak	kt	kt
V	.	.	ak	ak	ak	ak	ak	.	.	ak	ak	ak	kt	kt
46	.	.	ak	ak	ak	ak	ak	.	.	ak	ak	ak	kt	kt
449	.	.	ak	ak	-	ak	ak	.	.	ak	ak	ak	kt	kt
87	.	.	ak	ak	.	ak	ak	.	.	ak	ak	.	kt	kt
91	.	.	ak	ak	kk	ak	ak	.	.	ak	ak	.	kt	kt
490	.	.	ak	ak	kk	ak	ak	.	.	ak	ak	.	kt	kt
49	.	.	ak	ak	kk	ak	ak	.	.	ak	ak	kt	kt	kt
90	.	.	ak	ak	kk	ak	ak	.	.	ak	ak	kt	kt	kt
764	.	.	ak	ak	kk	ak	ak	.	.	ak	ak	kt	kt	kt
130	.	.	ak	ak	kk	ak	ak	.	.	ak	ak	kt	kt	kt
233	.	.	ak	ak	kk	ak	ak	.	.	ak	ak	kt	kt	kt
534	-	.	ak	ak	kk	ak	ak	.	.	ak	ak	kt	-	kt
239	.	.	.	ak	kk	ak	ak	.	.	ak	ak	kt	kt	kt
306	.	.	.	ak	kk	ak	ak	.	.	ak	ak	kt	kt	kt
403	.	.	.	.	kk	ak	ak	.	.	.	ak	kt	kt	kt
613	.	.	.	.	kk	ak	ak	.	.	.	ak	kt	kt	kt
La: W Tyc 3	o	.	.	.	.	.	.	.	.	.	.	.	kt	kt
;	.	.	.	.	o	o	o	o	o	o	o	o	o	o
Form	DB	CC	NE	NE	NE	NE	NE	MS	CC	KM	NE	KM	MS	MS

237

| Ch. | 20. | 20. | 20. | 20. | 20. | 20. | 20. | 20. | 20. | 20. | 20. | 20. | 20. | 20. |
Vs:	12	19	20	26	27	30	31	33	36	38	39	40	42	44a
MT	.	kt	kt	.	ak	ak	ak	ak	ak	.	ak	ak	.	.
B	.	kt	kt	–	.	.	.	.	.	kk	kk	kk	.	.
967	kt	kt	kt	–	.	.	.	.	.	.	.	.	.	.
Bo	.	kt	kt	.	.	kkt	.	.	.	.	ak	ak	.	.
A	.	kt	kt	.	.	kkt	.	ak	kt	kt	kk	kk	.	.
26	.	kt	kt	.	.	kt	.	.	kt	kt	kkt	kk	.	.
106	.	kt	kt	.	ak	kk	.	ak	kk	.	kk	kk	kt	kt
410	.	kt	kt	.	ak	kt	.	ak	kt	kt	kkt	kk	.	.
544	.	kt	kt	.	.	kkt	.	.	kkt	kt	kkt	kk	.	.
Aeth	.	kt	kt	.	ak	kk	.	ak	kk	.	kk	kk	.	.
Arab	.	kt	kt	.	ak	kkt	.	ak	kkt	kt	kk	kk	.	.
Q	.	kt	kt	.	ak	kk	ak	ak	kk	.	kk	kk	.	.
88	.	kt	kt	.	ak	kk	ak	ak	kk	.	kk	kk	.	.
Syh	.	kt	kt	.	ak	kk	ak	ak	kk	.	kk	kk	.	.
62	.	kt	kt	.	ak	ak	ak	ak	ak	.	ak	ak	.	.
147	.	kt	.	.	ak	.	ak	ak	kk	.	kk	kk	.	.
407	.	kt	kt	.	ak	kk	ak	ak	.	.	kk	kk	.	.
22	.	kt	kt	.	ak	ak	ak	ak	ak	.	ak	ak	.	.
36	.	kt	kt	.	ak	ak	ak	ak	ak	.	ak	ak	.	.
48	.	kt	kt	.	ak	ak	ak	ak	ak	.	ak	ak	.	.
51	.	kt	kt	.	ak	ak	ak	ak	ak	.	ak	ak	.	.
96	.	kt	kt	.	ak	ak	ak	ak	ak	.	ak	ak	.	.
231	.	kt	kt	.	ak	ak	ak	ak	ak	.	ak	ak	.	.
763	.	kt	kt	.	ak	ak	ak	ak	ak	.	ak	ak	.	.
311	.	kt	kt	.	ak	ak	ak	ak	ak	.	ak	ak	.	.
538	.	kt	kt	.	ak	ak	ak	ak	ak	.	ak	ak	.	.
V	.	kt	kt	.	ak	ak	ak	ak	ak	.	ak	ak	.	.
46	.	kt	kt	.	ak	ak	ak	ak	ak	.	ak	ak	.	.
449	.	kt	kt	.	ak	ak	ak	ak	ak	.	ak	ak	.	.
87	.	kt	kt	.	ak	kt	ak	ak	kt	kt	kkt	kk	.	.
91	.	kt	kt	.	ak	kt	ak	ak	kt	kt	kt	kk	.	.
490	.	kt	kt	.	ak	kt	ak	ak	kt	kt	kkt	kk	.	.
49	.	kt	kt	.	ak	kt	ak	ak	kt	kt	kkt	kk	.	.
90	.	kt	kt	.	ak	kt	ak	ak	kt	kt	kkt	kk	.	.
764	.	kt	kt	.	ak	kt	ak	ak	kt	kt	kkt	kk	.	.
130	.	kt	kt	.	ak	kkt	ak	ak	kkt	kt	kkt	kk	.	.
233	.	kt	kt	.	ak	kkt	ak	ak	kkt	kt	kkt	kk	.	.
534	.	kt	kt	.	ak	kt	ak	ak	kt	kt	kk	kk	.	.
239	.	kt	kt	.	ak	kkt	ak	ak	kkt	kt	kkt	kk	.	.
306	.	kt	kt	.	ak	kkt	ak	ak	kkt	kt	kkt	kk	.	.
403	.	kt	kt	.	.	kkt	ak	.	kkt	kt	kkt	kk	.	.
613	.	kt	kt	.	.	kkt	ak	.	kkt	kt	kkt	kk	.	.
La:														
W														
Tyc	o	o	o	o	o	o	.	.	.	.	o	o	o	o
S	.	kt	kt	–	.	.	.	.	.	.	.	.	.	.
C	o	kt	kt	–	o	.	.	.	.	.	.	.	.	.
Form	YD	MS	YD	YD	KM	KM	NE	NE	NE	YD	KM	NE	YD	YD

Table B.1

Ch. Vs.	20. 44b	21. 1	21. 3a	21. 3b	21. 4	21. 5	21. 6	21. 8	21. 10	21. 12	21. 13	21. 18	21. 22	21. 23
MT	ak	.	.	ak	.	ak	.	.	.	ak	.	ak	.	.
B	.	.	.	kk	.	kk	.	—	.	kk	.	kk	.	.
967	.	.	.	.	.	.	.	.	.	.	.	.	.	.
Bo	.	.	.	kti	.	.	.	ak	.	akt	.	.	.	.
A	ak	.	.	kti	.	kk	.	kt	.	kt	.	kk	.	.
26	kk	.	.	kkt	.	kk	.	kt	.	kkt	.	kk	.	.
106	ak	.	.	kk	.	kk	.	—	.	kk	.	kk	.	.
410	ak	.	.	kt	.	kk	.	kt	.	kk	.	kk	.	.
544	.	.	.	*	.	kk	.	kt	.	kkt	.	kk	.	.
Aeth	ak	.	.	kk	.	kk	.	kt	.	kkt	.	kk	.	.
Arab	ak	.	.	*	.	kk	.	.	.	kt	.	kk	.	.
Q	ak	.	.	kk	.	kk	.	kk	.	kk	.	kk	.	.
88	ak	.	.	.	.	kk	.	kk	.	kk	.	kk	.	.
Syh	ak	.	.	ak	.	kk	.	kk	.	kk	.	kk	.	.
62	.	.	.	ak	.	ak	.	.	.	ak	.	ak	.	.
147	ak	.	.	kk	.	kk	.	kk	.	kk	.	kk	.	.
407	ak	.	.	kk	.	kk	.	.	.	kk	.	kk	.	.
22	ak	.	.	ak	.	ak	.	ak	.	ak	.	ak	.	.
36	ak	.	.	ak	.	ak	.	akt	.	ak	.	ak	.	.
48	ak	.	.	ak	.	ak	.	ak	.	ak	.	ak	.	.
51	ak	.	.	ak	.	ak	.	ak	.	ak	.	ak	.	.
96	ak	.	.	ak	.	ak	.	ak	.	ak	.	ak	.	.
231	ak	.	.	ak	.	ak	.	ak	.	ak	.	ak	.	.
763	ak	.	.	ak	.	ak	.	ak	.	ak	.	ak	.	.
311	ak	.	.	ak	.	ak	.	ak	.	ak	.	ak	.	.
538	ak	.	.	ak	.	ak	.	ak	.	ak	.	ak	.	.
V	ak	.	.	ak	.	ak	.	ak	.	ak	.	ak	.	.
46	ak	.	.	ak	.	ak	.	ak	.	ak	.	kk	.	.
449	ak	.	.	ak	.	ak	.	ak	.	ak	.	ak	.	.
87	ak	.	.	kkt	.	kk	.	kt	.	kkt	.	kk	.	.
91	ak	.	.	kkt	.	kk	.	kt	.	kkt	.	kk	.	.
490	ak	.	.	kkt	.	kk	.	kt	.	kkt	.	kk	.	.
49	ak	.	.	kkt	.	kk	.	kt	.	kkt	.	kk	.	.
70	ak	.	.	kkt	.	kk	.	kt	.	kkt	.	kk	.	.
764	ak	.	.	kkt	.	kk	.	kt	.	kkt	.	kk	.	.
130	ak	.	.	kkt	.	kk	.	kt	.	kkt	.	kk	.	.
233	ak	.	.	kkt	.	kk	.	akt	.	kkt	.	kk	.	.
534	ak	.	.	kt	.	kk	.	kt	.	kt	.	kk	.	.
239	ak	.	.	*	.	kk	.	kt	.	kkt	.	kk	.	.
506	ak	.	.	*	.	kk	.	kt	.	kkt	.	kk	.	.
403	.	.	.	*	.	kk	.	kt	.	kt	.	kk	.	.
513	.	.	.	*	.	kk	.	kt	.	kt	.	kk	.	.
.a:														
yc	o	.	_	.	.	.	.	.	.	o	o	o	o	o
	.	.	—	.	o	o	o	o	o	o	o	o	o	o
orm	NE	CC	CC	KM	MS	AD	CC	KM	YD	NE	CC	NE	DB	CC

239

The Greek Text of Ezekiel

Ch. Vs.	21. 29	21. 31	21. 33	21. 37	22. 1	22. 3	22. 12	22. 14	22. 16	22. 17	22. 19	22. 22	22. 23	22. 28a
MT	ak	ak	ak	.	.	ak	ak	.	.	.	ak	.	.	ak
B	.	.	.	.	.	kk	.	.	.	.	.	.	.	.
967	.	.	.	—	.	.	.	.	.	.	.	.	.	.
Bo	kkt	.	.	.	.	.	.	.	.	.	.	.	.	.
A	kkt	kkt	kt	.	.	kkt	kk	.	.	.	kkt	.	.	.
26	kkt	.	kkt	.	.	kkt	.	.	.	.	kkt	.	.	.
106	kkt	kk	kk	.	.	kkt	kk	.	.	.	kk	.	.	.
410	kkt	kkt	kk	.	.	kt	kk	.	.	.	kkt	.	.	.
544	kkt	kkt	kkt	.	.	kkt	.	.	.	.	kt	.	.	.
Aeth	akk	kk	kk	.	.	kk	kk	.	.	.	kk	.	.	ak
Arab	kkt	kkt	kt	.	.	kkt	kk	.	.	.	kkt	.	.	ak
Q	kk	kk	kk	.	.	kk	kk	.	.	.	kk	.	.	ak
88	kk	kk	kk	.	.	kk	kk	.	.	.	kk	.	.	ak
Syh	kk	kk	kk	.	.	kk	kk	.	.	.	kk	.	.	ak
62	ak	ak	ak	—	.	ak	.	.	.	.	✱	.	.	ak
147	akk	kk	kk	—	.	kk	kk	.	.	.	kk	.	.	ak
407	kk	kk	kk	.	.	kk	ak	.	.	.	kk	.	.	ak
22	ak	ak	ak	.	.	ak	.	.	.	.	.	.	.	.
36	ak	ak	ak	.	.	ak	.	.	.	.	.	.	.	.
48	ak	ak	ak	.	.	ak	.	.	.	.	.	.	.	.
51	ak	ak	ak	.	.	ak	.	.	.	.	.	.	.	.
96	ak	ak	ak	.	.	ak	.	.	.	.	.	.	.	.
231	ak	ak	ak	.	.	ak	.	.	.	.	.	.	.	.
763	ak	ak	ak	.	.	ak	.	.	.	.	.	.	.	.
311	ak	ak	ak	.	.	ak	.	.	.	.	.	.	.	.
538	ak	ak	ak	.	.	ak	.	.	.	.	.	.	.	.
V	ak	ak	ak	.	.	ak	ak	.	.	.	ak	.	.	ak
46	ak	ak	ak	.	.	ak	ak	.	.	.	ak	.	.	.
449	ak	ak	ak	.	.	ak	ak	.	.	.	ak	.	.	ak
87	kkt	kk	kkt	.	.	kkt	kk	.	.	.	kk	.	.	ak
91	kkt	kk	kkt	.	.	kkt	kk	.	.	.	kk	.	.	ak
490	kkt	.	kkt	.	.	kkt	kk	.	.	.	kk	.	.	ak
49	kkt	kk	kkt	kk	kk	kkt	kk	.	.	.	kk	.	.	.
90	kkt	kk	kkt	.	.	kkt	kk	.	.	.	kk	.	.	.
764	kkt	kka	kkt	.	.	kkt	kk	.	.	.	kk	.	.	.
130	kkt	kk	kkt	.	.	kkt	kk	.	.	.	kk	.	.	.
233	kkt	kk	kkt	.	.	kkt	kk	.	.	.	kk	—	.	.
534	kt	kk	kt	.	.	kt	kk	.	.	.	kk	.	.	.
239	kkt	kkt	kkt	.	.	kkt	kk	.	.	.	kk	.	.	.
306	kkt	kk	kkt	.	.	kkt	kk	.	.	.	kk	.	.	.
403	kkt	kkt	kkt	.	.	kkt	.	.	.	.	kkt	.	.	.
613	kkt	kkt	kkt	.	.	kkt	.	.	.	.	kkt	.	.	.
La: W Tyc S C	.	.	.	.	.	.	o	o	o	o	o	o	o	o
Form	KM	KM	KM	DB	CC	KM	NE	DB	YD	CC	KM	DB	CC	K

Table B.1

Ch. Vs.	22. 28b	22. 31	23. 1	23. 22	23. 28	23. 32	23. 34	23. 35	23. 36	23. 46	23. 49	24. 1	24. 3	24. 6
MT	.	ak	.	ak	ak	ak	ak	ak	.	ak	ak	.	ak	ak
B	.	kk	.	.	kk	.	.	.	.	kk	.	.	.	.
967	-	.	.	.	.	.	.	.	-	.	.	.	kt	.
Bo	.	.	.	.	.	.	.	.	.	.	.	.	.	kk
A	.	kk	.	kkt	kkt	*	kkt	ak	.	ak	.	.	ak	ak
26	.	.	.	kkt	kkt	akt	kkt	ak	.	ak	.	.	ak	ak
106	.	kk	.	kk	kk	ak	-	.	.	kk	.	.	akk	ak
410	.	kk	.	kkt	kkt	kkt	kkt	ak	.	kk	.	.	ak	ak
544	.	kk	.	kkt	kkt	kkt	ak	ak	.	ak	.	.	ak	ak
Aeth	.	kk	.	kk	ak	.	ak	.	.	kk	.	.	kk	ak
Arab	.	kk	.	kk	kk	kk	ak	ak	.	kk	.	.	ak	kk
Q	.	kk	.	kk	kk	kk	ak	ak	.	kk	.	.	kk	ak
88	.	kk	.	kk	kk	kk	ak	ak	.	kk	kk	.	kk	ak
Syh	.	kk	.	kk	kk	kk	ak	ak	.	kk	kk	.	kk	ak
62	.	.	.	ak	ak	ak	.	.	.	ak	.	.	ak	.
147	.	ak	.	kk	kk	kk	ak	ak	.	kk	.	.	kk	ak
407	.	ak	.	.	kk	kk	ak	ak	.	kk	.	.	kk	ak
22	.	.	.	.	.	.	.	.	.	.	.	.	.	.
36	.	.	.	.	.	kk	ak	ak	.	.	kk	.	.	.
48	.	.	.	.	.	.	.	.	.	.	.	.	.	.
51	.	.	.	.	.	.	.	.	.	.	.	.	.	.
96	.	.	.	.	.	.	.	.	.	.	.	.	.	.
231	.	.	.	.	.	.	.	.	.	.	.	.	.	.
763	.	.	.	.	.	.	.	.	.	.	.	.	.	.
311	.	.	.	.	.	.	.	.	.	.	.	.	.	.
538	.	.	.	.	.	.	.	.	.	.	.	.	.	.
V	.	ak	.	ak	ak	ak	ak	ak	.	ak	ak	.	ak	ak
46	.	ak	.	ak	ak	ak	ak	-	.	ak	kk	.	ak	ak
449	.	ak	.	ak	ak	ak	ak	ak	.	ak	ak	.	ak	ak
87	.	kk	.	kk	kk	kk	ak	-	.	kk	kk	.	kk	ak
91	.	kk	.	kk	kk	kk	ak	ak	.	kk	kk	.	kk	ak
490	.	kk	.	kk	kk	kk	ak	ak	.	kk	kk	.	kk	ak
49	.	kk	.	kk	kk	kk	ak	ak	.	kk	kk	.	kk	ak
90	.	kk	.	kk	kk	kk	ak	ak	.	kk	kk	.	kk	ak
764	.	kk	.	kk	kk	kk	ak	-	.	kk	kk	.	kk	ak
130	.	kk	.	kk	kk	kk	ak	ak	.	kk	kk	.	kk	ak
233	.	kk	.	kk	kk	kk	ak	ak	.	kk	kk	.	kk	ak
534	.	kk	.	kk	kk	kk	ak	ak	.	kk	kk	.	.	ak
239	.	kk	.	kk	kk	kk	ak	ak	.	kk	kk	.	kk	ak
306	.	kk	.	kk	kk	kk	ak	ak	.	kk	kk	.	kk	ak
403	.	kk	.	kkt	kkt	kkt	kkt	ak	.	kk	kk	.	ak	ak
613	.	kk	.	kkt	kkt	kkt	kkt	ak	.	kk	kk	.	ak	ak
La: W	o	o	o	o	o	o	o	o	o	o	o	o	o	.
Tyc S	o	o	o	o	o	o	kt	.	.	.	.	.	.	.
Form	MS	NE	CC	KM	KM	KM	NE	KM	AM	KM	YD	CC	KM	KM

Ch. Vs.	24. 9	24. 14a	24. 14b	24. 15	24. 20	24. 21	24. 24	24. 27	25. 1	25. 3a	25. 3b	25. 5	25. 6	25. 7
MT	ak	.	ak	.	.	ak	ak	.	.	ak	ak	.	ak	.
B	.	.	.	.	.	.	.	.	.	.	.	.	.	.
967	kt	.	.	.	.	.	.	.	.	.	.	.	.	.
Bo	.	.	.	.	.	.	.	.	.	.	.	.	.	.
A	ak	.	ak	.	*	kkt	.	.	.	.	ak	.	kt	.
26	ak	.	ak	.	.	*	.	.	.	.	ak	.	kt	.
106	ak	.	ak	.	.	kk	ak	.	.	.	.	.	kt	.
410	ak	.	ak	.	.	kkt	ak	.	.	.	ak	.	kt	.
544	ak	.	ak	.	.	kkt	.	.	.	.	ak	.	kt	.
Aeth	ak	.	ak	.	.	kk	.	.	.	ak	ak	.	kk	.
Arab	ak	.	ak	.	.	kk	.	.	.	ak	ak	.	kk	.
Q	ak	.	ak	.	.	kk	ak	.	.	ak	ak	.	kk	.
88	ak	.	ak	.	.	kk	ak	.	.	ak	-	.	kk	.
Syh	ak	.	ak	.	.	kk	ak	.	.	ak	ak	ak	ak	.
62	.	.	ak	.	.	ak	.	.	.	.	.	.	.	.
147	ak	.	ak	.	.	kk	ak	.	.	ka	ak	.	kk	.
407	ak	.	ak	.	.	kk	ak	.	.	.	ak	-	kk	.
22	ak	.	.	.	.	.	.	.	.	.	.	.	.	.
36	ak	.	.	.	.	.	ak	.	.	.	ak	.	kk	.
48	ak	.	.	.	.	.	.	.	.	.	.	.	.	.
51	ak	.	.	.	.	.	.	.	.	.	.	.	.	.
96	ak	.	.	.	.	.	.	.	.	.	.	.	.	.
231	ak	.	.	.	.	.	.	.	.	.	.	.	.	.
763	ak	.	.	.	.	.	.	.	.	.	.	.	.	.
311	.	.	ak	.	.	.	.	.	.	.	.	.	.	.
538	.	.	ak	.	.	.	.	.	.	.	.	.	.	.
V	ak	.	ak	.	.	ak	ak	ak	.	ak	ak	ak	ak	ak
46	ak	.	ak	.	.	ak	ak	ak	.	ak	ak	ak	ak	ak
449	ak	.	ak	.	.	ak	ak	ka	.	ak	ak	ak	ak	ak
87	ak	.	.	.	.	.	ak	.	.	ak	ak	.	kk	.
91	ak	.	ak	.	.	kk	ak	.	.	ak	ak	.	kk	.
490	ak	.	ak	.	.	kk	ak	.	.	ak	ak	.	kk	.
49	ak	.	ak	.	.	kk	ak	.	.	ak	ak	.	kk	.
90	ak	.	ak	.	.	kk	ak	.	.	ak	ak	.	.	.
764	ak	.	ak	.	.	kk	ak	.	.	ak	ak	.	kk	.
130	ak	.	ak	.	.	kk	ak	.	.	ak	ak	.	kk	.
233	ak	.	ak	.	.	kk	ak	.	.	ak	ak	.	.	.
534	ak	.	ak	.	.	.	ak	.	.	ak	ak	.	kk	.
239	ak	.	ak	.	.	.	ak	.	.	ak	ak	.	kk	.
306	ak	.	ak	.	.	.	ak	.	.	ak	ak	.	kk	.
403	ak	.	ak	.	.	kkt	.	.	.	ak	ak	.	kt	.
613	ak	.	ak	.	.	kkt	.	.	.	ak	ak	.	kt	.
La:														
W	.	.	.	.	.	.	o	o	o	o	o	o	o	o
Tyc														
S	.	.	.	.	o	o	o	.	.	.	.	o	o	o
C	o	o	o	o	o	o	o	.	.	.	.	.	.	.
Form	KM	DB	NE	CC	CC	KM	YD	YD	CC	CC	KM	YD	KM	YD

242

h.s:	25.8	25.11	25.12	25.13	25.14	25.15	25.16	25.17	26.1	26.3	26.5	26.6	26.7	26.14a
T	ak	.	ak	ak	ak	ak	ak	.	.	ak	ak	.	ak	.
67	.	.	.	.	.	.	.	.	.	.	.	.	.	—
o	.	.	.	.	.	.	.	.	.	.	.	.	.	.
6	ak	.	ak	ak	.	ak	ak	.	.	ak	kk	.	ak	—
06	ak	.	ak	ak	ak	ak	ak	ak	.	ak	kk	.	ak	—
10	ak	.	ak	ak	ak	ak	ak	.	.	ak	kk	.	ak	—
44	ak	.	ak	ak	.	ak	ak	.	.	ak	kk	.	ak	—
eth	ak	.	ak	ak	ak	ak	ak	ak	.	ak	kk	.	ak	—
rab	ak	.	ka	ak	ak	ak	ak	ak	.	ak	kk	.	ak	—
8	ak	.	ak	ak	ak	ak	ak	ak	.	ak	kk	.	ak	—
yh	ak	.	ak	ak	ak	ak	ak	ak	.	ak	kk	.	ak	—
2	.	.	.	.	.	.	.	.	n	.	.	.	.	—
47	ak	.	ak	ak	ak	ak	ak	ak	.	ak	kk	.	ak	—
07	ak	.	ak	ak	ak	ak	ak	ak	.	ak	kk	.	ak	—
2	.	.	.	.	.	.	.	.	.	.	.	.	.	—
56	.	.	.	ak	.	.	.	.	.	.	.	.	.	—
8	.	.	.	.	.	.	.	.	.	.	.	.	.	—
1	.	.	.	.	.	.	.	.	.	.	.	.	.	—
6	.	.	.	.	.	.	.	.	.	.	.	.	.	—
31	.	.	.	.	.	.	.	.	.	.	.	.	.	—
63	.	.	.	.	.	.	.	.	.	.	.	.	.	—
11	.	.	.	.	.	.	.	.	.	.	.	.	.	—
38	.	.	.	.	.	.	.	.	.	.	.	.	.	—
	ak	.	ak	ak	ak	ak	ak	ak	.	ak	ak	.	ak	--
6	ak	.	ak	ak	ak	ak	ak	ak	.	ak	ak	.	ak	—
49	ak	.	ak	ak	ak	ak	ak	ak	.	ak	ak	.	ak	—
7	ak	.	ak	ak	ak	ak	ak	ak	.	ak	kk	.	ak	—
1	ak	.	ak	ak	ak	ak	ak	ak	.	ak	kk	.	ak	—
90	ak	.	ak	ak	ak	ak	ak	ak	.	ak	kk	.	ak	—
9	ak	.	ak	ak	ak	ak	ak	ak	.	ak	kk	.	ak	—
0	ak	.	ak	ak	ak	ak	ak	ak	.	ak	kk	.	ak	—
764	ak	.	ak	ak	ak	ak	ak	ak	.	ak	kk	.	ak	—
30	ak	.	ak	ak	ak	ak	ak	ak	.	ak	akk	.	ak	—
233	ak	.	ak	ak	ak	.	ak	ak	.	ak	kk	.	ak	—
34	ak	.	ak	ak	ak	ak	ak	ak	.	ak	akk	.	ak	—
239	ak	.	ak	ak	ak	ak	ak	ak	.	ak	akk	.	ak	—
06	ak	.	ak	ak	ak	ak	ak	ak	.	ak	akk	.	ak	—
03	ak	.	ak	ak	.	ak	ak	.	.	ak	.	.	ak	—
13	ak	.	ak	ak	.	ak	ak	.	.	ak	.	.	ak	—
a: W Tyc	o	o	o	o	o	o	o	o	o	o	o	o	o	—
B C	.	.	.	.	o	o	o	o	o	o	o	o	o	—
Form	KM	YD	KM	KM	NE	KM	KM	YD	CC	KM	NE	YD	KM	DB

243

Ch. Vs.	26. 14b	26. 15	26. 19	26. 21	27. 1	27. 3	28. 1	28. 2	28. 6	28. 10	28. 11	28. 12	28. 20	28. 2
MT	ak	ak	ak	ak	.	ak	.	ak	ak	ak	.	ak	.	a
B	.	kk	kk	kk	.	.	.	.	.	.	.	kk	.	.
967	.	−	.	.	.	.	.	.	.	.	.	.	.	.
Bo	.	.	.	.	.	.	.	kt	kt	.	.	−	.	.
A	.	akk	kk	kkt	.	akk	.	kt	kkt	.	.	.	.	.
26	.	ak	kk	kk	.	ak	.	kt	kt	.	.	ak	.	a
106	ak	kk	kk	kk	.	kk	.	kk	kk	ak	.	kk	.	a
410	ak	.	kk	kt	.	kk	.	kt	kk	ak	.	ak	.	a
544	.	ak	kk	kkt	.	akk	.	kt	kkt	.	.	ak	.	a
Aeth	ak	akk	akk	akk	.	kk	.	kk	kk	ak	.	kk	.	a
Arab	ak	kk	kk	kk	.	.	.	kk	kkt	ak	.	kk	.	a
Q	ak	kk	kk	kk	.	kk	.	kk	kk	ak	.	kk	.	a
88	ak	kk	kk	kk	.	kk	.	kk	kk	ak	.	kk	.	a
Syh	ak	kk	kk	kk	.	kk	.	kk	kk	ak	.	kk	.	a
62	.	.	ak	.	.	.	.	.	.	.	.	ak	.	a
147	ak	ak	ak	.	.	.	.	.	.	.	.	ak	.	a
407	ak	ak	kk	.	.	kk	.	.	kk	ak	.	kk	.	a
22	.	.	.	.	.	.	.	ak	ak	ak	.	ak	.	a
36	.	ak	kk	.	.	kk	.	ak	ak	ak	.	ak	.	a
48	.	.	.	.	.	.	.	ak	ak	ak	.	ak	.	a
51	.	.	.	.	.	.	.	ak	ak	ak	.	ak	.	a
96	.	.	.	.	.	.	.	ak	ak	ak	.	ak	.	a
231	.	.	.	.	.	.	.	ak	ak	ak	.	ak	.	a
763	.	.	.	.	.	.	.	ak	ak	ak	.	ak	.	a
311	.	.	.	.	.	−	.	ak	ak	ak	.	ak	.	a
538	.	.	.	.	.	−	.	ak	ak	ak	.	ak	.	a
V	ak	ak	ak	ak	.	ak	.	ak	ak	ak	.	ak	.	a
46	ak	ak	ak	ak	.	.	.	ak	ak	ak	.	ak	.	a
449	ak	ak	ak	ak	.	ak	.	ak	ak	ak	.	ak	.	a
87	ak	kk	kk	kk	.	kk	.	kk	kk	ak	.	kk	.	a
91	ak	kk	kk	kk	.	kk	.	kk	kk	ak	.	kk	.	a
490	ak	kk	kk	kk	.	kk	.	kk	kk	ak	.	kk	.	a
49	ak	kk	kk	kk	.	kk	.	kk	kk	ak	.	kk	.	a
90	ak	kk	kk	kk	.	kk	.	kk	kk	ak	.	kk	.	a
764	ak	kk	kk	kk	.	kk	.	kk	kk	ak	.	kk	.	a
130	ak	kk	kk	kk	.	kk	.	kk	kk	ak	.	kk	.	a
233	ak	kk	kk	kk	.	kk	.	kk	kk	ak	.	kk	.	a
534	ak	kk	kk	kk	.	.	.	kk	kk	ak	.	kk	.	a
239	ak	akk	kk	kk	.	kk	.	kk	kk	ak	.	kk	.	a
306	ak	akk	kk	kk	.	kk	.	kk	kk	ak	.	kk	.	a
403	.	ak	akk	kkt	.	ak	.	kt	kkt	.	.	ak	.	.
613	.	ak	akk	kkt	.	ak	.	kt	kkt	.	.	ak	.	.
La: W	.	.	.	−	.	.	o	o	o	o	o	o	o	o
Tyc	o	.	o	o	o	o	o	o	.	.	.	.	o	o
S														
C	.	.	.	.	.	.	o	.	.	.	.	−	o	o
Form	NE	KM	KM	NE	CC	KM	CC	KM	KM	NE	CC	KM	CC	KM

244

Ch. Vs.	28. 22b	28. 23	28. 24	28. 25	28. 26	29. 1	29. 3	29. 6	29. 8	29. 9	29. 13	29. 16	29. 17	29. 19
MT	.	.	ak	ak	kt	.	ak	.	ak	.	ak	ak	.	ak
B	.	.	.	kk	kt	.	.	.	.	.	.	.	.	kk
967	.	.	.	.	kt	.	.	.	.	.	.	.	.	.
Bo	.	.	.	−	kt	.	.	.	.	.	.	.	.	.
A	.	.	kt	kkt	kt	.	kt	.	kt	.	kk	kt	.	ak
26	.	.	kt	kkt	kt	.	kt	.	kt	.	kk	kt	.	ak
106	.	.	ak	−	kt	.	kk	.	kk	.	kk	ak	.	kk
410	.	.	ak	ak	kt	.	kk	.	kk	.	kk	*	.	ak
544	.	.	kt	kkt	kt	.	kt	.	kt	.	.	kt	.	ak
Aeth	.	.	ak	ak	kt	.	kk	.	kk	.	kk	ak	.	kk
Arab	.	.	ak	akt	kt	.	kk	.	kk	.	kk	ak	.	kk
Q	.	.	ak	ak	kt	.	kk	.	kk	.	kk	ak	.	kk
88	.	.	ak	ak	kt	.	kk	.	kk	.	kk	ak	.	kk
Syh	.	.	ak	ak	kt	.	kk	.	kk	.	kk	ak	.	kk
62	.	.	.	.	kt	.	kk	.	.	.	.	.	.	.
147	.	.	.	.	kt	.	kk	.	.	.	.	.	.	.
407	.	.	ak	ak	kt	.	kk	.	kk	.	kk	ak	.	kk
22	.	.	ak	ak	kt	.	ak	.	ak	.	ak	ak	.	ak
36	.	.	ak	ak	kt	.	ak	.	ak	.	ak	ak	.	ak
48	.	.	ak	ak	kt	.	ak	.	ak	.	ak	ak	.	ak
51	.	.	ak	ak	kt	.	ak	.	ak	.	ak	ak	.	ak
96	.	.	ak	ak	kt	.	ak	.	ak	.	ak	ak	.	ak
231	.	.	ak	ak	kt	.	ak	.	ak	.	ak	ak	.	ak
763	.	.	ak	ak	kt	.	ak	.	ak	.	ak	ak	.	ak
311	.	.	ak	ak	kt	.	ak	.	ak	.	ak	ak	.	.
538	.	.	ak	ak	kt	.	ak	.	ak	.	ak	ak	.	ak
V	.	.	ak	ak	kt	.	ak	.	ak	.	ak	ak	.	ak
46	.	.	ak	ak	kt	.	ak	.	ak	.	ak	ak	.	ak
449	.	.	ak	ak	kt	.	ak	.	ak	.	ak	ak	.	ak
87	.	.	ak	ak	kt	.	kk	.	kk	.	kk	ak	.	kk
91	.	.	ak	ak	kt	.	kk	.	kk	.	kk	ak	.	kk
490	.	.	ak	ak	kt	.	kk	.	kk	.	kk	ak	.	.
49	.	.	kk	ak	kt	.	kk	.	kk	.	kk	ak	.	kk
90	.	.	kk	ak	kt	.	kk	.	kk	.	kk	ak	.	kk
764	.	.	kk	ak	kt	.	kk	.	kk	.	kk	ak	.	kk
130	.	.	ak	ak	kt	.	kk	.	kk	.	kk	ak	.	kk
233	.	.	ak	ak	kt	.	kk	.	kk	.	kk	ak	.	kk
534	.	.	kk	ak	kt	.	kk	.	.	kt	kk	ak	.	kk
239	.	.	ak	ak	kt	.	kk	.	kk	.	kk	ak	.	kk
306	.	.	ak	ak	kt	.	kk	.	kk	.	kk	ak	.	kk
403	.	.	kt	kkt	kt	.	*	.	kt	.	kk	kt	.	ak
613	.	.	kt	kkt	kt	.	*	.	kt	.	kk	kt	.	ak
La: W Tyc S C	o	o	o	o	o	o	o	o	o	o	o	.	.	o
Form	YD	YD	YD	KM	YD	CC	KM	YD	KM	YD	KM	YD	CC	KM

Ch. Vs.	29.20	29.21	30.1	30.2	30.3	30.6a	30.6b	30.8	30.10	30.12	30.13	30.19	30.20	30.22
MT	ak	.	.	ak	.	.	ak	.	ak	.	ak	.	.	ak
B	kk	.	.	.	.	—	.	.	kk	.	kk	.	.	kk
967	.	.	.	.	.	—	.	.	.	.	.	.	.	.
Bo	ak	.	.	.	.	—	.	.	.	.	kk	.	.	kk
A	ak	.	.	.	.	—	.	.	ak	.	ak	.	.	kk
26	ak	.	.	.	.	—	.	.	ak	.	ak	.	.	kk
106	kk	.	.	ak	.	—	ak	.	kk	.	kk	.	.	kk
410	ak	.	.	ak	.	—	ak	.	ak	.	kk	.	.	kk
544	ak	.	.	.	.	—	.	.	ak	.	ak	.	.	kk
Aeth	kk	.	.	akk	.	—	ak	.	kk	.	kk	.	.	kk
Arab	kk	.	.	ak	.	—	ak	.	kk	.	kk	.	.	kk
Q	kk	.	.	ak	.	ak	ak	.	kk	.	kk	.	.	kk
88	kk	.	.	ak	.	ak	ak	.	kk	.	kk	.	.	kk
Syh	kk	.	.	ak	.	ak	ak	.	kk	.	kk	.	.	kk
62	.	.	.	ak	.	.	.	.	.	.	.	.	.	ak
147	.	.	.	ak	.	.	.	.	.	.	.	.	.	.
407	kk	.	.	ak	.	ak	ak	.	kk	.	.	.	.	kk
22	ak	.	.	ak	.	ak	ak	.	ak	.	ak	.	.	ak
36	ak	.	.	ak	.	ak	ak	.	ak	.	ak	.	.	ak
48	ak	.	.	ak	.	ak	ak	.	ak	.	ak	.	.	ak
51	ak	.	.	ak	.	ak	ak	.	ak	.	ak	.	.	ak
96	ak	.	.	ak	.	ak	ak	.	ak	.	ak	.	.	ak
231	ak	.	.	ak	.	ak	ak	.	ak	.	ak	.	.	ak
763	ak	.	.	ak	.	ak	ak	.	ak	.	ak	.	.	ak
311	ak	.	.	ak	.	ak	ak	.	ak	.	ak	.	.	ak
538	ak	.	.	ak	.	ak	ak	.	ak	.	ak	.	.	ak
V	ak	.	.	ak	.	ak	ak	.	ak	.	ak	.	.	ak
46	ak	.	.	ak	.	ak	ak	.	ak	.	ak	.	.	ak
449	ak	.	.	ak	.	ak	ak	.	ak	.	ak	.	.	ak
87	kk	.	.	ak	.	—	ak	.	kk	.	kk	.	.	kk
91	kk	.	.	ak	.	—	ak	.	kk	.	kk	.	.	.
490	kk	.	.	.	.	—	ak	.	kk	.	kk	.	.	.
49	kk	.	.	ak	.	—	ak	.	kk	.	kk	.	.	kk
90	kk	.	.	ak	.	—	ak	.	kk	.	kk	.	.	kk
764	kk	.	.	ak	.	—	ak	.	kk	.	kk	.	.	kk
130	kk	.	.	ak	.	—	ak	.	kk	.	kk	.	.	kk
233	kk	.	.	ak	.	—	ak	.	kk	.	kk	.	.	kk
534	kk	.	.	ak	.	—	ak	.	kk	.	kk	kt	.	kk
239	kk	.	.	ak	.	—	ak	.	akk	.	kk	.	.	kk
306	kk	.	.	ak	.	—	ak	.	kk	.	kk	.	.	kk
403	ak	.	.	.	.	—	.	.	ak	.	ak	.	.	kk
613	ak	.	.	.	.	—	.	.	ak	.	ak	.	.	kk
La: W														
Tyc	o	o	o	o	.	o	o	o	o	o	o	o	o	o
S	o	o	o	o	o	o	.	.	.	o	o	.	.	.
C														
Form	NE	YD	CC	KM	MS	KM	NE	YD	KM	DB	KM	YD	CC	KM

Table B.1

Ch. Vs.	30. 25	30. 26	31. 1	31. 10	31. 15	31. 18	32. 1	32. 3	32. 8	32. 11	32. 14	32. 15	32. 16	32. 17
MT	.	.	.	ak	ak	ak	.	ak	ak	ak	ak	.	ak	.
B	.	.	.	.	kk	kk	.	.	kk	.	.	.	kk	.
967	.	.	.	.	.	.	.	.	.	.	.	.	.	.
Bo	.	.	.	.	.	ak	.	ak	ak	.	.	.	ak	.
A	.	.	.	ak	ak	kk	.	ak	kkt	ak	ak	.	kk	.
26	.	.	.	ak	ak	kk	.	ak	kt	ak	ak	.	kk	.
106	.	.	.	kk	ak	kk	.	kk	kk	kk	ak	.	kk	.
410	.	.	.	ak	ak	kk	.	ak	kkt	ak	ak	.	kk	.
544	.	.	.	ak	ak	kk	.	ak	kkt	ak	ak	.	kk	.
Aeth	.	.	.	.	kk	kk	.	kk	kk	kk	ak	.	.	.
Arab	.	.	.	kk	kk	kk	.	kk	kk	.	ak	.	ak	.
Q	.	.	.	kk	kk	kk	.	kk	kk	kk	ak	.	kk	.
88	.	.	.	kk	kk	kk	.	kk	kk	kk	ak	.	kk	.
Syh	.	.	.	kk	kk	kk	.	kk	kk	kk	ak	.	kk	.
62	.	.	.	ak	ak	kt	.	.	.	.	.	.	.	.
147	.	.	.	kk	kk	.	.	kk	.	.	.	.	.	.
407	.	.	.	kk	kk	kk	.	kk	kk	kk	ak	.	kk	.
22	.	.	.	ak	ak	ak	.	ak	ak	ak	ak	.	ak	.
36	.	.	.	ak	ak	ak	.	ak	ak	ak	ak	.	ak	.
48	.	.	.	ak	ak	ak	.	ak	ak	ak	ak	.	ak	.
51	.	.	.	ak	ak	ak	.	ak	ak	ak	ak	.	ak	.
96	.	.	.	ak	ak	ak	.	ak	ak	ak	ak	.	ak	.
231	.	.	.	ak	ak	ak	.	ak	ak	ak	ak	.	ak	.
7&3	.	.	.	ak	ak	ak	.	ak	ak	ak	ak	.	ak	.
311	.	.	.	ak	ak	ak	.	ak	ak	ak	ak	.	ak	.
538	.	.	.	ak	ak	ak	.	ak	ak	ak	ak	.	ak	.
V	.	.	.	.	kk	ak	.	ak	ak	ak	ak	.	ak	.
46	.	.	.	.	kk	ak	.	ak	ak	ak	ak	.	ak	.
449	.	.	.	ak	ak	ak	.	ak	ak	ak	ak	.	ak	.
87	.	.	.	kk	kk	kk	.	kk	kk	kk	ak	.	kk	.
91	.	.	.	kk	kk	kk	.	kk	kk	kk	ak	.	kk	.
490	.	.	.	kk	kk	kk	.	kk	kk	kk	ak	.	kk	.
49	.	.	.	kk	kk	kk	.	kk	kk	kk	ak	.	kk	.
90	.	.	.	kk	kk	kk	.	kk	kk	kk	ak	.	kk	.
764	.	.	.	kk	kk	kk	.	kk	kk	kk	ak	.	kk	.
130	.	.	.	kk	kk	kk	.	kk	kk	kk	ak	.	kk	.
233	.	.	.	kk	kk	kk	.	kk	kk	kk	ak	.	kk	.
534	.	.	.	kk	kk	kk	.	kk	kk	kk	ak	.	kk	.
239	.	.	.	kk	kk	akk	.	kk	kk	kk	ak	.	kk	.
306	.	.	.	kk	kk	akk	.	kk	kk	kk	ak	.	kk	.
403	.	.	.	ak	ak	kk	.	ak	kkt	ak	ak	.	kk	.
613	.	.	.	ak	ak	kk	.	ak	kkt	ak	ak	.	kk	.
La: W Tyc	o	o	o	o	o	o	o	.	.	.	.	.	o	o
S	o	o	o	.	o	o	o	o	o	o	o	o	o	o
C	o	o	o	o	o	o	o	o	.	o	o	o	o	o
Form	YD	YD	CC	KM	KM	NE	CC	KM	NE	KM	NE	YD	NE	CC

247

Ch. Vs.	32. 31	32. 32	33. 1	33. 11	33. 22	33. 23	33. 25	33. 27	33. 29	33. 30	34. 1	34. 2	34. 7	34. 8
MT	ak	ak	.	ak	.	.	ak	ak	.	.	.	ak	.	ak
B	kk	kk	.	.	.	.	kk	kk	.	.	.	kk	.	kk
967	.	−	.	.	.	.	.	.	.	.	.	.	.	.
Bo	ak	kk	.	.	.	.	.	.	.	.	.	ak	.	.
A	kt	kkt	.	ak	.	.	ak	kk	.	.	.	kk	.	kk
26	kt	kkt	.	.	.	.	ak	kk	.	.	.	.	.	kk
106	kk	kk	.	ak	.	.	ak	.	.	.	.	kk	.	kk
410	kk	kk	.	.	.	.	ak	kk	.	.	.	kk	.	kk
544	kt	kkt	.	.	.	.	ak	kk	.	.	.	kk	.	kk
Aeth	kk	kk	.	ak	kk	kk	ak	akk	.	.	.	kk	.	kk
Arab	kk	kk	.	ak	.	.	ak	kk	.	.	.	.	.	kk
Q	kk	kk	.	ak	.	.	kk	ak	.	.	.	kk	.	ak
88	kk	.	.	ak	.	.	kk	ak	.	.	.	kk	.	ak
Syh	kk	kk	.	ak	.	.	kk	ak	.	.	.	kk	.	ak
62	ak	ak	.	ak	.	.	ak	ak	.	.	.	ak	.	ak
147	ak	ak	.	.	.	.	ak	kk	.	.	.	kk	.	kk
407	kk	kk	.	ak	.	.	ak	.	.	.	.	kk	.	ak
22	ak	ak	.	ak	.	.	ak	ak	.	.	.	ak	.	ak
36	ak	ak	.	ak	.	.	ak	ak	.	.	.	ak	.	ak
48	ak	ak	.	ak	.	.	ak	ak	.	.	.	ak	.	ak
51	ak	ak	.	ak	.	.	ak	ak	.	.	.	ak	.	ak
96	ak	ak	.	ak	.	.	ak	ak	.	.	.	ak	.	ak
231	ak	ak	.	ak	.	.	ak	ak	.	.	.	ak	.	ak
763	ak	ak	.	ak	.	.	ak	ak	.	.	.	ak	.	ak
311	ak	ak	.	ak	.	.	ak	ak	.	.	.	ak	.	ak
538	ak	ak	.	ak	.	.	ak	ak	.	.	.	ak	.	ak
V	ak	ak	.	ak	.	.	ak	ak	.	.	.	ak	.	ak
46	ak	ak	.	ak	.	.	ak	ak	.	.	.	ak	.	ak
449	ak	ak	.	ak	.	.	ak	ak	.	.	.	ak	.	ak
87	kk	kk	.	ak	.	.	ak	kk	.	.	.	kk	.	kk
91	kk	kk	.	ak	.	.	ak	kk	.	.	.	kk	.	kk
490	kk	kk	.	ak	.	.	ak	kk	.	.	.	kk	.	kk
49	kk	kk	.	ak	.	.	ak	kk	.	.	.	kk	.	kk
90	kk	kk	.	ak	.	.	ak	kk	.	.	.	kk	.	kk
764	kk	kk	.	ak	.	.	ak	kk	.	.	.	kk	.	kk
130	kk	kk	.	ak	.	.	ak	kk	.	.	.	kk	.	kk
233	kk	kk	.	ak	.	.	ak	kk	.	.	.	kk	.	kk
534	kk	kk	.	ak	.	.	ak	kk	.	.	.	kk	.	ak
239	kt	kk	.	ak	.	.	ak	kk	.	.	.	kk	.	kk
306	kt	kk	.	ak	.	.	ak	kk	.	.	.	kk	.	kk
403	kt	kkt	.	ak	.	.	ak	kk	.	.	.	kk	.	kk
613	kt	kkt	.	ak	.	.	ak	kk	.	.	.	kk	.	kk
La: W Tyc														
S	o	o	o	.	.	.	−	.	.	.	.	.	−	.
C	.	o	o	.	.	.	−	.	.	o	o	o	−	−
Form	NE	NE	CC	NE	CC	CC	KM	KM	YD	MS	CC	KM	CC	NE

248

Table B.1

Ch.	34.9	34.10	34.11	34.15	34.17	34.20	34.24a	34.24b	34.27	34.30a	34.30b	34.31	35.1	35.3
MT	.	ak	ak	ak	ak	ak	.	.	.	kt	ak	ak	.	ak
B	—	kk	.	kk	kk	kk	.	.	.	kt	.	kk	.	kk
967	—	.	.	.	kt	.	.	.	.	kt	.	.	.	.
Bo	—	.	.	.	ak	.	.	.	.	kt	ak	ak	.	ak
A	.	ak	kkt	kk	kk	kkt	.	.	.	kt	kk	kk	.	.
26	.	ak	kkt	kk	kk	kkt	.	.	.	kt	kk	kk	.	.
106	.	kk	kk	kk	kk	kk	.	.	.	kt	kk	.	.	kk
410	.	ak	kk	kk	kk	kk	.	.	.	kt	kk	kk	.	kk
544	.	ak	kkt	.	kk	kkt	—	.	.	kt	kk	kk	.	.
Aeth	.	kk	kk	kk	kk	kk	.	.	.	kt	kk	kk	.	kk
Arab	.	ak	kkt	kk	kk	kkt	.	.	.	kt	kk	kk	.	kk
Q	.	kk	kk	kk	kk	kk	.	.	.	kt	kk	kk	.	kk
88	.	kk	kk	kk	kk	kk	.	.	.	kt	kk	.	.	kk
Syh	.	kk	kk	kk	kk	kk	.	.	.	kt	kk	kk	.	kk
62	.	ak	ak	ak	ak	ak	.	.	.	kt	ak	kk	.	ak
147	.	ak	ak	ak	ak	ak	.	.	.	kt	ak	kk	.	ak
407	.	.	kk	kk	kk	kk	.	.	.	kt	kk	kk	.	kk
22	.	ak	ak	ak	ak	ak	.	.	.	kt	ak	ak	.	ak
36	.	ak	ak	ak	ak	ak	.	.	.	kt	ak	ak	.	ak
48	.	ak	ak	ak	ak	ak	.	.	.	kt	ak	ak	.	ak
51	.	ak	ak	ak	ak	ak	.	.	.	kt	ak	ak	.	ak
96	.	ak	ak	ak	ak	ak	.	.	.	kt	ak	ak	.	ak
231	.	ak	ak	ak	ak	ak	.	.	.	kt	ak	ak	.	ak
763	.	ak	ak	ak	ak	ak	.	.	.	kt	ak	ak	.	ak
311	.	ak	ak	ak	ak	ak	.	.	.	kt	ak	ak	.	ak
538	.	ak	ak	ak	ak	ak	.	.	.	kt	ak	ak	.	ak
V	.	ak	ak	ak	ak	ak	.	.	.	kt	ak	ak	.	ak
46	.	ak	ak	.	ak	ak	.	.	.	kt	ak	ak	.	ak
449	.	ak	ak	ak	ak	ak	.	.	.	kt	ak	ak	.	ak
87	.	kk	kk	kk	kk	kk	.	.	.	kt	kk	kk	.	kk
91	.	kk	kk	kk	kk	kk	.	.	.	kt	kk	kk	.	kk
490	.	kk	kk	kk	kk	kk	.	.	.	kt	kk	kk	.	kk
49	.	kk	.	kk	kk	kk	.	.	.	kt	kk	kk	.	kk
90	.	kk	.	kk	kk	kk	.	.	.	kt	kk	kk	.	kk
764	.	kk	.	kk	kk	kk	.	.	.	kt	kk	kk	.	kk
130	.	kk	kk	kk	kk	kk	—	.	.	kt	kk	kk	.	kk
233	.	kk	kk	kk	kk	kk	.	.	.	kt	kk	kk	.	kk
534	.	kk	kk	kk	kk	kk	.	.	.	kt	kk	kk	.	kk
239	.	kk	.	kk	kk	kk	.	.	.	kt	kk	kk	.	kk
306	.	kk	.	kk	kk	kk	.	.	.	kt	kk	kk	.	kk
403	.	ak	kkt	kk	kk	kkt	.	.	.	kt	kk	kk	.	.
613	.	ak	kkt	kk	kk	kkt	.	.	.	kt	kk	kk	.	.
La: W	o	o	o	o	.	.	.	.	.	.	—	.	.	.
Tyc														
S	.	.	.	.	kt	.	o	o	o	o	o	o	o	o
C	.	.	.	o	o	o	o	o	o	o	o	o	o	o
Form	CC	KM	KM	NE	KM	KM	MS	DB	YD	YD	NE	NE	CC	KM

Ch. Vs.	35. 4	35. 6	35. 9	35. 10	35. 11	35. 12	35. 14	35. 15	36. 1	36. 2	36. 3	36. 4a	36. 4b	36. 5
MT	.	ak	.	.	ak	.	ak	.	.	ak	ak	ak	ak	ak
B	.	kk	.	.	.	.	.	kt	.	kk	kk	.	.	kk
967	.	.	.	.	.	.	.	kt	.	.	.	.	.	.
Bo	.	ak	.	.	✱	.	kk	kt	.	-	.	.	.	.
A	.	kk	.	.	kk	.	.	kt	.	kk	kkt	.	.	.
26	.	kk	.	.	kk	.	.	kt	.	kk	kkt	.	.	kk
106	.	kk	.	.	kk	.	kk	kt	.	kk	kk	.	kk	kk
410	.	kk	.	.	kk	.	.	kt	.	kk	kt	.	kk	kk
544	.	kk	.	.	kk	.	.	kt	.	kk	kkt	.	.	kk
Aeth	.	kk	.	.	kk	.	kk	kt	.	kk	kk	.	.	kk
Arab	.	kk	.	.	kk	.	.	kt	.	kk	kkt	.	.	.
Q	.	kk	.	.	kk	.	kk	kt	.	kk	kk	ak	kk	kk
88	.	kk	.	.	kk	.	kk	kt	.	kk	kk	ak	kk	kk
Syh	.	kk	.	.	kk	.	kk	kt	.	kk	kk	ak	kk	kk
62	.	ak	.	.	ak	.	.	kt	.	ak	ak	ak	ak	.
147	.	ak	.	.	kk	.	kk	kt	.	kk	kk	kk	kk	kk
407	.	kk	.	.	kk	.	kk	kt	.	kk	kk	ak	kk	kk
22	.	ak	.	.	ak	.	ak	kt	.	ak	ak	.	ak	ak
36	.	ak	.	.	ak	.	ak	kt	.	ak	ak	.	ak	ak
48	.	ak	.	.	ak	.	ak	kt	.	ak	ak	.	ak	ak
51	.	ak	.	.	ak	.	ak	kt	.	ak	ak	.	ak	ak
96	.	ak	.	.	ak	.	ak	kt	.	ak	ak	.	ak	ak
231	.	ak	.	.	ak	.	ak	kt	.	ak	ak	.	ak	ak
763	.	ak	.	.	ak	.	ak	kt	.	ak	ak	.	ak	ak
311	.	ak	.	.	ak	.	ak	kt	.	ak	ak	.	ak	ak
538	.	ak	.	.	ak	.	ak	kt	.	ak	ak	.	ak	ak
V	.	ak	.	.	ak	.	ak	kt	.	ak	ak	.	ak	ak
46	.	ak	.	.	ak	.	.	kt	.	ak	ak	.	ak	ak
449	.	ak	.	.	ak	.	ak	kt	.	ak	ak	.	ak	ak
87	.	kk	.	.	kk	.	kk	kt	.	kk	kk	kk	.	kk
91	.	kk	.	.	kk	.	kk	kt	.	kk	kk	kk	kk	kk
490	.	kk	.	.	kk	.	kk	kt	.	kk	kk	kk	kk	kk
49	.	kk	.	.	kk	.	kk	kt	.	kk	kk	kk	kk	kk
90	.	kk	.	.	kk	.	kk	kt	.	kk	kk	kk	kk	kk
764	.	kk	.	.	kk	.	kk	kt	.	kk	kk	.	kk	kk
130	.	kk	.	.	kk	.	kk	kt	.	kk	kk	kk	kk	kk
233	.	.	.	.	kk	.	kk	kt	.	.	kk	.	kk	kk
534	.	ak	.	.	kk	.	kk	kt	.	kk	kk	.	kk	kk
239	.	kk	.	.	kk	.	kk	kt	.	kk	kk	.	kk	kk
306	.	kk	.	.	kk	.	kk	kt	.	kk	kk	.	kk	kk
403	.	kk	.	.	.	.	.	kt	.	kk	kkt	.	.	kk
613	.	kk	.	.	.	.	.	kt	.	kk	kkt	.	.	kk
La: W Tyc S C	.	o	o	o	o	o	o	o	o	o	o	o	o	o
Form	YD	NE	YD	MS	NE	YD	KM	YD	CC	KM	KM	CC	KM	KM

250

Table B.1

Ch. Ms.	36.6	36.7	36.11	36.13	36.14	36.15	36.16	36.20	36.22	36.23a	36.23b	36.32	36.33	36.36a
MT	ak	ak	.	ak	ak	ak	.	.	ak	.	ak	ak	ak	.
B	.	—	.	kk	kk	kk	.	.	.	.	—	kk	ak	.
967	.	—	:	.	.	.	.	.	.	.	—	—	—	—
O	kk	—	.	kk	ak	ak	.	.	.	.	—	.	.	.
A	ak	—	.	ak	ak	kt	.	.	ak	.	ak	kt	kt	.
26	ak	—	.	ak	akt	kt	.	.	ak	.	ak	kk	ak	.
106	kk	—	.	kk	kk	kk	.	.	kk	.	ak	kk	kk	.
410	ak	—	.	ak	ak	kk	.	.	ak	.	ak	kt	kt	.
544	ak	—	.	ak	akt	kt	.	.	kk	.	ak	kt	kt	.
Aeth	kk	—	.	kk	kk	kk	.	.	kk	.	ak	kk	kk	.
Arab	ak	—	.	kk	ak	kt	.	.	ak	.	ak	kt	kt	.
L	kk	ak	.	kk	kk	kk	.	.	kk	.	ak	kk	kk	.
88	kk	ak	.	kk	kk	kk	.	.	kk	.	ak	kk	kk	.
Syh	kk	ak	.	kk	kk	kk	.	.	kk	.	ak	kk	ak	.
62	ak	ak	.	ak	ak	ak	.	.	ak	.	ak	ak	ak	.
147	kk	—	.	kk	kk	kk	.	.	ak	.	ak	ak	ak	.
407	kk	ak	.	kk	kk	kk	.	.	kk	.	ak	kk	kk	.
22	ak	ak	.	ak	ak	ak	.	.	ak	.	ak	ak	ak	.
56	ak	ak	.	ak	ak	ak	.	.	ak	.	ak	ak	ak	.
48	ak	ak	.	ak	ak	ak	.	.	ak	.	ak	ak	ak	.
51	ak	ak	.	ak	ak	ak	.	.	ak	.	ak	ak	ak	.
96	ak	ak	.	ak	ak	ak	.	.	ak	.	ak	ak	ak	.
231	ak	ak	.	ak	ak	ak	.	.	ak	.	ak	ak	ak	.
763	ak	ak	.	ak	ak	ak	.	.	ak	.	ak	ak	ak	.
311	ak	ak	.	ak	ak	ak	.	.	ak	.	ak	ak	ak	—
538	ak	ak	.	ak	ak	ak	.	.	ak	.	ak	ak	ak	.
V	ak	ak	.	ak	ak	ak	.	.	ak	.	ak	ak	ak	.
46	ak	ak	.	ak	ak	ak	.	.	ak	.	—	ak	ak	.
449	ak	ak	.	ak	ak	ak	.	.	ak	.	ak	ak	ak	.
37	kk	—	.	kk	kk	kk	.	.	kk	.	ak	kk	kk	.
91	kk	—	.	kk	kk	kk	.	.	kk	.	ak	kk	kk	.
490	kk	—	.	kk	kk	kk	.	.	kk	.	ak	kk	kk	.
49	kk	—	.	kk	kk	kk	.	.	kk	.	ak	kk	kk	.
90	kk	—	.	kk	kk	kk	.	.	kk	.	ak	kk	kk	.
764	kk	—	.	kk	kk	kk	.	.	kk	.	ak	kk	kk	.
130	kk	—	.	kk	kk	kk	.	.	kk	.	ak	kk	kk	.
233	kk	—	.	kk	kk	kk	.	.	kk	.	ak	kk	kk	.
534	kk	—	.	kk	kk	.	.	.	kk	.	ak	kk	kk	.
239	kk	—	.	kk	kk	kk	.	.	kk	.	ak	kk	kk	.
306	kk	—	.	kk	kk	kk	.	.	kk	.	ak	kk	kk	.
403	ak	—	.	ak	akt	kt	.	.	ak	.	ak	kt	kt	.
613	ak	—	.	ak	akt	kt	.	.	ak	.	ak	kt	kt	.
La:														
W														
Tyc	.	—	o	o	o	o	.	.	.	o	—	.	ak	.
S														
C														
Form	KM	KM	YD	KM	NE	NE	CC	CC	KM	YD	NE	NE	KM	Y

251

Ch. Vs.	36.36b	36.37	36.38	37.1a	37.1b	37.3	37.4	37.5	37.6	37.9	37.12	37.13	37.14a	3·1
MT	.	ak	.	.	.	ak	.	ak	.	ak	ak	.	.	.
B	.	ak	.	.	.	.	.	.	.	.	.	.	.	.
967	–	–	–	.	.	kt	.	kt	.	kt	.	.	.	.
Bo	.	.	.	.	.	*	.	ak	.	ak	ak	.	.	a
A	kk	kkt	.	.	.	kk	.	kk	.	kk	ak	.	.	k
26	.	kk	.	.	.	kk	.	kk	.	kk	ak	.	.	.
106	.	kk	.	.	.	kk	.	kk	.	kk	kk	.	.	k
410	.	kt	.	.	.	kk	.	kk	.	kk	ak	.	.	k
544	kk	kkt	.	.	.	kk	.	kk	.	kk	ak	.	.	k
Aeth	.	kk	.	.	.	kk	.	kk	.	kk	kk	.	.	k
Arab	kk	kkt	.	.	.	kk	.	kk	.	kk	kk	.	.	k
Q	.	kk	.	.	.	kk	.	kk	.	kk	kk	.	.	k
88	.	kk	.	.	.	kk	.	kk	.	kk	kk	.	.	k
Syh	.	kk	.	.	.	kk	.	kk	.	kk	kk	.	.	k
62	.	ak	.	.	.	ak	.	ak	.	ak	ak	.	.	a
147	.	ak	.	.	.	ak	.	ak	.	ak	ak	.	.	a
407	.	kk	.	.	.	kk	.	kk	.	kk	kk	.	.	k
22	.	ak	.	.	.	kt	.	ak	.	ak	ak	.	.	a
36	.	ak	.	.	.	kt	.	ak	.	ak	ak	.	.	a
48	.	ak	.	.	.	kt	.	ak	.	ak	ak	.	.	a
51	.	ak	.	.	.	kt	.	ak	.	ak	ak	.	.	a
96	.	ak	.	.	.	kt	.	ak	.	ak	ak	.	.	a
231	.	ak	.	.	.	kt	.	ak	.	ak	ak	.	.	a
763	.	ak	.	.	.	kt	.	ak	.	ak	ak	.	.	a
311	.	ak	.	.	.	kt	.	ak	.	ak	ak	.	.	a
538	.	ak	.	.	.	kt	.	ak	.	ak	ak	.	.	a
V	.	ak	.	.	.	kt	.	ak	.	ak	ak	.	.	a
46	.	ak	.	.	.	kt	.	ak	.	ak	ak	.	.	a
449	.	ak	.	.	.	akt	.	ak	.	ak	ak	.	.	a
87	.	kk	.	.	.	kk	.	.	.	kk	kk	.	.	kk
91	.	kk	.	.	.	kk	.	kk	.	kk	kk	.	.	kk
490	.	kk	.	.	.	kk	.	kk	.	kk	kk	.	.	kk
49	.	kk	.	.	.	kk	.	kk	.	kk	kk	.	.	kk
90	.	kk	.	.	.	kk	.	kk	.	kk	kk	.	.	kk
764	.	kk	.	.	.	kk	.	kk	.	kk	kk	.	.	kk
130	.	kk	.	.	.	kk	.	kk	.	kk	kk	.	.	kk
233	.	kk	.	.	.	kk	.	.	.	kk	kk	.	.	kk
534	.	kk	.	.	.	kk	.	kk	.	kk	kk	.	.	kk
239	.	kk	.	.	.	kk	.	kk	.	kk	kk	.	.	kk
306	.	kk	.	.	.	kk	.	kk	.	kk	kk	.	.	kk
403	.	kt	.	.	.	kk	.	kk	.	kk	ak	.	.	kk
613	.	kt	.	.	.	kk	.	kk	.	kk	ak	.	.	kk
La: W Tyc S C	.	o	o	o	o	o	o	o	o	o	.	.	.	o
Form	DB	KM	YD	CC	CC	AD	CC	KM	YD	KM	KM	YD	YD	NE

Table B.1

Ch. Vs.	37. 15	37. 19	37. 21	37. 28	38. 1	38. 3	38. 10	38. 14	38. 17	38. 18	38. 21	38. 23	39. 1	39. 5
MT	.	ak	ak	.	.	ak	ak	ak	ak	ak	ak	.	ak	ak
B	.	.	kk	.	.	kk	kk	.	kk	kk	.	.	.	.
967	.	.	.	.	.	.	.	.	.	.	.	.	.	kt
Bo	.	ak	ak	.	.	ak	ak	ak	ak	ak	ak	.	ak	ak
A	.	ak	akt	.	.	ak	kkt	kkt	akt	kkt	kk	.	kk	kk
26	.	ak	akt	.	.	.	kt	kkt	kkt	kkt	kk	.	kk	kk
106	.	akk	kk	.	.	kk	kk	kk	kk	kk	kk	.	kk	kk
410	.	ak	akt	.	.	ak	kt	kt	kt	kkt	kk	.	kk	kk
544	.	ak	akt	.	.	ak	kkt	kkt	akt	kt	kk	.	kk	kk
Aeth	.	kk	kk	.	.	kk	kk	kk	kk	kk	kk	.	kk	.
Arab	.	ak	akt	.	.	ak	kkt	kkt	akt	kkt	kk	.	kk	kk
Q	.	kk	kk	.	.	kk	kk	kk	kk	kk	kk	.	kk	kk
88	.	kk	kk	.	.	kk	kk	kk	kk	kk	kk	.	kk	kk
Syh	.	kk	kk	.	.	kk	kk	kk	kk	kk	kk	.	kk	kk
62	.	ak	ak	.	.	ak	ak	ak	ak	ak	ak	.	ak	ak
147	.	ak	ak	.	.	kk	kk	kk	kk	kk	kk	.	kk	kk
407	.	.	kk	.	.	kk	kk	kk	kk	kk	kk	.	kk	kk
22	.	ak	ak	.	.	ak	ak	ak	ak	ak	ak	.	ak	ak
36	.	ak	ak	.	.	ak	ak	ak	ak	ak	ak	.	ak	ak
48	.	ak	ak	.	.	ak	ak	ak	ak	ak	ak	.	ak	ak
51	.	ak	ak	.	.	ak	ak	ak	ak	ak	ak	.	ak	ak
96	.	ak	ak	.	.	ak	ak	ak	ak	ak	ak	.	ak	ak
231	.	ak	ak	.	.	ak	ak	ak	ak	ak	ak	.	ak	ak
763	.	ak	ak	.	.	ak	ak	ak	ak	ak	ak	.	ak	ak
311	.	ak	ak	.	.	ak	ak	ak	ak	ak	ak	.	ak	ak
538	.	ak	ak	.	.	ak	ak	ak	ak	ak	ak	.	ak	ak
V	.	ak	ak	.	.	ak	ak	ak	ak	ak	ak	.	ak	ak
46	.	ak	ak	.	.	ak	ak	ak	ak	ak	ak	.	ak	ak
449	.	ak	ak	.	.	ak	ak	ak	ak	ak	ak	.	ak	ak
87	.	kk	kk	.	.	kk	kk	kk	kk	kk	kk	.	kk	kk
91	.	kk	kk	.	.	kk	kk	kk	kk	kk	kk	.	kk	kk
490	.	kk	kk	.	.	kk	kk	kk	kk	kk	kk	.	kk	kk
49	.	kk	kk	.	.	kk	kk	kk	kk	kk	kk	.	kk	kk
90	.	kk	kk	.	.	kk	kk	kk	kk	.	kk	.	kk	kk
764	.	kk	kk	.	.	kk	kk	kk	kk	kk	kk	.	kk	kk
130	.	kk	kk	.	.	kk	kk	kk	kk	kk	kk	.	kk	kk
233	.	kk	kk	.	.	kk	kk	kk	kk	kk	kk	.	kk	kk
534	.	kk	kk	kt	.	kk	.	kk	kk	kk	kk	.	kk	kk
239	.	kk	kk	.	.	kk	kk	kk	kk	kk	kk	.	kk	kk
306	.	kk	kk	.	.	kk	kk	kk	kk	kk	kk	.	kk	kk
403	.	ak	akt	.	.	ak	kkt	kkt	akt	kt	kk	.	kk	kk
613	.	ak	akt	.	.	ak	kkt	kkt	akt	kt	kk	.	kk	kk
La: W	o	o	.	.	o	o	.	.	.	.	o	o	o	o
Tyc	o	o	.	.	o	o	o	o	o	o	o	o	o	o
S	o	o	o	o	o	o	o	.	.	.	.	.	.	.
C														
Form	CC	KM	KM	YD	CC	KM	KM	KM	KM	NE	NE	YD	KM	NE

253

| Ch. | 39. | 39. | 39. | 39. | 39. | 39. | 39. | 39. | 39. | 39. | 39. | 40. | 40. | 41. |
Vs.	6	7	8	10	13	17	20	22	25	28	29	1	46	22
MT	.	.	ak	ak	ak	ak	ak	kt	ak	kt	ak	.	.	.
B	.	.	kk	.	.	.	.	kt	kk	kt	kk	.	.	.
967	.	.	.	.	.	.	.	kt	.	kt	kt	.	.	.
Bo	.	.	ak	ak	ak	ak	ak	kt	ak	kt	ak	.	.	.
A	.	kk	kkt	.	.	.	kk	kt	kkt	kt	kk	.	.	.
26	.	.	kkt	.	kk	.	kk	kt	kt	kt	kk	.	.	.
106	.	.	kk	kk	kk	.	kk	kt	kk	kt	kk	.	.	.
410	.	.	kt	kk	kk	kk	kk	kt	kkt	kt	kk	.	.	.
544	.	kk	kkt	.	.	.	kk	kt	kkt	kt	kk	.	.	.
Aeth	.	.	kk	kk	kk	kk	kk	kt	kk	kt	kk	.	.	.
Arab	.	.	kkt	.	.	.	kk	kt	kkt	kt	kk	.	.	.
Q	.	.	kk	kk	kk	kk	kk	kt	kk	kt	kk	.	.	.
88	.	.	kk	kk	kk	kk	kk	kt	kk	kt	kk	.	.	.
Syh	.	.	kk	kk	kk	kk	kk	kt	kk	kt	kk	.	.	.
62	.	.	ak	ak	ak	ak	ak	kt	ak	kt	ak	.	.	.
147	.	.	kk	kk	kk	kk	kk	kt	ak	kt	ak	.	.	.
407	.	.	kk	kk	kk	kk	kk	kt	kk	kt	kk	.	.	.
22	.	.	ak	ak	ak	ak	ak	kt	ak	kt	ak	.	.	.
36	.	.	ak	ak	ak	ak	ak	kt	ak	kt	ak	.	.	.
48	.	.	ak	ak	ak	ak	ak	kt	ak	kt	ak	.	.	.
51	.	.	ak	ak	ak	ak	ak	kt	ak	kt	ak	.	.	.
96	.	.	ak	ak	ak	ak	ak	kt	ak	kt	ak	.	.	.
231	.	.	ak	ak	ak	ak	ak	kt	ak	kt	ak	.	.	.
763	.	.	ak	ak	ak	ak	ak	kt	ak	kt	ak	.	.	.
311	.	.	ak	ak	ak	ak	ak	kt	ak	kt	ak	.	.	.
538	.	.	ak	ak	ak	ak	ak	kt	ak	kt	ak	.	.	.
V	.	.	ak	ak	ak	ak	ak	kt	ak	kt	ak	.	.	.
46	.	.	ak	ak	ak	ak	ak	kt	ak	kt	ak	.	.	.
449	.	.	ak	ak	ak	ak	ak	kt	ak	kt	ak	.	.	.
87	.	.	kk	kk	kk	kk	kk	kt	kk	kt	kk	.	.	.
91	.	.	kk	kk	kk	kk	kk	kt	kk	kt	kk	.	.	.
490	.	.	kk	kk	kk	kk	kk	kt	kk	kt	kk	.	.	.
49	.	.	kk	kk	kk	kk	kk	kt	kk	kt	kk	.	.	.
90	.	.	kk	kk	kk	kk	kk	kt	kk	kt	kk	.	.	.
764	.	.	kk	kk	kk	kk	kk	kt	kk	kt	kk	.	.	.
130	.	.	kk	kk	kk	kk	kk	kt	kk	kt	kk	.	.	.
233	.	.	kk	kk	kk	kk	kk	kt	kk	kt	kk	.	.	.
534	.	.	kk	kk	kk	kk	kk	kt	kk	kt	kk	.	.	.
239	.	.	kk	kk	kk	kk	kk	kt	kk	kt	kk	.	.	.
306	.	.	kk	kk	kk	kk	kk	kt	.	kt	kk	.	.	.
403	.	.	kkt	.	.	.	kk	kt	kkt	kt	kk	.	.	.
613	.	.	kkt	.	.	.	kk	kt	kkt	kt	kk	.	.	.
La:														
W	o	o	o	o	o	o	o	o	o	o	o	o	.	-
Tyc														
S	.	.	.	.	.	.	.	kt	.	kt	.	.	o	o
C														
Form	YD	YD	NE	NE	NE	KM	NE	YD	KM	YD	NE	CC	MS	MS

Table B.1

Ch. Vs.	42. 13	43. 4	43. 5	43. 18	43. 19	43. 24a	43. 24b	43. 27	44. 2a	44. 2b	44. 3	44. 4a	44. 4b	44. 5a
MT	.	.	.	ak	ak	.	.	ak	.	kti	.	.	.	.
B	.	.	.	kti	kt	.	.	.	.	kti	.	—	.	.
967	.	.	.	.	.	.	.	.	.	kti	.	.	.	.
Bo	.	.	.	kti	kk	.	.	kk	.	kti	.	—	.	.
A	.	.	.	kti	kt	.	.	.	.	kti	.	—	.	.
26	.	.	.	kti	kt	.	.	.	.	kti	.	—	.	.
106	.	.	.	kti	kt	.	.	.	.	kti	.	—	.	.
410	.	.	.	kti	kkt	.	.	.	.	kti	.	—	.	.
544	.	.	.	kti	kt	.	.	.	.	kti	t	—	.	.
Aeth	.	o	o	kt	kt	o	o	o	.	kti	o	o	o	o
Arab	.	.	.	kti	kt	.	.	kk	.	kti	.	—	.	.
Q	.	.	.	kk	kk	.	.	kk	.	kti	.	.	.	.
88	.	.	.	kk	kk	.	.	kk	.	kti	.	.	.	.
Syh	.	.	.	kk	kk	.	.	kk	.	kti	.	.	.	.
62	.	.	.	kti	ak	.	.	ak	.	kti	.	—	.	.
147	.	.	.	kti	ak	.	.	kk	.	kti	.	—	.	.
407	.	.	.	kti	kt	.	.	kk	.	kti	.	—	.	.
22	.	.	kk	ak	ak	.	.	ak	.	kti	.	—	.	.
36	.	.	kk	ak	ak	.	.	ak	.	kti	.	.	.	.
48	.	.	kk	ak	ak	.	.	ak	.	kti	.	.	.	.
51	.	.	kk	ak	ak	.	.	ak	.	kti	.	.	.	.
96	.	.	kk	ak	ak	.	.	ak	.	kti	.	.	.	.
231	.	.	.	ak	ak	.	.	ak	.	kti	.	.	.	.
763	.	.	kk	ak	ak	.	.	ak	.	kti	.	.	.	.
311	.	.	kk	ak	ak	.	.	ak	.	kti	.	.	.	.
538	.	.	kk	ak	ak	.	.	ak	.	kti	.	.	.	.
V	.	.	kk	ak	ak	.	.	ak	.	kti	.	.	.	.
46	.	ki	.	kti	ak	.	.	kk	.	kti	.	—	.	.
449	.	.	kk	kti	ak	.	.	ak	.	kti	.	.	.	.
87	.	.	.	kti	kk	.	.	kk	.	kti	.	—	.	.
91	.	.	.	kti	kk	.	.	kk	.	kti	.	—	.	.
490	.	.	.	kti	kk	.	.	kk	.	kti	.	—	.	.
49	.	.	.	kti	kk	.	.	kk	.	kti	.	.	—	.
90	.	.	.	kti	kk	.	.	kk	.	kti	.	.	—	.
764	.	.	.	*	kk	.	.	kk	.	kti	.	.	—	.
130	.	.	.	kti	kt	.	.	kk	.	kti	.	—	.	.
233	.	.	.	kti	kt	.	.	kk	.	kti	.	—	.	.
534	.	.	.	*	kt	.	.	kk	.	kti	.	—	.	.
239	.	.	.	kti	kk	.	.	kk	—	kti	.	—	.	.
306	.	.	.	kti	kk	.	.	kk	.	kti	.	—	.	.
403	.	.	.	kti	kt	.	.	.	.	kti	.	—	.	.
613	.	.	.	kti	.	.	.	ak	.	kti	.	—	.	.
La: W	.	o	o	o	o	o	o	o	o	o	o	o	o	o
Tyc														
S														
C	o	o	o	o	o	.	.	.	.	kti	.	.	.	.
Form	MS	CC	CC	KM	NE	MS	MS	NE	AM	MS	MS	CC	CC	AM

255

Ch.	44.	44.	44.	44.	44.	44.	45.	45.	45.	45.	45.	45.	45.	4...
Vs.	5b	6	9	12	15	27	1	4	9a	9b	15	18	23	1
MT	.	ak	ak	ak	ak	ak	.	.	ak	ak	ak	ak	.	a
B	.	kt	kt	kt	kt	kt	.	.	kt	kt	kt	kt	.	k
967	.								.					
Bo	.	kt	kt	kt	kt	kt	.	.	kt	kt	kt	kt	.	k
A	.	kt	kt	kt	kt	kt	.	.	kt	kt	kt	kt	.	k
26	*	kt	kt	kt	kt	kt	.	.	kt	kt	kt	kt	.	k
106	.	kt	kt	kt	kt	kt	.	.	kt	kt	kt	kt	.	k
410	.	kkt	kt	kt	kt	kt	.	.	kt	kt	kt	kt	.	k
544	.	kt	kt	kt	kt	kt	.	.	kt	kt	kt	kt	.	k
Aeth	o	o	kt	kt	kt	o	o	o	kt	kt	o	kt	o	k
Arab	.	kt	kt	kt	kt	kt	.	.	kt	kt	kt	kt	.	k
Q	.	kk	kt	kt	kt	kt	.	.	kk	kt	kt	kt	.	k
88	.	kk	kk	kt	kt	kt	.	.	kk	kt	kt	kt	.	k
Syh	.	kk	kk	kt	kt	kt	.	.	kk	kt	kt	kt	.	k
62	.	ak	kt	kt	kt	kt	.	.	ak	ak	ak	ak	.	a
147	.	kti	kk	kti	kt	kt	.	.	kti	kt	kt	kt	.	k
407	.	kti	kk	kti	kk	kt	.	.	kti	kt	kt	kt	.	k
22	.	akt	ak	ak	ak	ak	.	.	ak	ak	ak	ak	.	a
36	.	akt	ak	ak	ak	ak	.	.	ak	ak	ak	ak	.	a
48	.	akt	ak	ak	ak	ak	.	.	ak	ak	ak	ak	.	a
51	.	akt	ak	ak	ak	ak	.	.	ak	ak	ak	ak	.	a
96	.	akt	ak	ak	ak	ak	.	.	ak	ak	ak	ak	.	a
231	.	akt	ak	ak	ak	ak	.	.	ak	ak	ak	ak	.	a
763	.	akt	ak	ak	ak	ak	.	.	ak	ak	ak	ak	.	a
311	.	akt	ak	ak	ak	ak	.	.	ak	ak	ak	ak	.	a
538	.	akt	ak	ak	ak	ak	.	.	ak	ak	ak	ak	.	a
V	.	akt	ak	ak	ak	ak	.	.	ak	ak	ak	ak	.	a
46	.	akt	ak	ak	ak	ak	.	.	ak	ak	ak	ak	.	a
449	.	kt	ak	ak	ak	ak	.	.	ak	ak	ak	ak	.	a
87	.	kk	kt	kt	kt	kt	kk	kk	kk	kt	kt	kt	kk	k
91	.	kk	kt	kt	kt	kt	.	.	.	kt	kt	kt	.	k
490	.	kk	kt	kt	kt	kt	.	.	.	kt	kt	kt	.	k
49	.	kk	kt	kt	kt	kt	.	.	.	kt	kt	kt	.	k
90	.	kk	kt	kt	kt	kt	.	.	.	kt	kt	kt	.	k
764	.	kk	kt	kt	kt	kt	.	.	.	kt	kt	kt	.	k
130	.	kt	kt	kt	kt	kt	.	.	kk	kt	kt	kt	.	k
233	.	kt	kt	kt	kt	kt	.	.	.	kt	kk	kt	.	k
534	.	kk	kt	kt	kt	kt	.	.	.	kt	kt	kt	.	k
239	.	kk	kt	kkt	kt	kt	.	.	.	kt	kt	kt	.	k
306	.	kk	kt	kt	kt	kt	.	.	kt	kt	kt	kt	.	k
403	.	kk	kt	kt	kt	kt	.	.	kt	kt	kt	kt	.	k
613	.	.	ak	ak	kt	ak	.	.	.	kt	ak	ak	.	a
La:														
W	o	o	o	o	o	o	o	.	kt	kt	.	kt	.	k
Tyc														
S														
C	o	o	o	o	o	kt	.	o	o	o	o	o	o	o
Form	CC	KM	KM	NE	NE	NE	MS	MS	KM	NE	NE	KM	MS	K

Table B.1

Ch. Vs.	46. 3	46. 4	46. 9	46. 12	46. 13	46. 14	46. 16	47. 13	47. 23	48. 9	48. 10	48. 14	48. 29	48. 35
MT	.	.	.	.	.	.	ak	ak	ak	.	.	.	ak	.
B	.	.	.	.	.	.	kt	kt	kt	.	—	.	kt	—
967	.	.	.	.	.	.	.	.	.	.	—	.	.	—
Bo	.	.	.	.	.	.	kk	kt	kt	.	—	.	kt	.
A	.	.	.	.	.	.	ak	kt	kt	.	—	.	kt	.
26	.	.	.	.	.	.	akt	kt	kt	.	—	.	kt	.
106	.	.	.	—	.	.	akt	kt	kt	.	—	.	kt	—
410	.	.	.	.	.	.	akt	kt	kt	.	—	.	kt	—
544	.	.	.	.	.	.	akt	kt	kt	.	—	.	kt	.
Aeth	.	.	.	—	.	.	o	kt	o	.	—	.	kt	.
Arab	.	.	.	.	.	.	ak	kt	kt	.	—	.	kt	.
Q	.	.	.	.	.	.	kt	kt	kt	.	—	.	kt	.
88	.	.	.	.	.	.	kk	kt	kt	.	—	.	kt	.
Syh	.	.	.	.	.	.	ak	kt	kt	.	—	.	kt	.
62	.	.	.	.	.	.	ak	ak	ak	.	.	.	ak	.
147	.	.	.	.	.	.	kt	kt	ak	.	.	.	kt	.
407	.	.	.	.	.	.	kt	kt	kt	.	—	.	kt	.
22	.	.	.	.	.	.	ak	kt	ak	.	.	.	ak	—
36	.	.	.	.	.	.	ak	kt	ak	.	.	.	ak	.
48	.	.	.	.	.	.	ak	kt	ak	.	.	.	ak	—
51	.	.	.	.	.	.	ak	kt	ak	.	.	.	ak	—
96	.	.	.	.	.	.	ak	kt	ak	.	.	.	ak	.
231	.	.	.	.	.	.	ak	kt	ak	.	.	.	ak	—
763	.	.	.	.	.	.	ak	o	o	o	o	o	o	o
311	.	.	.	.	.	.	ak	kt	ak	.	.	.	ak	.
538	.	.	.	.	.	.	ak	kt	ak	.	.	.	ak	.
V	.	.	.	.	.	.	ak	kt	ak	.	.	.	ak	.
46	.	.	.	.	.	.	ak	kt	kt	.	—	.	kt	.
449	.	.	.	.	.	.	ak	akt	ak	.	.	.	ak	.
87	.	.	.	.	.	.	kk	kt	kt	.	—	.	kt	.
91	.	.	.	.	.	.	kk	kt	kt	.	—	.	kt	.
490	.	.	.	.	.	.	kk	kt	kt	.	—	.	kt	.
49	.	.	.	.	.	.	kk	kt	kt	.	—	.	kt	.
90	.	.	.	.	.	.	kk	kt	kt	.	—	.	kt	.
764	.	.	.	.	.	.	kk	kt	kt	.	—	.	kt	.
130	.	.	.	.	.	.	kk	kt	kt	.	—	.	kt	.
233	.	.	.	.	.	.	kk	kt	kt	.	—	.	kt	.
534	.	.	.	.	.	.	kk	kt	kt	.	—	.	kt	.
239	.	.	.	.	.	.	kk	kt	kt	.	—	.	kk	.
306	.	.	.	.	.	.	kk	kt	kt	.	—	.	kk	.
403	.	.	.	.	.	.	akt	kt	kt	.	—	.	kt	.
513	.	.	.	.	.	.	kk	kt	ak	.	.	.	kt	.
La: J	.	.	.	o	o	o	o	o	o	o	o	o	kt	—
yc }	o	o	o	o	o	o	o	o	o	o	—	.	kt	.
;	o	o	o	.	.	.	o	kt	o	o	o	o	kt	.
Form	MS	MS	MS	MS	MS	MS	KM	KM	NE	MS	CC	MS	NE	MS

257

APPENDIX C

The Hebrew Fragment 4QEz/a

10.17   [עמדם יעמדו ובברומם ירומו אתם

10.18   [ד יהוה מעל מפתן הבית ויעמד על הכרובים

10.19   [ם וירומו מן הארץ לעיני בצאתם והאופנים

             יהוה הקדמוני וכבוד אל [שראל

10.20   [אתי תחת אלהי ישראל בנהר כב]

10.21   לאחד וארבעה כנפים לא]

10.22   ]ניהם המה הפנים א]

           ש] אל עבר פנוו ילכו

1.1   [קדמוני הפונה קד]

          ביוכם את יא]ז

1.2   שבים או ן היצצי]

1.3   בתים היא הס]

1.5   ותפל עלי רוח

       ישראל ומפלות

1.6   ]ת ומלאתם

1.7   שמתם בתוכה

.8   חרב יראתם

.9   מתוכה

.10   ]לו

otographs of the fragment are given on the endpapers of both
lumes of the English edition of Zimmerli's commentary on
ekiel (1979 + 1983; cf. p. xlvi of vol 1).

APPENDIX D

Vocabulary Common to S1 and S3

D.1 Vocabulary Common to All Three Sections

The list below contains all the Hebrew terms (apart
from prepositions and particles) which are common in S1, S2
and S3.

The third column shows what sort of agreement exists
among all the sections. If there is no appreciable translation
difference between sections, and one rendering predominates
(i.e. it appears in at least half of the cases in each
section), then that rendering is given. If there is no
appreciable difference between sections, but no one rendering
predominates, then a (4) is given.

The fourth and fifth columns note whether there is a
difference of translation between S1 and S3, and S2 and S3
respectively. If there is a translation difference then a "<"
is given. If there is an influencing factor to be taken into
consideration, then a number is cited after the angular
bracket. The number refers to the influencing factors
mentioned in Chapter II: 1 — Vorlage, 2 — context, 3 —
textual integrity, 4 — frequency and distribution, 5 — the
translator's vocabulary, and 6 — the progression of the
translation.

A "16" or "36" means that the Hebrew term is found only
in ch.16 within S1 or in 36.23c-38 within S2.

1	אב	πατηρ		
2	אבן		<2,4	<3
3	אדם	ανθρωπος		
4	אדני		<3	<3
5	אח	αδελφος		
6	איש	(4)		
7	אכל (ק.)	εσθιειν		
8	אלהים	θεος		
9	אמר	λεγειν/ειπειν		
10	אף			<1,3
11	ארץ	γη		
12	אשה	γυνη		
13	בגד		<2	
14	בדל (ה.)	διαστελλειν		
15	בהמה	κτηνος		
16	בוא (ק.)	(4)		
17	בוא (ה.)	(4)		
18	בית	οικος		
19	במה		<1,3	<1,3
20	בן	υιος		
21	בקר	πρωι		
22	ברית	διαθηκη		
23	בשר		<2	<2
24	בת	θυγατηρ		
25	גבה (1)	υψος		
26	גבה (2)	υψηλος		
27	גבול	τα ορια		
28	גדול	μεγας		
29	גלול	(4)		
30	גלות	αιχμαλωσια		
31	דבר	λεγειν/ειπειν		
32	דם	αιμα		
33	דרך		<2	<2
34	היה (ק.)	(4)		
35	הר	ορος		

36	זבח		<3	
37	(.ק) זרק	36	<2	[<]
38	חגר			<1,3
39	חדש		<2	<2
40	חוץ		<2	<2
41	חטאת		<2	<2
42	חטה			<
43	חי		<2	<2
44	חיה	ζην		
45	(.פ) חלל	βεβηλουν		
46	חמס		<	<
47	חק	36		[<]
48	חקה	προσταγμα		
49	טהור	36 (καθαρος)		
50	(.פ) טהר		<1,3	
51	(.פ) טמא		<2	
52	(.הת) טמא	μιαινειν		
53	יד	χειρ		
54	(.ה) ידע			<
55	יהודה	ιουδας		
56	יהוה		<3	
57	יום	ημερα		
58	(.ק) יכל		<1,3	
59	ים		<2,4	
60	(.ק) יצא	εξερχεσθαι		
61	(.ה) יצא	εξαγειν		
62	ישראל	ισραηλ		
63	(.ק) ישב		<4	
64	(.נ) יתר		<2	<2
65	כבוד	δοξα		
66	כלי	σκευος		
67	(.נ) כלם	16		
68	כלמה	16		
69	כסא	θρονος		
70	כף		<1,2	<2

71	כפיר	λεων		
72	כרוב	χερουβ(ιν)		
73 (.ק) כתב			<2	<2
74	כתף		<2	<2
75	לב	καρδια		
76 (.ק) לבש				<
77	לקח	λαμβανειν		
78	מאד	σφοδρα		
79	מושב	κατοικια		
80	נים	υδωρ		
81 (.ק) מכר			<5	<3
82 (.ק) מלא				<
83 (.פ) מלא				<
84	מלא		<1,2,3	<1,2,3
85	מלך		<2	<
86	מעשה		<2	<1,3
87	מקדש	τα αγια		
88	מקום	τοπος		
89	משפט	(4)		
90	מתנים	οσφυς		
91	נאם	λεγει		
92 (.ה) נגד			<2	<2
93	נהר	ποταμος		
94 (.ה) נוח			<2	
95	נחשת			<
96 (.ק) נפל		πιπτειν		
97 (.ה) נפל			<2	
98	נפש	ψυχη		
99 (.ק) נשא		(4)		
100	נשיא		<3	<
101 (.ק) נתן		διδοναι		
102 (.נ) נתן		διδοσθαι		
103 (.ה) סבב			<1,3	<1,3
104	סביב			<
105 (.ה) סור		(4)		

264

#	Hebrew	Greek		
106	עבד (ק.)		<2	<2
107	עבר (ק.)	(4)		
108	עבר (ה.)		<1,2,4	
109	עולם			<4
110	עוו			<
111	עין		<3	
112	עיר	πολις		
113	עלה (ק.)	αναβαινειν		
114	עלה (ה.)		<3	<2
115	עם			<2
116	עמד (ק.)	ιστανσι		
117	עץ		<2	<2
118	ערב	εσπερα		
119	עשה (ק.)	ποιειν		
120	פנה (ק.)			<2
121	פנה		<2,3	<2,3
122	פרי	καρπος		
123	פתח (ק.)	ανοιγνυναι		
124	פתח (נ.)	ανοιγνυσθαι		
125	פתח		<	<
126	צאן	τα προβατα		
127	צדקה	ξικαιοσυνη		
128	צפון	βορρα		
129	קדים		<2,4	<2
130	קדמוני		<	<
131	קדש (פ.)	αγιαζειν		
132	קדש	αγιος		
133	קול	φωνη		
134	קומה		<2	<2
135	קיר			<3
136	קצה		<2	<2
137	קרב (ק.)		<2	
138	קרוב			<
139	ראה (ק.)	οραν/ιξειν		
140	ראש	κεφαλη		

141	רב	πολυς		
142	רגל	πους		
143	רוח		<2	<2
144 (ק.)	שׂים			<
145	שׂפה		<2	<2
146	שׁבט	φυλη		
147 (ק.)	שׁוב		<2,3	<2,3
148 (ה.)	שׁוב	(4)		
149	שׁחת		<1,3	<1,3
150	שׁכן		<2	<2
151 (פ.)	שׁלח			<2
152	שׁלחן	τραπεζα		
153 (ה.)	שׁלך		<1,2	<1,2
154	שׁם	ονομα		
155	שׁמן	ελαιον		
156 (ק.)	שׁמע	ακουειν		
157 (ק.)	שׁמר	φυλασσειν		
158	שׁנה	ετος		
159	שׁער	πυλη		
160 (ק.)	שׁפט	κρινειν		
161 (ק.)	שׁתה	πινειν		
162	תועבה			<
163	תמים		<2	

D.2 Vocabulary Common to S1 and S3

The list below contains all the terms (apart from prepositions and particles) which are common only to S1 and S3 in the MT. The conventions used are the same as those used in D.1. The third column in this case shows the relationship between S1 and S3.

1	אוז	ους
2	אחות	αδελφη
3	אחר	ετερος
4	אילם/אולם	αιλαμ
5	אלמנה	χηρα
6	אם	μητηρ
7	אציל	<2
8	בקר	βους
9	ברך	μηρος
10	בתולה	παρθενος
11	גב	<2
12	גדר	<5
13	גור (ק.)	<
14	גר	προσηλυτος
15	דרום	<2
16	היכל	ναος
17	הין	ιν
18	זנות	πορνεια
19	זרע	σπερμα
20	חיצון	εξωτερος
21	חלק (פ.)	<2
22	חצי	16
23	חצר	αυλη
24	טמא (ק.)	μιαινειν
25	טמא	ακαθαρτος
26	טרפה	θηριαλωτος

27	ילד (ה.)	γενναν
28	ימני	δεξιος
29	ינה (ה.)	καταδυναστευειν
30	כבר	χοβωρ
31	כהן	ιερευς
32	כלה (פ.)	συντελειν
33	כפר	16
34	לחם	αρτος
35	מאזנים	ζυγος
36	מאכל	<2
37	מוצא	<2
38	מזבח	θυσιατηριον
39	מכשול	κολασις
40	מפתן	αιθριον
41	מראה (1)	ορασις
42	מראה (2)	ορασις
43	מרי	παραπικραινειν
44	מת	<1,2
45	מתנה	δομα
46	נבלה	θνησιμαιον
47	נגב	<2
48	נגש (ק.)	εγγιζειν
49	נסך	σπονδη
50	סבב (ה.)	<2
51	סגר (נ.)	<2
52	סלת	16
53	צליון	<
54	צמה (לצמות)	(4)
55	עצם	<2
56	עשה (נ.)	(4)
57	עשור	δεκατος
58	פאר	<2
59	פגר	<1,3
60	פנימי	(4)
61	פרר (ה.)	παραβαινειν

62	צדק	<2
63	קטן	16
64	קרב (ה.)	<2
65	קרבן	<1,3
66	ראה (ה.)	δεικνυναι
67	ראשית	(4)
68	רבע	μερος
69	רום (ה.)	<2
70	רחק (ק.)	<
71	רצה (ק.)	προσδεχεσθαι
72	שערה	κριθη
73	שרף	(4)
74	שתב	σαββατα
75	השתחוה	προσκυνειν
76	שחט (ק.)	σφαζειν
77	שרת (פ.)	<2
78	תורה	<2
79	תימן	(4)
80	תמם (ק.)	εκλειπειν
81	תעה (ק.)	πλανασθαι
82	תרומה	απαρχη

D.3 Summary of Lists

Distribution of Hebrew Terms in the MT:

	S1/S2/S3	S1/S3	Total
Number of terms common to all sections :	163	82	245
Number of terms common to all sections : (excluding ch.16)	161	78	239
Number of terms common to all sections : (excluding 16 and 36.23c-38)	158	78	236
Number of terms with approximately the : same translation in all sections*	80	49	129
Number of terms with variety of : rendering*	10	6	16
Number of terms whose translations in : S1 and S3 agree against those in S2*	18	-	18
Number of terms where S1 and S3 differ*:	50	23	73
: Number of terms where S1 and S3 : differ and are affected by factors other than context*	22	4	26
: Number of terms where context : change is significant (and S1 differs from S3)*	25	16	41
: Number of terms where context : change necessitates translation change*	13	7	20
: Number of terms where context : change could justify translation change*	12	9	21
: Number of terms where there is : translation change and no apparent influencing factors*	3	3	6

* excluding ch.16 and 36:23c-38.

BIBLIOGRAPHY

Aejmelaeus A.
1982a   Parataxis in the Septuagint. A Study of
               the Renderings of the Hebrew Coordinate
               Clauses in the Greek Pentateuch.
               Helsinki, Suomalainen Tiedeakatemia.

1982b   Participium Coniunctum as a Criterion of
               Translation Technique.
               VT 32: 385-393.

Aland K.
1976   Repertorium der griechischen christlichen
               Papyri. Vol I.
               Patristische Texte und Studien 18
               Berlin/ New York, De Gruyter.

Aly Z. and Koenen L.
1980   Three Rolls of the Early Septuagint:
               Genesis and Deuteronomy.
               Bonn, Rudolf Habelt Verlag.

Arndt W.F. & Gingrich F.W.
1952   A Greek-English Lexicon of the New
               Testament and Other Early Christian
               Literature.
               Chicago, University of Chicago Press.

Barr J.
1979   The Typology of Literalism
               in Ancient Biblical Translations.
               (Mitteilungen des Septuaginta-
               Unternehmens XV)
               Göttingen, Vandenhoeck & Ruprecht.

Barthélemy D.
1963   Les Devanciers d'Aquila.
               Leiden, Brill.

1978   Études d'Histoire du Texte de l'Ancien
               Testament.
               Göttingen, Vandenhoeck & Ruprecht.

Baudissin W.W.
1929   Kyrios als Gottesname im Judentum und
               seine Stelle in der Religionsgeschichte.
               4 vols., hrgb. von O. Eissfeldt.
               Giessen, Töpelmann.

Baumgärtel F.
1923a   Zu den <<'dny yhwh>> Stellen bei Ezechiel.
               BWAT nF 5 (= Baumgärtel and Herrmann
               1923): 81-95.

1923b   Zu den Gottesnamen im Pentateuch.
               BWAT nF 5 (= Baumgärtel and Herrmann
               1923): 96-97.

271

1961a   Die Formel <<n'm yhwh>>
             ZAW 73: 277–290.

1961b   Zu den Gottesnamen in der Büchern
             Jeremia und Ezechiel.
             Verbannung und Heimkehr: 1–29
             (See Kuschke 1961).

Baumgärtel F. and Herrmann J.
    1923   See Herrmann and Baumgärtel.

Baumgartner W.
    1953   See Koehler L. and Baumgartner W.

Bedodi F.
    1974   I <<nomina sacra>> nei papiri greci
             vetero-testamentari precristiani.
             StP 13: 89–103.

Bertholet A.
    1897   Das Buch Hesekiel.
             (Kurzer Hand-Commentar zum alten
             Testament XII).
             Freiburg, Mohr.

Blaquart J.-L.
    1977   Parole de Dieu et prophètes d'Amos à
             ézéchiel.
             Le Point Théologique 24: 15–30.

Blass F., Debrunner A., Funk R.W.
    1961   A Greek Grammar of the New Testament and
             Other Early Christian Literature.
             Chicago and London, University of Chicago
             Press.

Boadt L.
    1975   The A:B:B:A Chiasm of Identical Roots in
             Ezekiel.
             VT 25: 693–699.

    1978   Textual Problems in Ezekiel and Poetic
             Analysis of Paired Words.
             JBL 97: 489–499.

Bodine W.R.
    1980   The Greek Text of Judges:
             Recensional Developments.
             Chico, California, Scholars Press.

Bogaert P.-M.
    1978a   Le témoignage de la Vetus Latina dans
             l'étude de la tradition des Septante.
             ézéchiel et Daniel dans le Papyrus 967.
             Bib 59: 384–395.

Bibliography

1978b	Review of Tov E., "The Septuagint Translation of Jeremiah and Baruch". RTL 9: 342-347.
1981a	Le Livre de Jérémie: Le prophète et son milieu: les oracles et leur transmission. Leuven University Press.
1981b	L'Orientation du parvis du sanctuaire dans la version greque de l'Exode. L'Antiquité Classique 50: 79-85.

Briggs C.A.
1974 See Brown F., Driver S.R., and Briggs C.A.

Brock S.
1969 The Phenomenon of Biblical Translation in Antiquity. Alta (The University of Birmingham Review) II, 8: 96-102.

1972 The Phenomenon of the Septuagint. OTS 17: 11-36.

1979 Aspects of Translation Technique in Antiquity. GRBS 20: 69-87.

Brock S., Fritsch C.T., Jellicoe S.
1973 A Classified Bibliography of the Septuagint. Leiden, Brill.

Brown F., Driver S.R., and Briggs C.A.
1974 A Hebrew and English Lexicon of the Old Testament. Oxford, Clarendon Press. First Published 1907.

Brown S.
1970 Concerning the Origin of the Nomina Sacra. StP 9: 7-19.

Brownlee W.H.
1963 The Scroll of Ezekiel from the Eleventh Qumran Cave. RevQ 4: 11-28.

Burkitt F.C.
1894 The Book of Rules of Tyconius. Cambridge, Cambridge University Press. (=Texts and Studies vol. III, no. 1).

1897 Fragments of the Books of Kings according to the Translation of Aquila. Cambridge University Press.

Camilo dos Santos E.
        1973   An Expanded Hebrew Index for the Hatch-
                        Redpath Concordance to the Septuagint.
                        Jerusalem, Dugith.

Carley K.W.
        1974   The Book of the Prophet Ezekiel.
                        Cambridge University Press.

Cerfaux L.
        1931a   Le nom divin <<Kyrios>> dans la bible
                        grec.
                        RSPT 20: 27-51.

        1931b   Adonai et Kyrios.
                        RSPT 20: 417-452.

Cooke G.A.
        1936   A Critical and Exegetical Commentary on
                        the Book of Ezekiel.
                        Edinburgh, T & T Clark.

Cornill C.H.
        1886   Das Buch des Propheten Ezekiel.
                        Leipzig, Hinrichs.

Dalman G.H.
        1889   Der Gottesname Adonaj und seine
                        Geschichte.
                        Berlin, Reuther.

Danielsmeyer, W.
        1936   Neue Untersuchungen zur Ezechiel-
                        Septuaginta. (Dissertation).
                        Münster.

Debrunner A.
        1961   See Blass F., Debrunner A., Funk R.W.

Denniston J.D.
        1954   The Greek Particles (second edition).
                        Oxford, Clarendon Press.

Driver S.R.,
        1974   See Brown F., Driver S.R., and Briggs C.A

Dunand F.
        1966   Papyrus grecs bibliques. (Papyrus
                        F. Inv. 266). Volumina de la
                        Genèse et du Deutéronome. (Introduction).
                        Cairo. L'Institut Français d'Archéologie
                        Orientale.

        1971   Papyrus grecs bibliques: Volumina de la
                        Genèse et du Deutéronome. (Text and
                        plates).
                        études de Papyrologie 9: 81-150
                        (+ 15 plates).

Bibliography

Ehrlich A.B.
1912   Randglossen zur hebräischen Bibel.
               Vol. 5.
               Leipzig, Hinrichs.
               (Reprinted: Hildesheim, Olms, 1968).

Eichrodt W.
1970   Ezekiel. A Commentary.
               London, SCM. (Translated from: Der Prophet
               Ezekiel 1965/6).

Eissfeldt O.
1974   Adhon.
               TDOT 1: 59-72.

Elliger K.
1967   Liber Ezechiel. (Fasc. 9 of BHS)
               Stuttgart, Deutsche Bibelstiftung.

Filson F.V.
1943   The Omission of Ez 12.26-28 and 36.23b-38
               in Codex 967.
               JBL 62: 27-32.

Fitzmyer J.A.
1975/77   The Dead Sea Scrolls. Major Publications
               and Tools for Study.
               Missoula, Montana, Scholars Press.

Fohrer G.
1952   Die Hauptprobleme des Buches Ezechiel.
               Berlin, Töpelmann.

1955   Ezechiel. (Mit einem Beitrag von
               K. Galling).
               Tübingen, Mohr.

Fritsch C.T.
1973   See Brock, Fritsch, Jellicoe.

Foerster W. and Quell G.
1965   "Kurios".
               TDNT vol. 3: 1039-1095.

Funk R.W.
1961   See Blass F., Debrunner A., Funk R.W.

Galiano M.F.
1968   Notes on the Madrid Ezekiel Papyrus.
               BASP 5: 72.

1970   Notes on the Madrid Ezekiel Papyrus.
               Proceedings of the Twelfth International
               Congress of Papyrology (Toronto)
               pp. 133-138.

1971a   El papiro antinoopolitano de Ezequiel a la
         luz de las páginas matritenses de 967.
         Emerita 39: 51-61.

1971b   Nuevas páginas del códice 967 del A.T.
         griego. (Ez 28,19-43,9).
         StP 10: 5-77.

Gehman H.S.
    1938a   The Relations between the Hebrew Text of
             Ezekiel and that of the John H. Scheide
             Papyri.
             JAOS 58: 92-102.

    1938b   The Relations between the Text of the John
             H. Scheide Papyri and that of the other
             Greek MSS. of Ezekiel.
             JBL 57: 281-287.

Gehman H.S., Johnson A.C., Kase E.H.
    1938   See: Johnson, Gehman, Kase.

Gingrich F.W. and Arndt W.F.
    1952   See: Arndt W.F. and Gingrich F.W.

Gooding D.W.
    1959   The Account of the Tabernacle.
             Cambridge University Press.

    1967a   Review of "Die Infinitve in der
             Septuaginta" by I. Soisalon-Soininen.
             JTS (n.s.) 18: 451-455.

    1967b   Temple Specifications: A Dispute in
             logical Arrangement between the MT and
             the LXX.
             VT 17: 143-172.

Gooding D.W. and Walters P.
    1973   See: Walters P. and Gooding D.W.

Greenberg M.
    1978   The Use of the Ancient Versions for
             Interpreting the Hebrew Text.
             SVT 29: 131-148.

Grenfell B.P. and Hunt A.S.
    1904   The Oxyrhynchus Papyri: Part IV.
             London. Egypt Exploration Fund.

Halperin D.J.
    1982   Merkabah Midrash in the Septuagint.
             JBL 101: 351-363.

Harford J.B.
    1935   Studies in the Book of Ezekiel.
             Cambridge University Press.

Bibliography

Hatch E. and Redpath H.A.
    1897   A Concordance to the Septuagint and the
                other Greek Versions of the Old
                Testament (including the Apocryphal
                Books).
                Oxford, Clarendon Press. (Reprinted in
                1975 by Akademische Druck- u. Verlags-
                anstalt, Graz.)

Heinisch P.
    1923   Das Buch Ezechiel.
                Bonn, Hanstein.

Helbing R.
    1907   Grammatik der Septuaginta Laut- und
                Wortlehre.
                Göttingen, Vandenhoeck & Ruprecht.

    1928   Die Kasussyntax der Verba bei den
                Septuaginta.
                Göttingen, Vandenhoeck & Ruprecht.
                Reprinted 1979.

Herrmann J.
    1913   Die Gottesnamen im Ezechieltexte.
                BWAT (o.s.) 13: 70-87. (BWAT 13 =
                Altestamentliche Studien, Rudolf zum
                60. Geburtstag dargebracht).

    1923   Die Septuaginta zu Ezechiel das Werk
                dreier übersetzer.
                BWAT (nF/n.s.) 5: 1-19. (BWAT nF 5 =
                Herrmann, Baumgärtel 1923).

    1924   Ezechiel.
                Leipzig, Deichert.

Herrmann J. and Baumgärtel F.
    1923   Beiträge zur Entstehungsgeschichte der
                Septuaginta (=BWAT nF 5).
                Berlin/Stuttgart/Leipzig.

Hockey S.M.
    1980   A Guide to Computer Applications in the
                Humanities.
                London, Duckworth.

Holladay W.L.
    1976   A Concise Hebrew and Aramaic Lexicon of
                the Old Testament.
                Grand Rapids, Michigan, Eerdsmans.

Hunt A.S.
    1910   The Oxyrhynchus Papyri: Part VII.
                London. Egypt Exploration Fund.

Hunt A.S. and Grenfell B.P.
    1904   See Grenfell B.P. and Hunt A.S.

Irwin W.I.
1943   The Problem of Ezekiel.
        Chicago, The University of Chicago Press.

Jacques X.
1972   List of Septuagint Words Sharing Common
        Elements.
        Rome, Biblical Institute Press.

Jahn G.
1905   Das Buch Ezechiel auf Grund der
        Septuaginta hergestellt.
        Leipzig, Pfeiffer.

Jahn L.G.
1972   Der griechische Text des Buches Ezekiel.
        Bonn, Habelt.

Jankowski S.
1977   I "nomina sacra" nei papiri dei LXX.
        StP 16: 81-116.

Janzen J.G.
1973   Studies in the Text of Jeremiah.
        Cambridge, Massachusetts, Harvard
        University Press.

Jellicoe S.
1968   The Septuagint and Modern Study.
        Oxford, Clarendon Press.

1973   See: Brock, Fritsch, Jellicoe.

1974   Studies in the Septuagint: Origins,
        Recensions and Interpretations.
        New York, KTAV.

Johannessohn M.
1925   Der Gebrauch der Präpositionen in der
        Septuaginta.
        Göttingen.

Johnson A.C., Gehman H.S. and Kase E.H.
1938   The John H. Scheide Biblical Papyri,
        Ezekiel.
        Princeton, Princeton University Press.

Kahle P.E.
1959   The Cairo Genizah (2nd edn.).
        Oxford, Blackwell.

Kase E.H.
1938   See Johnson, Gehman, Kase.

Bibliography

Katz P. (See also Walters P.)
    1954   Zur Textgestaltung der Ezechiel
                   Septuaginta.
                   Bib 35: 29-39. (Also in Ziegler
                   1971: 415-425).

    1956a   Septuagintal Studies in the Mid-Century.
                   Their Links with the Past and Their
                   Present Tendencies.
                   Pp. 176-208 of the C. H. Dodd festschrift
                   "The Background of the New Testament and
                   Its Eschatology", Cambridge University
                   Press.

    1956b   Zur übersetzungstechnik der Septuaginta.
                   Die Welt des Orients 2: 267-273.

Kenyon F.G.
    1933a   Nomina Sacra in the Chester Beatty Papyri.
                   Aegyptus 13: 5-10.

    1933b   The Chester Beatty Biblical Papyri.
                   Descriptions and Texts of Twelve
                   Manuscripts on Papyrus of the Greek Bible.
                   Fasciculus 1. General Introduction.
                   London, Emery Walker Ltd.

    1937   The Chester Beatty Biblical Papyri.
                   Fasc. 7. Ezekiel, Daniel, Esther: Text.
                   London, Emery Walker Ltd.

    1938   The Chester Beatty Biblical Papyri.
                   Fasc. 8. Ezekiel, Daniel, Esther: Plates.
                   London, Emery Walker Ltd.

    1975   The Text of the Greek Bible. (Third
                   Edition).
                   London, Duckworth.

Koehler L. and Baumgartner W.
    1953   Lexicon in Veteris Testamenti Libros.
                   Leiden, Brill.

    1958   Supplementum ad Lexicon in Veteris
                   Testamenti Libros.
                   Leiden, Brill.

Koenen L. and Aly Z.
    1980   See Aly Z. and Koenen L.

Kraetzschmar R.
    1900   Das Buch Ezechiel.
                   (Handkommentar zum alten Testament).
                   Göttingen, Vandenhoeck & Ruprecht.

Kraft R.A. (Editor)
    1972   1972 Proceedings for the International
                   Organization for Septuagint and Cognate
                   Studies and the Society of Biblical Liter-
                   ature Pseudepigrapha Seminar. (=Septuagint
                   and Cognate Studies, Number Two.)
                   Society of Biblical Literature.

Kuhn K.G.
          1960   Konkordanz zu den Qumrantexten.
                    Göttingen, Vandenhoeck & Ruprecht.

Kuschke A.
          1961   Verbannung und Heimkehr. (Festschrift).
                    Tübingen, J. C. B. Mohr.

Lee J.A.L.
          1983   A Lexical Study of the Septuagint Version
                    of the Pentateuch.
                    (Septuagint and Cognate Studies 14).
                    Chico, California, Scholars Press.

Lennox R.
          1947   The Theological Character of the Book of
                    Ezekiel in the Septuagint. (Dissertation).
                    Princeton.

Lewis N.
          1974   Papyrus in Classical Antiquity.
                    Oxford. Clarendon Press.

Lust J.
          1968   <<Mon Seigneur Jahweh>> dans le texte
                    hébreu d'ézéchiel.
                    ETL 44: 482-488.

          1981a   Ezekiel 36-40 in the Oldest Greek
                    Manuscript.
                    CBQ 43: 517-533. (Originally published
                    as "De sammenhang van Ez. 36-40" in
                    Tijdschrift voor Theologie 20 (1980):
                    26-39).

          1981b   <<Gathering and Return>> in Jeremiah and
                    Ezekiel.
                    Pp. 119-142 of "Le Livre de Jérémie",
                    edited by P.-M. Bogaert.

Marcus R.
          1931/32   Divine Names and Attributes in Hellenistic
                    Jewish Literature.
                    Proceedings of the American Academy for
                    Jewish Research 3: 43-120.

Martin R.A.
          1960   Some Syntactical Criteria of Translation
                    Greek.
                    VT 10: 295-310.

          1974   Syntactical Evidence of Semitic Sources i
                    Greek Documents.
                    Septuagint and Cognate Studies, Number
                    Three, Society of Biblical Literature.

Mercati G.
          1958   Psalterii Hexapli Reliquiae.
                    Vatican Library.

Bibliography

Metzger B.M.
1968 The Text of the New Testament. (2nd ed.).
Oxford, Clarendon Press.

1981 Manuscripts of the Greek Bible.
New York/Oxford, Oxford University Press.

Muraoka T.
1972a The Greek Texts of Samuel-Kings:
Incomplete Translations or Recensional
Activity?
Published in Kraft 1972: 90-107.

1972b A Re-examination of the two-translator
theory of a Septuagint Book. (Summary)
BIOSCS 5: 9.

1973 Literary Device in the Septuagint.
Textus 8: 20-30.

Nestle E.
1878 Jakob von Edessa über den Schem
hammephorasch und andere Gottesnamen.
ZDMG 32: 465-508, 735-6.

Nida E.A.
1964 Toward a Science of Translating.
Leiden, Brill.

O'Connell K.G.
1972 The Theodotionic Revision of the Book of
Exodus.
Cambridge, Massachusetts, Harvard
University Press.

Orlinsky H.M.
1975 The Septuagint as Holy Writ and the
Philosophy of the Translators.
HUCA 46: 89-114.

Paap A.H.R.E.
1959 Nomina Sacra in the Greek Papyri of the
First Five Centuries.
Leiden.

Panyik A.
1938 A Critical and Comparative Study of the
Old Latin Texts of the Book of Ezekiel
and the Minor Prophets. (Thesis).
Princeton University.

Payne J.B(arton)
1949 The Relationship of the Chester Beatty
Papyri of Ezekiel to Codex Vaticanus.
JBL 68: 251-265.

Pietersma A.
1984   Kyrios or Tetragram: A Renewed Quest for
            the Original Septuagint.
            Pp. 85-101 of: De Septuaginta. Studies
            in Honour of John William Wevers on His
            Sixty-Fifth Birthday.
            Ontario, Benben Publications.

Procksch O.
1910   Studien zur Geschichte der Septuaginta -
            Die Propheten.
            Leipzig, Hinrichs.

Rabin Ch.
1968   The Translation Process and the Character
            of the Septuagint.
            Textus 6: 1-26.

Radday Y.T., Shore H., Pollatschek M.A., and Wickmann D.
1982   Genesis, Wellhausen and the Computer.
            ZAW 94: 467-481.

Rahlfs A.
1935   Septuaginta   Vols. I and II.
            Stuttgart, Württembergische Bibelanstalt.

Ranke E.
1871   Par Palimpsestorum Wirceburgensium.
            Vindobonae, Braumüller.

Redpath H.A.
1897   See Hatch, Redpath.

1907   The Book of the Prophet Ezekiel.
            London, Methuen.

Revell E.J.
1976   A Note on Papyrus 967.
            StP 15: 131-136.

Reynolds L.D. and Wilson N.G.
1974   Scribes and Scholars.(2nd edition)
            Oxford, Clarendon Press.

Rife J.M.
1933   The Mechanics of Translation Greek.
            JBL 52: 244-252.

Roberts C.H.
1950   The Antinoopolis Papyri. Part 1.
            London, Egypt Exploration Society.

1979   Manuscript, Society and Belief in Early
            Christian Egypt. (The Schweich Lectures o
            the British Academy 1977.)
            London, Oxford University Press.

Bibliography

Sanders J.A.
1979   Text and Canon: Concepts and Method.
                        JBL 98: 5-9.

Schäfers J.
1909   Ist das Buch Ezechiel in der Septuaginta
                        von einem oder mehreren Dolmetschern
                        übersetzt?
                        Theologie und Glaube 1: 289-291.

Shenkel J.D.
1968   Chronology and Recensional Development
                        in the Greek Text of Kings.
                        Cambridge, Massachusetts, Harvard
                        University Press.

Skehan P.W.
1980   The Divine Name at Qumran, in the Masada
                        Scroll, and in the Septuagint.
                        BIOSCS 13: 14-49.

Smith M.
1967   Another Criterion for the <<kaige>>
                        Recension.
                        Bib 48: 443-5.

Soisalon-Soininen I.
1965   Die Infinitive in der Septuaginta.
                        Helsinki, Suomalainen Tiedeakatemia.

Sollamo R.
1979   Renderings of Hebrew Semiprepositions in
                        the Septuagint.
                        Helsinki, Suomalainen Tiedeakatemia.

Spottorno M.V.
1981a   La omisión de Ez. 36, 23b-38 y la
                        transposición de capítulos en el papiro
                        967.
                        Emerita 50: 93-99.

Stalker D.M.G.
1968   Ezekiel (Torch Bible Commentary).
                        London, SCM.

Swete H.B.
1914   An Introduction to the Old Testament in
                        Greek (2nd edition, revised by
                        R.R. Ottley).
                        Cambridge, Cambridge University Press.
                        (Reprinted in 1968 by KTAV, New York).

Taylor C.
1900   Hebrew-Greek Cairo Genizah Palimpsests
                        from the Taylor-Schechter Collection.
                        Cambridge University Press.

Taylor J.B.
    1969   Ezekiel. An Introduction and Commentary. London, Tyndale Press.

Thackeray H.St.J.
    1903a   The Greek Translators of Jeremiah. JTS (o.s.) 4: 245–266.

    1903b   The Greek Translators of Ezekiel. JTS (o.s.) 4: 398–411.

    1903c   The Greek Translators of the Prophetical Books. JTS (o.s.) 4: 578–585.

    1907a   The Greek Translators of the Four Books of Kings. JTS (o.s.) 8: 262–278.

    1907b   The Bisection of Books in Primitive Septuagint MSS. JTS (o.s.) 9: 88–98.

    1909   A Grammar of the Old Testament in Greek. Cambridge, Cambridge University Press. (Reprinted in 1978 by Olms, Hildesheim/ New York.)

    1915   "Septuagint". International Standard Bible Encyclodpedia vol. 4: 2722–32.

    1921   The Septuagint and Jewish Worship. The Schweich Lectures 1920. London, Oxford University Press.

Tov E.
    1973   Transliterations of Hebrew Words in the Greek Versions of the Old Testament. Textus 8: 78–92.

    1975   Review of "A Classified Bibliography of the Septuagint" (Brock, Fritsch, Jellicoe 1973). VT 25: 803–810.

    1976   The Septuagint Translation of Jeremiah and Baruch. Missoula, Montana, Scholars Press.

    1978   Studies in the Vocabulary of the Septuagint – The Relation between Vocabulary and Translation Technique. Tarbiz 47: 120–138 (Hebrew) + I–II (English summary).

    1979   Loanwords, Homophony and Transliterations in the Septuagint. Bib 60: 216–236.

    1981   The Text-critical Use of the Septuagint in Biblical Research. (Jerusalem Biblical Studies 3) Jerusalem, Simor.

Bibliography

Toy C.H.
1899   The Book of the Prophet Ezekiel.
            London, Clarke.

Treu K.
1970   Christliche Papyri II.
            APF 20: 145-152.

1974   Christliche Papyri IV.
            APF 22/23: 367-395.

Turner E.G.
1968   Greek Papyri. An Introduction.
            Oxford, Clarendon Press.

1971   Greek Manuscripts of the Ancient
            World.
            Oxford. Clarendon Press.

Turner N.
1956   The Greek Translators of Ezekiel.
            JTS (n.s.) 7: 12-24.

1963   A Grammar of New Testament Greek (by
            J. H. Moulton). Vol. III.
            Edinburgh, T. & T. Clark.

Turner P.D.M.
1970   The Septuagint Version of Chapters i-xxxix
            of the Book of Ezekiel. (Thesis).
            Oxford University.

Vaccari A.
1965   The Hesychian Recension of the Septuagint.
            Bib 46: 60-66. Reprinted in:
            Jellicoe (1974): 336-342.

Van Haelst J.
1976   Catalogue des papyrus littéraires juifs
            et chrétiens.
            Paris, Sorbonne.

Vermes G.
1968   The Dead Sea Scrolls in English
            (2nd edn.).
            Middelsex, England, Penguin.

Waddell W.G.
1944   The Tetragrammaton in the LXX.
            JTS 45: 158-161.

Walters P. (See also P. Katz)
1973   The Text of the Septuagint. (Edited by
            D.W.Gooding).
            Cambridge, Cambridge University Press.

Wevers J.W.
1951   Evidence of the Text of the John
            H. Scheide Papyri for the Translation of
            the Status Constructus in Ezekiel.
            JBL 70: 211-216.

1969   Ezekiel. (The Century Bible).
            London, Nelson.

Wilson N.G.
1974   See Reynolds L.D. and Wilson N.G.

Würthwein E.
1980   The Text of the Old Testament.
            London, SCM. (U.S. edition: Grand Rapids,
            Eerdmans, 1979).

Yadin Y.
1978   Masada: Herod's Fortress and the Zealots'
            Last Stand.
            London, Sphere.

Ziegler J.
1934   Untersuchen zur Septuaginta des Buches
            Isaias.
            (Alttestamentliche Abhandlungen XII)
            Münster, Aschendorff.

1934/5   Die Einheit der Septuaginta zum
            Zwölfprophetenbuch.
            Beilage zum Vorlesungsverzeichnis der
            Staatlichen Akademie zu Braunsberg
            pp. 1-16 (= Ziegler 1971: 29-42).

1939   Septuaginta vol. XIV, Isaias.
            Göttingen, Vandenhoeck & Ruprecht.

1943   Septuaginta vol XIII, Duodecim prophetae.
            Göttingen, Vandenhoeck & Ruprecht.

1946   Die Bedeutung des Chester Beatty-Scheide
            Papyrus 967 für die Textüberlieferung
            der Ezechiel-Septuaginta.
            ZAW 61 (1945-48): 76-94. Reprinted in:
            Ziegler 1971: 321-339.

1952   Septuaginta vol XVI,1, Ezechiel.
            Göttingen, Vandenhoeck & Ruprecht.

1953   Zur Textgestaltung der Ezechiel-
            Septuaginta.
            Bib 34: 435-455. Reprinted in: Ziegler
            1971: 394-414.

1954   Septuaginta vol XVI,2, Susanna, Daniel,
            Bel et Draco.
            Göttingen, Vandenhoeck & Ruprecht.

1957   Septuaginta vol XV, Ieremias-Baruch-
            Threni-Epistula Ieremiae.
            Göttingen, Vandenhoeck & Ruprecht.

Bibliography

1959   Die Vorlage der Isaias-LXX und die erste Isaias-Rolle von Qumran 1QIs/a. JBL 78: 34-59. Reprinted in: Ziegler 1971: 484-509.

1971   Sylloge. Gesammelte Aufsätze zur Septuaginta. (= Mitteilungen des Septuaginta-Unternehmens X). Göttingen, Vandenhoeck & Ruprecht.

1977   Septuaginta vol XVI,1, Ezechiel (2nd ed.), mit einem Nachtrag von Detlef Fraenkel. Göttingen, Vandenhoeck & Ruprecht.

Zimmerli W.

1969   Ezechiel. 2 vols. Biblischer Kommentar Altes Testament, Band XIII/1 + Band XIII/2. Neukirchen-Vluyn, Neukirchener Verlag des Erziehungsvereins GmbH.

1979   Ezekiel 1. Philadelphia, Fortress Press.

1983   Ezekiel 2. Philadelphia, Fortress Press.

INDEXES

GREEK

See also Appendix D.

289

λατρευω 170
λεγω 105-111,134,189
λειτουργεω 170-1
λιθοβολεω 186
λικμαω 118
λιψ 176
λοιμος 120
λοιπον 172
λουω 185

μακροθεν 184
μαναα 32
μαστος 185
μαχαιρα 101-105,134,189
μεγαλαυχεω 189
μεγεθος 173
μεθη 184
μετα 152,189
μηρος 179
μιαινω 169-170
μισεω 186
μισθωμα 190
μισος 185
μοιχαλις 186
μοιχαομαι 186
μοιχευω 185-6
μοχθος 185
μυκτηρ 28,186
μυκτηριζω 28

ναγεβ 175
νεμω 98
νεομηνια 184
νεοτης 185
νηπιοτης 189
νομιμα (τα) 174

νομος 174
νοτος 174-6
νωτος 27,28,173

ξιφος 102,105,186,189

οικημα 190
οικος 40
ολεθρος 119
ομορεω 189
ονος 185
οπισω 152-3,189
ορασις 24,155
οργη 28,29
οροφωμα 28
οτι 12,97-101,134
οφθαλμος 155-7,191
οχλος 116,134
οψις 24,155

παιδευω 185
παραδεισος 191
παραπικραινω 24
παραπτωμα 127,134
παρεξ 42
παροδευομαι 187,191
παροδος 183,187,189
παροικος 161
πατρις 185
πελτη 185
περι 33,34
περιβαλλω 150,167
περικυκλος 139-142
περισσος 172
περιτιθημι 190
περιφερες 141

INDEXES

HEBREW

See also Appendix D.